WE DARED THE ANDES

WE DARED THE ANDES

*Three journeys
into the unknown*

GUSTAF BOLINDER

Translated by Elsa Kruuse

THE ADVENTURERS CLUB

LONDON

THE ADVENTURERS CLUB
178–202 Great Portland Street,
London, W.1

*This book has been set in Baskerville type
face. It has been printed in Great Britain on
Antique Wove paper by Taylor Garnett
Evans & Co. Ltd., Watford, Herts, and
bound by them*

Contents

Illustrations

between pages 96 and 97

Introduction

THIS is the story of three expeditions which my wife, Esther, and I made to the mysterious mountain fastnesses of the much feared Indian tribes which live in that magnificent spur of the Andes separating Colombia from Venezuela.

We were very young. When we left Sweden the first time, in 1915, we were expecting our first child and were not very well prepared for the adventures ahead of us. But the fascination of journeying into the unknown was strong in both of us. No one in the world up to that time knew anything of the habits and culture of the Indians in those mountains except that they were warlike Caribs who, by their very name, were understood to be cannibals.

On our second trip five years later, we made the astounding discovery of the existence of a tribe of Pygmy Indians, who gradually became our friends. On our third expedition in 1936, we were able, with their help, to fulfil our dream of crossing the Andes, going from one country to the other and thereby becoming the first white people ever to do so.

Colombia is the only country in South America having a Pacific and an Atlantic coastline. Beginning at its southern border, the Sierra Nevada de Merida come heaving up from Peru and, bending 200 miles northeast, bear off into the Caribbean coastal range. Between the Orinoco savannas and the Maracaibo lowlands, these mighty mountains rise to perpetually snow-capped peaks over 15,000 feet high.

Forking east at the Venezuelan border, the northern branch becomes the Sierra de Perijá. And in them are the Serrania de Motilones, the mountains of the dreaded Motilon Indians who had never seen white people before that day in 1915 when we stood in a little mountain cornfield face to face.

We made our headquarters for all three expeditions in the charming old town of Valledupar which dates from Spanish colonial days. 'Upar' was believed to be an Indian word meaning 'valley' which would seem to make the town's name 'Valley-Valley'. It lies buried in a wooded section not far from the roaring Guatapuri River. In the centre of the town was a huge grassy plaza surrounded by white-washed one-storey adobe houses. Two small churches besides – and that was all there was to the town when we first saw it against its backdrop of blue mountains raising their glittering peaks into the sky.

It was there we confirmed the fact that no expedition had been able to cross from Colombia into Venezuela, chiefly because of the Indians' hostility. Here, the warnings of those wiser than we were repeated. The Indians were 'tame' only in a few scattered sections, they assured us. Yet we were at last able, with the help of our diminutive friends, to conquer the jungle, where no trails existed, climbing slowly and often painfully across these mysterious and hitherto unknown mountains.

There are still two groups of Indians in the area with whom neither we nor anyone else have been able to make friends. They live in the forests around the Rio Catatumbo and the Rio de Oro at the Andes' feet. These are the tribes which are still resisting the efforts of the big oil companies to prospect for petroleum. The rich Barranca Bermeja oil fields are a major part of Colombia's economy today and are second only to Venezuela's. But these Indians continue to defy further exploration and the powerful oil concerns have never been able to reach an understanding with them.

Our discovery of the Pygmy Maraca tribe on our second trip caused quite a stir. It is well known that there are Pygmies in Africa and in some countries bordering on the Pacific. But we were met by complete scientific consternation on our return with the news of our discovery, until we showed the photographs we had brought back to an American scientific convention which was meeting in Gothenburg. Such well-known men as Rivet, Gusinde and Erland Nordenskjöld studied our photographs with great interest. Then, the latter showed me an ancient map he had turned up in his subsequent research on which the word 'pigmeos' was written very clearly over the mountains of the Maraca Indians.

It is now forty years since we met the Motilon Indians for the first time but little has changed in their mountains since then. Down on the plains where the Creoles live, time had stood still for centuries. But for them new winds have begun to blow away the dusty idyl, so fascinating to the historian and sociologist. The Creoles of Valledupar therefore have a special chapter to themselves.

GUSTAF BOLINDER

8

BOOK ONE

CHAPTER ONE

THE first journey into the unknown had begun. It was a modest caravan which pushed through the forest at the foot of the Andes. A few pack mules were led along by some half-blood peons riding more of these patient, respectable beasts. They sat cross-legged on saddles made of wood and straw, with forked *garabato'n* in one hand – a stick which they used both as a whip and spurs.

My wife, Esther, and I also rode mules. Anything but fiery steeds, they stumbled along the narrow, winding trail. We couldn't be very proud of our caravan but we were very happy, even though we'd had to scrape the bottom of the cash box to get it together. Let's say we were not travelling according to the rules. Certain things are expected of white travellers down there. For us, the main thing was that we were now on our way south where exciting experiences were awaiting us and, if we were successful, a rich reward for our scientific curiosity and efforts. We meant to uncover the secrets of these primeval mountains and their people.

We were young. We had a right to be adventurous. In addition, we were one little family. Our baby daughter, Sif, slept in a little hammock around my neck. We saw nothing strange in travelling like that. Others did the same in this primitive country. As a matter of fact, our baby was also a native, in a way, for she had been born in this country only a few months before! The natives, the Indians, whom we were determined to get to know, trusted right from the start a man who travelled with his wife and child – a man leaves his family at home when his intentions are not friendly.

The forest began to be taller and thicker – more impenetrable. The trail was very narrow and we had to bend down closer to our saddles as the jungle reached out at us from every direction. The broad-bladed machetes flashed almost continuously now, cutting back the vines and branches in our path. At times we had to lie almost flat on our mules' necks to pass under half-fallen trees hanging over the trail, and it wasn't always easy for me, carrying the baby in her little hammock slung around my neck.

Soon the path became so narrow that the branches scraped the mules' sides and the riders' legs, but since we were wearing leggings of jaguar and cow skin, we were protected.

9

We had to be alert every minute, however, in order not to get hurt. Some of those vines cause unpleasant cuts which don't heal – and we had to be quick to slip out of the saddle and slide under treacherous branches. We were continually attacked by insects the worst of which were the ticks which crawled under our clothes and dug themselves into the skin. At night we pulled them off after soaking the skin in alcohol or oil, which made them loosen their grip.

Here and there a tree had fallen right across the trail and the huge trunk blocked our way. This was a seldom used trail and whoever came along it had to clear it as best he could. Since no one could move them, it meant making his way around the roots or the crown. This made the trail still longer and more crooked. Here was another fallen tree. Our peons were ordered to cut a path around it, which they began to do only after a long discussion as to the easiest way to go about it.

For our part, we called a halt and dismounted as it was time for the baby to eat. I handed her over to her mother, then unfastened a camp stool from the mule pack and put it in a comfortable place for her. I stood a moment, then, leaning against the saddle, and looked at my young wife, as blonde and lovely as a northern summer's day, surrounded by the green depths of this tropical forest. The child's head was like a white flower on her mother's breast.

A single flower was growing nearby, a large red cup, flaming in the greenness. I went over to pick it for her but stopped. It was covered with ants and the petals fell as soon as I touched it. Quickly I drew back my hand, and just in time. The stalk of the flower suddenly came alive and reached out for me – flat, shiny brown and thin, edged with a moving fringe of legs with jaw-like claws! It was a poisonous millipede, one of the dreaded myriapods. In the forests of this hot country it was best to remember the 'look-but-don't-touch' warnings we'd been given! Compared to a millipede, a scorpion is almost cosy to have around. I put an end to the disgusting thing with a few lashes of my whip.

The path was cleared now and we could go on. In no time we came to a glen where we found ourselves facing the typical tropic rain forest. It was mightier and more imposing in its luxuriant growth than I had dreamed possible before seeing it with my own eyes. I have to admit I had been dubious about reports I had heard. But standing there. I understood that none of them had been exaggerated in the slightest degree. People shrink here and become no bigger than the ants.

One also gets this feeling in a huge Gothic cathedral where there is the same reaching for the sky in the shadowy silence under arches pointing to heaven. But the cathedral is cool and peaceful. Man has given it its beautifully exact proportions. The primeval forest is boundless – gigantic, frightening. Here the trees grew as high as we could see, some of enormous girth as though sculptured of grey clay; others thin and straight as arrows. Vines clung around the naked tree trunks and wove between them in a kind of basketry of twisted green ropes.

Liana vines snaked through the protective green mass and cast themselves in bold loops from tree to tree. An emerald dusk bathed everything beneath it, although it was a little paler at the top. Only a few single flowers stood out against every variation of tones of green. In order to see the beauty of these jungle flowers, one had to bend down closely or else climb a tree higher than any of the others.

It was completely quiet at that time of day. A few little sounds like a bird's beak drumming on a stump or the faint whistle of a tapir were soon swallowed up again in the great silence. But this quiet was only on the surface. The fight for survival continued unabated all around us. The wild cat hunted the tapir, monkey and giant anteater. Birds of prey cruised about for favourite morsels. Poisonous snakes slithered across the forest floor and along the branches of trees. Strangler vines rose up from the luxuriant undergrowth to throw their arms around young trees, get a grip on them and then climb them, sucking out their life-giving sap until only the dry trunks remained to bear up these parasites as they sought out other victims.

This eruptive vegetation breeds on decay. Vapours hover under the vast arches of the trees and it is hard to breathe. Our thin clothes stuck to our bodies. During long jungle expeditions you are surprised to find that you long for a northern spring, for nature's rebirth, the way it is at home. Here there is no fresh, new growth. Everything looks as though it had burst out ready grown and over-ripe.

The primeval forest has no room for man. All those forces, which otherwise would be fighting each other, join in turning against man. A caravan is in constant danger and all too many have fallen victim to the jungle's might. Neither is there much to eat and there is no fodder for horses or pack mules.

Nevertheless, it wasn't here that sudden death usually lay in wait. The danger was greatest where the forest thinned, the trees stood shorter and the sun's rays began to pierce through the ceiling of leaves. Everyone was conscious of that danger now. We had to hurry on – get to a village where we could put up for the night.

We could have set up a camp, of course. We had tents and the peons were used to sleeping under the open sky. But the mules and burros had to have food and there was none in the forest. We weren't too well equipped, either. Ants and other bugs could get

11

into our sleeping bags on the ground if we camped out. But those were minor reasons. Our peons knew as well as we did why we didn't want to spend the night in the jungle. They walked along very cautiously and now and again reined in their mules and listened. They were afraid.

It's true that death always waits in the jungle's green depths. Fever mosquitoes buzz in the shadows, leaves hang heavy with poisonous creeping things, snakes rustle in the bushes. At night the jaguars sneak out and, in the forest's murky waters, crocodiles, stinging rays and rapacious fish lurk. But those dangers weren't what they were thinking about. We were used to them. We met them everywhere. No. There was something else they feared even more. They were going along in constant dread that, at any minute, arrows would come whizzing out of the bushes.

We had reached a tract which had long been avoided because of hostile Indian attacks. Several wayfarers were known to have been overpowered and killed here, but, as the whole purpose of our expedition was to try to come into contact with these Indians, I had to calm the peons.

These Indians are called Motilons by the whites and Creoles. They live in the chain of mountains which form the border between the sister countries, Colombia and Venezuela, the Sierra de Perijá. We were now in Colombia on the west side of the Andes. After the conquest, the whites had settled on the plains on each side of the mountains but they had never succeeded in conquering the mountain tops. For hundreds of years, the Indians had looked down over these plains at the villages of their white enemies who were no longer really white, of course, as they had several generations of intermarriage with descendants of Negro slaves behind them.

In any case, the Motilon Indians were war-like and courageous and just the mention of their name made the people in the plains tremble. Not only were there battles with the Creoles whenever they tried to push up the mountain sides, but the Indians attacked wayfarers in the valleys, raided farms and stole cattle. The over-hanging threat of their raids and not infrequent revolutions had thinned out the population of whole tracts of land in the area.

Recently however, we were told, the Indians in some sections had apparently given up their raids. If so, we hoped it would be possible to make contact with them and get to know these people about whom even the anthropologists knew very little.

We really had planned to return to Sweden after a year's research farther north. Our money was almost gone. But we couldn't resist this opportunity to try to meet the Motilons. Go back when it was only a few days' march to the mountain holdout of these wild natives and the chances of making contact with them were better than ever? No! We decided to risk it. We didn't want to tell anyone at home about our plan, though, until we succeeded. If we failed, we would talk very quietly about our little 'extra expedition' to what the map still called *region inexplorado*.

We weren't quite as rash as a good many people thought, however. We knew very well that we had to take into account one thing – caution. On an expedition such as the one we were contemplating, caution and patience would be at a premium if we were to get to know hostile Indians and live to tell about it. We hoped for the best.

By that time we were in an area which had been considered a danger zone for some time. However, the Indians had not made any raids for a couple of years, in fact, hadn't even shown their faces. Apparently they were on the move a lot and probably had gone over to other sections of the mountain jungles. One day, they'd be back, of course. For some time, the government had been providing armed escorts for travellers, but it wasn't considered necessary in this section any longer. Nevertheless, the peons were uneasy and moved along so quietly they didn't even swear at the mules or shout and sing dirty songs as they usually did. In fact, they were going along much too slowly and I had to hustle them up.

'We've got to go faster if you don't want to sleep in the forest,' I told them. 'It's still a good way to the nearest village.'

I had a map. It was old but there was no other kind. Our goal was the village of Codazzi, named for a well-known cartographer who had died down here somewhere before finishing his work. Among the people, however, the village was still called Pueblito, 'the little town'. I knew we couldn't reach it before the next day. According to the map, though, there were two still smaller villages on the way to it. The nearest, Palmira, was the one I hoped to reach before nightfall, although I didn't know exactly how far away it was. I couldn't rely on the map and the information I had secured about the distance to Pueblito had also been pretty vague. They measure in 'long miles' and 'short miles', according to the condition of the roads and trails.

The path now made the going very difficult. It was slippery, stony, winding, and the vegetation was even thicker than before. The peons had all they could do to clear it and force the mules on. The poor beasts were tired now and balky, I had to be on constant guard against branches and vines as I had the baby to think of and, all in all, we forgot about the Indians completely for quite a while.

We were reminded of them in an unexpected way. The forest suddenly became lighter and we came out into a glen. Amazed, we reined in the animals. Before us, the slanting rays of the afternoon sun fell across some crumbled clay walls between which lay some half-burned logs, swarming with insects. Low bushes had grown up in the remnants of the walls and here and there a tree leaned over the ruins.

There was no doubt about it. This was – or rather had been – Palmira! I suddenly recalled reports that the Indians had sacked two Creole villages a year or so earlier. No one had said anything about Palmira, not even the monks, who had given us letters of introduction to the Capucine brothers in Pueblito, which I began to think might be the only one of these villages still left standing. Just the same, the map showed one more village on our way – El Jobo.

The peons were getting nervous again. They looked anxiously about them as if expecting to be surrounded by wild men any minute. I didn't want to stay there either, I had to admit. It wasn't a good camp site. There was hardly any grass for the animals and termites and leaf-cutting ants had completely taken over the ruins. To make matters worse, the stream which had supplied water to the inhabitants was completely dried up.

The peons willingly agreed that we should continue. There were a couple of hours left of daylight and perhaps there were people in El Jobo. At any rate, it couldn't be worse than Palmira. When I pointed out that the signs we had seen of Indians being nearby were not very recent ones and that no Indians had been seen on this side of Pueblito for some time, the peons were pacified.

We rode and rode. Even the mules now seemed as anxious as we were that we'd arrive somewhere soon. They were hungry and thirsty and I noticed they had begun to increase their pace of their own accord without prodding.

We kept telling ourselves that we weren't in any danger here but the memory of those forlorn ruins remained with us and we couldn't help but think what ideal conditions this terrain provided for scouts and snipers, with its thick bushes and trees rubbing branches with each other. We also disliked the prospect of spending the night in a ruined village like Palmira. We had not met a soul all day long. The forest stood silent and undisturbed without a sign that we were approaching a habitation of any kind.

The trail was getting worse than ever, if that were possible. The sun would soon be going down and, when it did, everything would be completely blacked out. It was already dusk. Had I been right or wrong in leaving that ruined village?

Just then the forest thinned again. Relieved, we rode a little faster. And then we saw it – the same sight we had already seen. El Jobo, too, lay in ruins! The two places looked so much alike, in fact, that for a moment I thought we had been riding in a circle.

The youngest of the peons, Francisco, rode the smartest mule. The animal sniffed the air a moment and then dashed off all by itself, chased by Francisco, who disappeared behind a clay wall.

In the next instant he let out such a shriek that we all froze in our tracks. I grabbed my revolver and was about to approach the wall when a strange, high little voice called out, '*Quien es?*' We all heaved sighs of relief. Someone else was with Francisco and he spoke Spanish!

Francisco reappeared followed by a man, on a moth-eaten donkey, wearing a torn khaki uniform and holding an old-fashioned rifle across his knees. I had to laugh because, though I saw he was a gendarme, he looked more like a reincarnation of Sancho Panza.

Francisco's steed had picked up the scent of the gendarme's mount which was the reason it had taken off with such sudden interest.

The gendarme had hidden behind some bushes when he heard our voices and it was when he looked out between the branches that Francisco had seen his face and screamed. At last we had met a wayfarer who also planned to spend the night here! But the gendarme had even better news for us.

There were people living nearby, he told us, and he and another gendarme were stationed here to protect them. A new village was being built, he said, by a white man from the interior. Señor Olivella, who was planning to stake out a ranch there since the Indians seemed to have deserted the area. The gendarme offered to show us the way to the man's camp.

Arrived there, we found Olivella with about twenty workers. A house with the usual clay walls and palmleaf roof was under construction. Olivella lived with his workmen in a temporary shelter – a roof held up by posts and without walls.

He had seen us coming while we were still quite far away – he'd been careful to set his shelter a bit above the savanna – and hurried towards us with surprise written all over his face.

He apologized that he couldn't offer us anything better than the shelter, which we would have to share with several others. 'But everything I have is yours,' he told us, adding: 'You can trust me completely in little things and big, both night and day. My servants are at your disposition, my cook, my dogs. Don't ever hesitate to ask for what you want.'

Of course, these were the customary courtesies of the Creole and were not to be taken too literally but it is certainly nicer to be received in a friendly way like that than to be met with sullen faces and rudeness. And there are still a few countries where the latter is the fashion.

Here, hospitality is all the warmer among those who don't have much of anything themselves. Even the well-to-do live frugally by our standards. At least Olivella had a cook, Beatrice, who prepared his food, while the peons made their own; though it wasn't much different from that of the master of the house. We had some canned goods with us, among them a tin of sardines which we proffered our host to enliven the evening meal. We also invited him to share a bottle of beer which, at that time, was a rare drink in remote South American villages and still may be in El Jobo.

Beatrice turned out to be an ugly white-spotted Negro woman. Such spotted Negroes are fairly common here. A skin disease, *jovero,* leaves pigmentless spots. At first it is unpleasant to have such a poor spotted soul handle food, but one gets used to it. The disease is not considered dangerous and does not attack white people. Behind Beatrice's ample skirts, hid a shy ten-year-old girl, whose skin didn't have a single spot.

I once saw a pair of such spotted Negro girls at a country fair in Sweden where they were billed as the Jaguar Girls of the Jungle. They had come from a bawdy house in some tropical island, however, and had never seen the jungle.

With our host, we walked over to the peons who were chatting with the others. They were just making their everlasting *sancocho,* a soup of whatever happens to be at hand. But out of the pot I saw a pair of hands sticking up – a frighteningly cannibalistic sight. They had just shot a monkey and put the whole beast in the pot. When they assured me it was about done and offered me a morsel, I was glad I didn't happen to be starving. Monkey meat is for bushwackers and Indians. The others were busy roasting two morocones, a kind of land turtle. The air smelled badly of burned horn. The poor beasts had been flung on the coals alive and are considered done when their shells are burned through. There *are* primitive ways of preparing food which are quite clever but this was not one of them. The meat tasted as sickening as it smelled.

Señor Olivella arranged to have half his peons move out from the shelter so that we could put up our hammocks there, and they left us plenty of room. Those evacuated moved over to the half-finished house whose roof was partly laid. They were used to living in shelters without walls, hammock to hammock. We planned, as in everything else, to follow the custom of the country so we did the same. We also knew that as soon as people stretch out in their hammocks they get to talking and we hoped to hear something about the Indians.

Everyone was apparently satisfied with his meal, particularly our host, who was delighted with the beer, even though it was warm. Directly after eating, each went to his hammock. Esther and I lay on the outside of the shelter with Sif between us while, out in the new house, the peons hung their hammocks criss-cross above and below each other to make room for them all. We were glad we could

16

get as much air as possible. After all, we were in one of the hottest parts of the world. At least we were protected from the rain – what more could one wish for?

I had doled out smokes to everyone – those small cigars which farm girls make by rolling them expertly on their bare thighs. They cost next to nothing, which is about all there is to say in their favour. Glowing cigar tips glimmered everywhere in the dark and moved like fireflies as the hammocks swung. Our host started to talk about the Indians.

'Their enmity towards whites goes back a long time,' Señor Olivella announced. 'But I don't think I'm wrong when I say it was the fault of the whites from the beginning. They say that at one time the Indians would come down here to trade, now and then, but it must have been a long time ago. Not in anyone's memory around here has there been peace. But, my good people,' and he turned his voice towards the peons, 'your forefathers didn't do the slightest thing to try to win the Indians' friendship.'

We waited for some reaction but as none developed, he went on. 'If they could hurt the Indians, destroy their cornfields, murder any women and children they came on, they did it at every opportunity. Fortunately, the Indians lived in almost inaccessible mountain forests where the terrain is the worst in the world. There they could lie in ambush, shoot a brace of silent arrows and disappear.'

Señor Olivella told us that several expeditions had tried to get through 'up there' – and he nodded towards the dark mountains – because they had an idea there were rich ore deposits there.

'That was what a certain Señor Munoz thought in his day,' mumbled an old greybeard from the depths of his hammock. 'I was along on that ill-fated expedition when I was a lad. But I trailed behind with the bearers. He was a nice man, that Señor, and he hired over sixty men for his expedition. We had to walk the whole way, cutting through the jungle. Because almost everybody was armed, they were sure the Indians wouldn't attack them.' He paused to pull on his cigar.

'If he hadn't had so many people along, nobody would have dared go with him though. They relied on each other. Señor Munoz had lots of presents with him for the Indians as he wanted to make friends. He had chosen a section where he was sure there weren't any Indians. But there were,' said the man, remembering. 'He had divided up the area for reconnaissance and some of his men found a couple of Indian huts and caught sight of a few children running away. They shot after them and set fire to the huts.

'When Señor Munoz learned what had happened he swore pretty loud and told them of the danger they were in, but he had hardly finished his warning when he was struck by an arrow. The darn

17

thing went right through him, he fell flat on his face and died right off. His men fled in every direction as more arrows whined through the air. When things quietened down, a couple of men went back and put some earth over Señor Munoz. After that, the whole crowd took off for home, most of them getting arrows in their backs, but they were just wounded.'

The old man was about to stop, but I wanted to keep him talking. 'What did you do?' I asked him.

'Well, you can bet I threw away my pack and ran as soon as I heard what had happened. And so did all the other bearers. The Indians salvaged all the stuff we had left behind. Some time later we heard that Señor Munoz was wearing a leather belt filled with gold money. That was lost too, if the Indians didn't find it. But what would they want with money?'

'Didn't the Indians keep to themselves in the mountains in the old days, Clemente?' another voice asked out of the darkness.

'Well, yes,' the old fellow replied. 'But after Munoz's and a few other people's expeditions up there, they began to avenge their dead by lying in ambush, attacking everybody who came along. It wasn't long before they dared come down to the villages, too, and whenever we had a revolution, they made the most of it. So many people left the villages at one time, there was hardly anybody left around here. Quick as a flash they'd come and then disappear again. It was on one of those raids when they burned down Palmira and El Jobo.

'Funny thing. They took everything made out of iron they could lay hands on, hinges, locks, and even keys, and left lots of stuff you'd think they'd want. Well, that's our punishment for all the harm we've done them, I guess. That's what the monks say, and I guess they're right.'

A young fellow spoke for the first time. 'It's not strange we Creoles wanted revenge, too, don't forget. There's hardly anybody living around here, or who used to live here I should have said, who hasn't lost somebody in his family because of those Indians. They've been getting bolder, too, as we civilized people get fewer and fewer. For a long time the women have been afraid to get water from the streams around Pueblito unless their men go along with guns. One Indian, I heard, managed to sneak right into the village and tried to shoot a pig. The arrow hit all right but the pig didn't die right away. It ran through the street squealing its head off, with the Indian after it. He caught it, too, and was off with it before the villagers could get down their old shotguns. Nobody wanted to go after him much, anyway, so he went free.'

'I know a pig story, too,' another man began, and giggled to himself a little before he started: 'It's about Alfonso Lopez. He

18

went outside the village a little way to sit – well, he was in a hurry, shall we say. And you know how the village pigs come down and stand around in a half-circle waiting at times like that? Oh, excuse me, Señora,' he said quickly in a belated apology to my wife, 'but I'm only stating the facts. Well, there squatted Alfonso, and the pig was coming nearer to him. But there also was an Indian hiding in the bushes. The Indian shot the pig and missed, but Lopez got an arrow in his seat. I'll never forget that day when he came galloping through the village yelling and holding up his pants as well as he could with the arrow sticking out behind. It was only a bird arrow with a wooden head, but he hasn't got over being mad yet, and I can't help laughing every time I think about it.'

As villages and small towns had no sanitation facilities, the people withdrew to the outskirts when necessary, but to have an Indian behind your bush would prove disconcerting, I had to agree.

'The Indians want meat,' a peon broke in, when the laughter had died down. 'They don't have any domestic animals of their own. They hunted ours when they came down from the mountains. When I was a boy I helped the herdsmen because it wasn't safe for children to herd the cows alone. As the Indians had a taste for meat, the herdsmen had to be grown men and armed.'

'Yes,' he went on, reminiscing, 'it was dangerous even to walk along the roads here before the government began sending out gendarme escorts. The Indians respect uniforms and guns, and since the monks have been putting gifts for the Indians up there in the mountains above Pueblito, they've stopped raiding the cattle. Maybe they'll let white people come up their mountains now. *Quien sabe?*'

It was beginning to get late. The cigars had gone out. The talk petered out, and a snore here and there indicated that soon we'd all be asleep.

CHAPTER TWO

We had scarcely gone to sleep when we were wakened by a piercing scream. We were on our feet like a shot. The gendarmes dashed out in their ragged cotton underwear, hair on end, their Remingtons in their hands. They really should have kept watch all night, but they'd gone to bed with the others. After all, it was a long time since any Indians had been seen around there.

It was still fairly dark. The scream was a woman's – probably Beatrice, our cook. Yes, she was lying in her hammock shaking, her hands over her eyes. When she came to her senses, she explained that she was afraid of everything supernatural. And just now, sure enough, she had seen two white donkeys and a black man right before her very eyes.

'White donkeys?' Señor Olivella asked again. 'We haven't got any such thing. Why wake up the whole camp with nonsense like that? The only people we have to be afraid of are Indians, and they haven't got any donkeys,' he thundered.

Beatrice wouldn't give in. 'I'm more scared of ghosts than Indians,' she insisted, 'even if the devils did kill my whole family.'

'The reason I brought her along,' my host explained in a hushed aside, 'is that she's really not afraid of Indians or any other living person. How was I to know she'd be frightened of ghosts!'

Remarking philosophically that we all have our failings, Señor Olivella assured us that she was a good worker and that as soon as work on the new house was finished, which would take a few days, we were welcome to take her along with us.

We really did need a cook, and Beatrice was willing. While talking to her we realized suddenly that the man she claimed she had seen in her dream might really have been a thief, and the white donkeys two of our mules he had stolen. When our men went out to make sure, they found that two of them were indeed missing. It developed, however, that they had got out of the compound alone, and the peons who went out to follow the hoofprints eventually located them and brought them back.

Beatrice came in with two cups of strong coffee. The peons were already seated in a circle around a fire. Sif, our little daughter, lay on her back, gurgling contentedly, so, leaving her a while, we walked around among the ruins while the mules were being shod.

The village was a wreck. Household goods lay strewn about — rusty enamel plates, spoons and pieces of pottery the Indians hadn't bothered with because they weren't made of iron or steel. Apparently they knew that this junk couldn't be used for arrowheads or knives. I was wondering how they went about smelting down the iron when my foot struck something metallic. I stopped to pick it up and showed it to Esther. 'Why it's an old stirrup,' she exclaimed. 'It's exactly like the one we bought!'

She was quite right. It was an old-fashioned thing in the shape of a shoe with the toe curved up in a point. It was made of brass and was similar to stirrups still used in this area where people often ride barefoot or wear slippers. It's easy to get cut by branches, vines, and cactus in the jungle, and the 'shoe' stirrups afford some protection. Newer models are now factory-made of aluminium, but in the old days they were beautifully worked by hand. Sometimes they were of silver, especially for the ladies. Others were made of brass, like this one.

We had bought an identical stirrup in a junk shop on the coast – the only one – and now had found its mate in El Jobo's ruins! Our host assured us that this was a sign of very good luck.

It was already midday when we pulled into Pueblito and found that it was indeed a 'little town'. Clay huts lined both sides of the only street leading to an open square. On one side, the only large building looked down on the others. This was the monks' mission. Pueblito lay at the very foot of the mountains and was protected by them on two sides. Towards the east stretched the broad savannas. Its situation was really ideal, but the village was very dirty and run down and the heat intolerable.

Brush and thickets grew right up to the houses – a good protection for prowling Indians, I thought. And, looking up from down there, we could make out some of their huts and cornfields, bright patches in the dark forest-clad heights.

Through the middle of the village ran a water trough where people fetched their water. As they also threw their garbage in it, whenever it dried up the street smelled to high heaven. However, the water had been led into the village so that the women would not have to go off to the stream and risk being attacked by the Indians.

We went over to the Capucines' headquarters – whitewashed and neat with flower borders in front and a little garden in back. We were received very graciously. All Europeans down here feel like compatriots when they meet and the monks were Spaniards. That we were 'unbelievers' didn't bother them a bit.

The monks were taking care of a group of Indian boys, although not from the Motilon mountains but from another part of the country. However, they were ready to start their mission work here as soon as friendly relations with these Indians could be established. There were also three nuns of the Order of the Sacred Heart who immediately took care of Esther and little Sif. The work of the monks, I found, was chiefly concentrated on orphan children among the inhabitants and they didn't concern themselves too much with the religious lives of the villagers.

After the abbot had wished us welcome, brown-cowled monks cleared out an adobe hut for us. It looked quite comfortable, but I noticed it had not been lived in. We discovered why a little later.

We got to know all the villagers very quickly and, as soon as we were settled into our house, began plans for our expedition to the Indians' mountains.

It was evident that things had been much quieter along the Indian border recently. There had been no attacks on the roads as travellers were given gendarme escorts in every section considered risky. Both the monks and the authorities had impressed on the people that they were not to shoot at the mere sight of an Indian and they forbade anyone to destroy the Indians' temporary camps and hunting shelters.

The greatest service along these lines had been done by Bishop Atanasio at the monastery, who later became one of our best friends in Colombia. We learned that he had once formed an expedition with hundreds of followers which had gone up into the mountains and set out gifts everywhere they found Indian huts or fields. His gifts were mostly small objects made of iron so the Indians would get so much of the stuff they wouldn't have to come down and steal it from the Creoles.

We heard that people had seen Indians from a distance – they retreated quickly when they knew they'd been seen – but no one had come into contact with them, which was just the way the monks like it. From the first, the bishop very rightly insisted that only the most trustworthy whites should make the first contact.

On that expedition, the bishop told us, they had passed several little villages which the Indians had deserted, but people were not allowed to touch anything and if a gate were broken or a hut needed fixing, it was done before they went on.

Since the bishop's peace offensive, it had been quiet in the region. But farther south the situation was different. There everyone knew that the Indians were *bravos* – hostile. Here, however, they were waiting until the Indians who were hiding out in the mountains above us should become completely *mansos,* as they called it – tame – so that people would dare pat them as they would good dogs!

We already knew that the Indians were divided into several small groups which the whites had named after the rivers in the region: the Casacará, Socomba, Milagru and others. We also discovered that nobody in the village believed that we had come merely to make friends with the Indians. They understood that that had to be done first before we could get into the mountains at all, but they were convinced we were looking for something very valuable up there. People didn't come all the way down here from Europe otherwise, they reasoned. The foreign señor (El Señor Mister, as they called me) certainly knew something! He had been called *sabio,* a learned man, in the government's letter of introduction, as the good abbot's secretary could testify – even though he had had some difficulty in spelling out the words. It was clear that I had come to search out the country's riches and exploit them.

Several of those who had taken part in the bishop's expedition had collected stones which looked strange, as if they had streaks of what might be gold or silver in them, and now a stream of people came to our temporary home to show us their finds and see if they were worth anything. They wouldn't say where they'd found them, though. Undoubtedly they wanted to be the only ones to profit from their secret treasures.

It didn't help much, of course, to assure them that I was not a geologist and didn't know anything about minerals. How could a learned one not know such things, they asked. Gradually, with the monks' help, we got free of those people. I believe they told the villagers that mineralogy had to come after real peace with the Indians was achieved.

But the people didn't stop talking. Wasn't it true that huge treasures were buried up in the mountains? The old conquerors, and later the revolutionaries, were known to have hidden vast riches somewhere up there. They were convinced that I had some secret instrument with me which would disclose where the treasure was buried.

As a matter of fact, I did know of an authentic case of just such hidden treasure, but I didn't think it wise to mention it just then. Later, I was to make use of my information under other circumstances.

My plan was to continue where the bishop left off and set out gifts for the Indians. Whatever happened, there was no thought of making it a large expedition and I knew there would be no difficulty in getting all the people I needed. Quite the contrary. The bishop's expedition had gone well, and now hidden treasure glimmered in the offing. But I couldn't afford to pay a lot of people either, and I didn't want any but the most trustworthy and fearless I could find. Therefore, I decided to select a few gendarmes. Even among them a large group volunteered, but I selected only two. My wife and child had to stay behind for the time being.

The first thing was to set out gifts of knives, glass beads, and bright lengths of cloth in the nearest fields and villages of the Milagru Indians, which lay at the foot of the mountain about four miles from Pueblito. The Indians would probably come soon as it was time for harvesting their corn. At such times, they used to live for a few days near each field to enjoy eating the fresh corn. Then they loaded their baskets with the rest of the unhusked corn and returned to their cool mountains. The people in Pueblito knew their ways.

I could ride a good bit of the way, I discovered. The others walked. My *mozo*, Francisco, an Indian from the mountains far to the north, took charge of my donkey where the path ended, and waited there for our return. We hoped to be back in the village by evening at the latest.

The weapons we carried couldn't be seen, but their holsters stuck out under the gendarmes' shirts just the same. I had borrowed

23

Esther's neat little Browning, which was easier to hide than my big one.

After a few hours, we reached the cornfield. It didn't look much like one of our cornfields. As usual, the men had felled the larger trees which had pulled down the smaller ones with them, breaking through the lianas and other vines. They had had to chop only a few big trees to bring down half the forest with them, and they then left them all where they fell. Towards the end of the dry season, the Indians set fire to the whole lot. The branches, bushes, and vines are burned up, but the big trunks lie half charred. Between these trunks the women plant the corn, digging one hole at a time and putting a few kernels in each. Corn grows best in little mounds of earth, and the charcoal helped. But to us it looked like any other burned-over forest.

For three to four years the corn would grow well but, as the Indians knew nothing about cultivation or fertilizers, they had to burn down another patch of forest when the earth in one field became fallow. At any rate, they had plenty of forest at hand.

We halted and one of the gendarmes climbed a tree from which he blew a series of blasts on a bugle. It is always safest to announce your approach when you don't mean any harm.

No one could be seen in the cornfield, but we set out our gifts in places where they couldn't fail to catch the eye. We carried on talking and calling to each other as we walked slowly to a group of huts on a little knoll, which we had only just noticed. Apparently there was no one in them either. Approaching them slowly, we saw they were nothing but slanting roofs covered with leaves. I thought they were the Indians' temporary camp, but the gendarmes assured me that they had never seen any better, even in the Indians' villages. If so, I reasoned, their real villages must be very high up in the mountains. After all, no white men had been able to penetrate very far in expeditions and it was probable they had never seen any but these temporary camps.

It was time to go back to Pueblito. To avoid returning to this field for nothing, we knew we must wait several days. It would take quite some time before the Indians came down to collect their gifts – and to leave gifts for us – that is, if they did! However, they had already shown a willingness to exchange gifts, which is always the beginning of a friendship. I knew, nevertheless, that some primitive people never get beyond a so-called 'silent barter', in which the respective parties never get to meet. It might continue that way for another hundred years, too, as far as I could tell.

But this had to be different! Just to come back with a few arrows and baskets would be ridiculous. We had come all this way and we were willing to take any risks, but not for the sake of a few cheap souvenirs. We wanted to study this absolutely unknown culture and, above all, we wanted to get to know these people and make friends with them. We liked Indians and were pretty certain we could get on good terms with them even if they were 'crude, hostile, and vulgar wild men', as one travel book put it.

At least, the Creoles themselves admitted that it wasn't entirely the fault of the Indians they were hostile, but that they too were to blame for beginning the state of war still being waged. I was confident that these 'wild men' wouldn't be so hard to get along with once we got to talk with them.

The older gendarme, Calderón, who was an expert guide, broke into my thoughts: 'The Indians will come today, I think. They've heard us and are probably following us some of the way right now, to see what we're up to. They can move silently in this undergrowth and no one can see or hear them if they don't want to be seen or heard. I'm used to the forest, but I can't tell if there are any Indians around unless I'm riding my donkey.'

'I know donkeys are alert and have a sixth sense,' I told him. 'They've often warned us of jaguars sneaking about. But I didn't know they could tell if Indians were around.'

He insisted, 'They sure can, Don Gustavo, you can bet on that! They get nervous, stamp around, and whinny – just the way they do when they know a puma or jaguar is lurking in the underbrush. I don't know how they can tell the difference between Indians and other people at such a distance – maybe they smell different from us. I guess that's it. I can smell Indians myself but, unfortunately, not from very far away.'

'Ha!' Pedro Lopez, the younger gendarme sniffed. 'You can smell them but not before it's too late, you mean. I prefer relying on my donkey!' Both of them were laughing when Calderón interrupted: 'You know, nobody dared laugh out loud in this forest a year ago. Thanks be to Saint Theresa, protector of the traveller, that no arrows are finding their mark from behind those bushes now.'

'Listen,' I said, 'when we come back to see if the Indians have left any gifts and taken ours, I'll bring along my donkey. The path wasn't so bad that we couldn't clear it for riding. And the donkey can tell us if there are any Indians around, if your story is true. Right now we don't know if they've seen us or even heard our trumpeting and singing.' I pretended not to hear a side remark that maybe they had and had been frightened away permanently.

The gendarmes were convinced, in any case, that our visit had not gone unnoticed. However that might be, the Indians had to come down the mountain pretty soon to harvest the corn which was just about ready to pick. If they didn't come they'd be stupid, because in another day or so the monkeys would have a field day eating it up.

We went back to hot, rotten-smelling Pueblito. My house stood on the outer rim of the village and Francisco and I stopped there, but the gendarmes went over to the plaza where they were immediately surrounded by a group of curious villagers. It was still regarded as somewhat of a sensation for anyone to go to 'Indian country' and come back.

When I walked into my house, I found Beatrice and her daughter installed. We now had two servants!

Francisco had worked for me a long time. An Indian from the Sierra Nevada, he went around in western shirt and pants and could speak Spanish. He called himself a Catholic, although he believed absolutely in the medicine men and other gods of his ancestral religion. In general, he didn't trust white men but he had attached himself to me. Maybe it was because I was so interested in Indian customs and his thoughts and didn't tease or ridicule him for his answers to my questions, as the others did. He was very particular that I should get a good impression of his own tribe and learn about its often extremely odd customs, which he regarded as good and necessary ones.

I bought Francisco's freedom from a plantation owner who was using him like an animal, and I never regretted that investment. Because he was an Indian, Francisco was able to go hungry if necessary and sleep whenever the opportunity arose – but always with one eye open. He never stole anything and, in addition, knew how to put on a packing on a mule better than anybody I've ever known.

Of course, Indians are fine when they're out in the woods, but not so good when they stay in one place very long. They take naturally to a wandering life and their need for freedom never leaves them. Plantation owners down there naturally don't know these things about Indians and aren't concerned about them either. What they want is a good labourer.

To go along on our peregrinations suited Francisco perfectly. Every day he was up before the sun, rekindled our fire and made coffee, which he then brought to us in our hammocks. He also had an inborn distrust of all Creoles, and a particular prejudice against Negroes and mulattoes. When in some village, a group of curious faces appeared in the doorway of our tent or shelter, Francisco always raised his thumb over his shoulder to them – Keep out! it said, and they did. 'They've only come to steal,' he'd tell us.

Francisco understood very well that we were travelling down here to get to know as much as we could about various tribes so that we could tell people back home how they lived. But when his tribe had its big feast, we always had to let him go home to take part

26

in it. We knew beforehand that he wouldn't get back very soon after one of those feasts, but whenever we did need him and sent for him he would walk day and night until he reached our camp – tired, hungry, and a little anxious that he'd be fired this time for sure.

Beatrice proved to be another necessity. Households are primitive and hard to take care of even in the villages. What was more we had run out of our canned goods and had to live exactly as the people did there. Our kitchen was a shed with a fire-place on the ground. Wood and water had to be carried, and corn pounded in a large wooden mortar, then ground into meal between stones.

Every morning the dough was formed into round cakes which were baked on hot coals and were eaten with dried pieces of meat, which were also grilled over the fire. Beatrice's service with the monks had made her especially useful, however. She could cook well and advised us on several culinary matters.

She recommended that we buy a pig – one of the black, long-legged beasts which made the environs of the village unpleasant and often rather dangerous. So we bought one pig and, after it was slaughtered, Beatrice skinned it and tried all the fat, which she poured into bottles. This was the process used in ancient times by the Iberians in Spain and the Celts in France before they learned about olive oil, and it was still going on here!

The meat was cut into strips, salted, and put to dry in the sun. When Beatrice announced that we had more lard than we could possibly use, I became conscious of another of her virtues. She opened her own shop, selling a large quantity of lard at a little lower than the current market value, and made a killing, as the product was somewhat scarce at the time.

One day, Beatrice made some excellent pastries of corn meal and pork, seasoned with caraway seeds, pepper, and pineapple vinegar, which she wrapped in leaves and baked. But the very next day the maggots got in them and, so far as we were concerned, Beatrice and Francisco could have them all to themselves. They were delighted. Washing out the maggots, they ate them all.

Beatrice, too, was used to travelling – she was married to an *arriero*, a mule driver, whom she seldom saw. Their little girl bore the distinguished name Trinidad Gregoria de los Tres Reyes, but was called Trina for short. She was a sweet child, serving as a help to her mother and baby-sitter for our little Sif when we needed her.

Whether we were living in a house or in a camp, we used to build a playpen of boxes on the floor or earth, spread out some blankets and let Sif crawl around to her heart's content under Trina's watchful eye – it wasn't safe to let a baby play on the bare floor or earth where we were. As for Trina, her mother would punish her by hitting her on the head with an iron cooking pot but it didn't seem to cause any ill effects.

All the members of the expedition were collected at our house for a conference. We were enjoying coffee made in a clay pot – coffee the way it should be made. While we sipped it slowly, we talked over our situation and our prospects. We knew it would take time before we succeeded, but in South America you learn patience.

There was only one problem – our supply of gifts was not unlimited and our finances were in the same predicament. Peace missions are expensive, no matter how unpretentious. The monks had no funds for further exploits, and we had to pay the gendarmes we'd been able to round up, even though they were volunteers and it was their job to provide safe conduct along these trails.

The government inspector at the boundary of this Indian territory, whose name was Londoño, was an energetic young fellow. He had long dreamed of collecting all the gendarmes – about thirty – and heading an expedition with these trusty men. That evening he came to talk it over with me. First of all, it was clear that patrolling the roads could not be stopped right away, so that meant fewer men for an expedition.

While we were in Pueblito we had asked to talk with every traveller coming through from the south. There were some Indian tribes along the Casacará and the Socomba Rivers, we knew. Well, some travellers said, the Casacará district was unsafe, but no reports of any attacks had come in for some time. Others told us that the Socomba River Indians were still considered *bravos* – warlike. They had shot arrows into the ground when they caught sight of a couple of cowherds. The latter had fled, yelling, and reached the village completely out of breath. When they could speak, they reported that the Indians had stolen a calf from them.

'It's not completely safe, shall we say?' Londoño remarked to me on the side, and added: 'It is being whispered around that the herders feasted on the calf themselves. But it's no secret the Indians love fresh meat.'

A few days later we decided it was time to go back up to the Motilon Indians' cornfield. We planned to cut a bridle path right through to the field, not so that I might ride instead of walk, but because we needed a beaten track in case we should succeed in becoming friendly with the Indians and decide to set up a base of operations there later. Also, we could test the mules' 'sixth sense'.

They are alert and careful beasts and travellers in South America soon learn to depend on them. As for horses, they are used in the tropics mostly for short rides and they are highly nervous. The mule is a contented animal and best for long trips. They get along even if they have only grass and have to do without their daily corn ration. Then there is their ability to sense danger – not only through their keen hearing and smell but by a kind of intuition which tells them, for example, that a certain part of a trail is not safe. We and many other travellers proved that mules can judge the conditions of a road better than the rider. If it refuses to go ahead, it is wiser to dismount and have a look at the road instead of forcing it on.

Once, when my wife was riding in the Sierra Nevada, she spurred her mule when he balked, refusing to go another step. In the next minute the whole path crumbled under them and she and the mule plummeted down the side of a cliff. Fortunately, neither was injured as bushes and hummocks of earth broke the fall. The powerful Bishop Atanasio had a similar experience during an expedition into the Sierras. He and his donkey rolled down a brush-covered cliffside and survived. The people took this as a matter of course – it was obvious that the saints had held their hands over such a high prelate. But, as my wife was a 'heathen', they were amazed that she survived and regarded her rescue as a miracle. The place where the bishop and all his belongings fell off the cliff has been called *Caida del Obispo*. It isn't certain whether those who christened it 'The Bishop's Fall' appreciated its double meaning or not.

CHAPTER THREE

WE started off for the Indians' cornfield before daybreak to clear a track for the pack mules so that we could get back to Pueblito the same day. None of the men had any great desire to spend the night near that cornfield, and maybe they were right.

It was harder to hack our way through than we had thought. It usually is. Even the most careful calculations get upset here because it is impossible to tell just how long any job will take. We consoled ourselves that the old Spanish conquerors had had the same problem because, even if there had been a trail through there the year before, it would now be just as thickly overgrown as this jungle we were cutting our way through. The Spaniards had brought horses along as well as mules because they found that the Indians respected riders – and it gave the conquerors some advantage over those on foot.

Not only must the path be wide but high enough too. A rider cannot sit hunched down on his beast's neck all the way, even though he has to often enough, no matter how much work has been done by the men going ahead with their matchetes. No matter how slight the incline, the path was so slippery or the stones so loose that my mule fell several times. But I managed to get it on its feet without further misadventure.

It was almost afternoon when we approached the cornfield again. Our arrival was well announced ahead of time by our hacking and slashing at the undergrowth. Then we found that we couldn't get up to the field – which was straight ahead of us – as the mules were unable to get any footing at all. That meant more hours of work, cutting a roundabout path for them uphill all the way. But eventually we saw a clearing and stood once more in the cornfield.

We hallooed in all directions and Calderón blew the bugle which hung over his shoulder. There was a complete silence.

Suddenly, however, my mule began to act up. It whinnied and pawed the ground and was determined to turn tail and go home.

'Don Gustavo,' Calderón whispered to me, 'I think the Indians have come!'

I dismounted, tied the animal firmly to a tree and walked slowly towards the bushes ahead. Calderón, who was behind me, laid a hand on my arm and pointed. On a branch I saw a bow hanging and a quiver of arrows. Further on we caught sight of a basket.

The Indians had taken our gifts and set out theirs – but were they still around there? The gendarmes were sure of it. We got together and shouted a welcome into the forest. There was no answer. Looking around, we saw that the Indians had harvested part of their field but not all. Had they gone home?

Despite the tenseness of the moment, I couldn't help stopping to examine the quiver which had immediately aroused my interest. It wasn't unusual at first glance – a long, narrow cylinder of braided grass out of which stuck a few arrows with wooden or iron heads. What interested me, from a professional point of view, was the fact that, as far as was known, these Indians didn't have quivers for their arrows, and to me this was an extremely valuable discovery. The arrows themselves were carefully fashioned, but I didn't have time to study them there in detail.

We collected in a pile everything the Indians had left for us and went towards the storage shelters, all the while shouting and calling as bravely as we could, although I think our voices sounded a little forced.

The huts stood on a low hillside and could be clearly seen from the cornfield. A camp has to be placed high up so that the rain water can drain off it and its inhabitants won't have to live in a lake. We noticed quite a few more articles hanging on branches around there, too, but saw no Indians and our calls got no answer.

We collected more bows and arrows and also found necklaces of black, red, or green seeds, some distaffs and woven cotton bags, and a couple of pipes with leather bowls and short wooden stems – a good start for my ethnographic collection. But although we shouted ourselves hoarse, no Indians were to be seen.

'They're either not here or they don't want to come out of hiding,' I told the men. 'Whatever happens, we have to think about the trip back. I'm going to set out a few more gifts for them.'

This time I had to be less generous with our knives and axes. The supply was getting low. But I put out some red handkerchiefs and strings of glass beads where they would glitter in the sun.

There was nothing left but to return. While I was hanging some elegant lengths of cotton cloth, which I'd bought from a travelling Syrian merchant, on some tree branches, Francisco went to get the mule.

He came racing back, breathless. 'The mule's gone!' he shouted. It had broken its tether and disappeared and, to judge from its tracks, in the direction of home. There was nothing for it but to descend the path on foot.

'I know it was afraid of the Indians,' Calderón confided. 'It knew they were around there and didn't like being left alone. Maybe it's gone home.'

I sincerely hoped it hadn't because it wasn't from Pueblito but from another village and it would be a nuisance to get it back again. However, after an hour's hike, we suddenly came upon the beast, standing alongside the path, quietly hanging its head in shame. Just as Francisco went up to it with a collection of Indian souvenirs, however, it backed away and snorted like a wild thing. As I didn't have any, I went over and managed to calm it enough to let me mount.

That these animals could smell Indians certainly was no 'old wives' tale', and I had occasion to appreciate their specialized sense of smell more than once. Now, however, our visit was over and I was on my way back to my little family.

CHAPTER FOUR

ALL the time we had been away, my wife had little to do but wait in that far from pleasant mud village of Pueblito. But she hadn't been idle. She had talked to the monks again and to everyone who had passed through from other villages about the Indians to the south, who lived around the Casacará and Socomba Rivers.

As far as the Casacará tribe was concerned, my wife got some valuable information from a few men who had taken part in the bishop's peace expedition. She reported that it would take us at least three days to get even to their first villages as they lived so high up in the mountains, and no one had any advice to offer on what we should do if they didn't welcome us. If they chose to attack, we'd be vastly outnumbered. Even the monks discouraged any plan to meet the Casacará.

The Socombas, then? Officially they were still *bravos* but it was known that, like the villagers above Pueblito, they had cornfields in the lowlands which made the prospect of getting near them less risky. First, however, we had to make contact with the Milagrus.

As I have already noted, I knew that our supply of peace offerings wouldn't last if this silent barter should continue any length of time, but I had an idea. There was nothing the Indians liked better than fresh meat. Why didn't we give them a good animal to slaughter?

My idea was met with consternation. Nobody had ever thought of it, neither the monks nor the Creoles. The Indians were addicted to stealing cattle. On top of that, should one really give them an animal?

'Why not?' I asked them. 'You've told me the Indians used to steal anything made of iron before it was given to them. Now they have so much metal junk up there they can soon set up shop right here in Pueblito and sell axes to you. It's the same principle with animals. If the Indians see that they can trade enough of their wares for a cow, they'll stop stealing them.'

I managed to convince them all. In fact, I overheard one man wonder why they hadn't thought of it before. However, I didn't tell them what I really thought about its working in the long run. The Creoles would soon tire of exchanging a good cow for a mess of bows and arrows, which was all the Indians really had to offer. But the villagers didn't think about that angle. What interested them most was who would be the lucky one to sell me a cow. I was aware that to a foreigner the price would be a good deal higher than its current market value.

For me the main difficulty was not in selecting the animal – there were many offers – but how to get it to the Indians. You couldn't tether a cow out in a cornfield for several days, in case the Indians decided not to show up sooner. There wasn't much for it to eat and, if it got loose, and ate up the harvest, the Indians would be angry and the whole plan a fiasco. Besides, who was to milk it? Most important of all, though, was to figure out how we were to let the Indians know it was a gift unless we were there to tell them so in sign language or in some other way.

I bought a reasonably well fed heifer (which solved the milking problem) at a fairly reasonable price under the circumstances. Now we were ready to start on our second expedition up the mountain. Only a day had elapsed since our first visit. The Indians certainly weren't far away since the corn was still waiting to be harvested.

The news that we were starting off again next day, taking a heifer with us, spread around the village like wildfire. I hired a boy from the mission to help with the animal and arranged that, if we decided to stay overnight up there, I would send the boy back with a message for my wife.

Although I had planned to return the same day, I took along a couple of days' provisions to be on the safe side.

It wasn't an easy job to get the cow (which my wife and I decided to call 'Peace Girl') on its way. The boy led it while Francisco switched at it from behind. My mule was also very resentful of its new companion and the boy from the mission wasn't always very efficient. On the other hand, the forest was so thick on either side of the path that there was nowhere for the heifer to go but forward, which limited any sudden attempt at side excursions. We let the boy and the heifer bring up the rear, following along as best they could while we went on ahead.

The trail was pretty good most of the way and I was able to get my mule to go a little faster. But before I knew it I was so far ahead that I was beyond hailing distance. I called out to the others but got no answer. It was best to wait for them to catch up, I decided, so I chose a spot in the shade of a tree where I dismounted and sat down. The mule found a bush with leaves it liked and that kept it busy quietly nibbling.

As I sat there thinking things over and trying to protect myself from the stinging sand flies, I watched endless columns of leaf-cutting ants marching along, each with a piece of a leaf flying like a banner over its head. These parts of South America are infested with stinging, biting, flying, crawling things. No matter how hot it is – and it's cooler at the Equator – people could still live here comfortably if it were not for this plague of insects against which you have to wage a continuous battle.

There they marched – the leaf-cutting ants – carrying their green flags. At their sides marched the warrior ants with huge jaws, ready to protect them. We often had to take precautions so that they wouldn't get into our supplies. When we stayed any length of time in one camp, we tried to smoke them out or blast their underground fortresses with a little gunpowder. But the results were never permanent. All the energy of this heavy tropical growth was needed, though, to repair the damage these ants did to everything that bore leaves. They ravaged any growing thing and it was small comfort to know that when the fat female ants swarm they are good to eat. They really are delicious and taste like honey, even though they are not particularly nutritious.

At last my little caravan hove in sight. When they saw me sitting staring at the ground they thought I had lost something. To be interested in watching ants was something they couldn't understand. As for myself, I knew a good deal about Indians but precious little about ants, and had been enjoying myself.

'Don Gustavo,' Calderón said, when he finally understood what I was doing, 'as a learned man, tell us how we can get rid of these damned bugs. They eat up all our fodder. It makes me sick just to look at them.'

But I couldn't tell him what to do. There weren't so many ant killers available then as there are today. He spat some tobacco juice into the nearest marching column, which stopped its progress temporarily and brought the 'soldiers' running from every direction.

The gendarmes looked very sceptical when I told them that the ants used the leaves they cut to cultivate mushrooms. I recognized that look. It was the same I had seen when I told them that cows in my country live in houses with glass windows. Here there was just one window pane in the whole village and that was in the mayor's house. One gendarme pointed out that the ants didn't have anything against a nice bit of cloth and they certainly couldn't use that to make mushroom beds of.

It was odd. It seemed as if the ants couldn't distinguish between leaves and cloth. If you're unlucky, they'll eat your mosquito net. Calderón had lost a mantilla he bought for his girl that way. He had spread it on a bush to dry after a heavy rain, on the way to see her, and that was the end of it.

'The worst of it was,' Calderón went on, 'my pal liked the same girl. He'd bought a big, gaudy kerchief for her. But the cloth was too thick for the ants. So the girl got the kerchief and my pal got my girl.' It was perfectly natural to Calderón, incidentally, that the girl's decision should hang on a gift.

Now Francisco spoke up and said they had been worried about my getting so far ahead of them. We hadn't thought about Indians up to that point but now the gendarmes, very politely but firmly, forbade me to run any more risks. Giving my promise, we started off again up towards the cornfield together.

As we got closer to the clearing, calling out as we went along, my mule stopped suddenly. It planted its small hooves firmly in the moss that covered the trail and refused to budge. It could mean only one thing. The Indians must have come!

I left Francisco to look after the animal, which once again showed signs of wanting to get away from there as fast as possible, and the rest of us went cautiously – but noisily – over to the field, shouting and singing at the top of our lungs. For my part, I chose our Students' Song, which young Swedish students sing when they pass their exams. I can't carry a tune but it didn't matter. Neither could they. The main thing was that we made our presence known.

The field was deserted but it was obvious that the Indians had been picking corn very recently. There was a basket full of cobs and, on top of it, a pair of woven straw fans such as they used to fan a fire and which later became very popular with white people.

Calderón whistled suddenly and pointed. Behind the bushes over by the camp huts we saw painted faces watching us!

Staring out at us through that green jungle, those Indians looked terrifying. Their sharp arrowheads glittered where the light struck them. I recognized those big arrows which could fell a man in an instant. We already had several of them which the Indians had exchanged for our gifts.

We just stood looking across the clearing – stood there, silent for once, our hands at our sides. Something had to be done.

I grabbed some exchange gifts. This time I had brought along a Swedish army knife with polished brass trim and a temporarily shiny blade. Drawing it out of its sheath, I swung it in the air so it would shine in the sun, then thrust it back in the sheath and threw the whole thing over in the direction of the huts.

We heard a murmur go up from behind the bushes.

Trying to keep an eye on them, I took one of the Indians' baskets and began to pull out long fringes of glass beads – the kind which were then used at home to trim lampshades. I had had to give a lot of them to the Creoles since they considered them too beautiful to give away to the Indians. As it turned out, the Indians didn't like them as well as other things – they preferred beads less gaudily coloured!

Nevertheless the bead fringes glittered enticingly in the sunshine and it was obvious that they had made an impression on our audience for, as I looked up, I saw that the Indians were now standing up. Slowly they came out from behind the bushes, their bowstrings held taut by arrows steadily aimed in our direction.

There were only men among them, dressed exactly and looking precisely as had been described; just as I had expected they would look. Their faces were painted with red designs, their hair was cut short and they wore long, sleeveless shirts of some course material. Each one was holding a fistful of arrows and I saw that their bows were quite straight and flat, like long rulers.

I suddenly remembered that I had heard there was one Indian word which they all understood – *Yacano* or *Yacuno* – meaning 'friend'. I was fairly sure it was the right word because the same word is found in several Caribbean languages and means someone close, a relation. Even in our country we call good family friends, 'uncle' and 'brother'.

I called out *'Yacano, yacano!'* as loudly as I was able while, at the

35

same time, Calderón blew a loud whistle on the muzzle of his gun, as one can by blowing on the open top of a bottle.

Suddenly the Indians began throwing away their weapons and calling out to us in their language. The risk of a clash between us seemed to have passed.

It still looked as though the Indians were not going to come any nearer, however. If only that blasted cow would get there, I thought, then we could take the initiative. As it was, I felt it wise to withdraw a little and go and get the cow, leaving the Indians, meanwhile, to pick up their presents and get on with the corn-harvesting.

Somehow we had to let them know that we would come back later in the day. We had to use sign language.

I stepped forward and pointed to myself and my followers and showed them how we would go away and then come back when the sun – I pointed to it – was down on the horizon. I indicated the gifts and got the idea across, apparently, that there would be more. Next, I tried to tell them about the cow – that we would be bringing with us a four-legged animal. Gendarme Pedro Lopez played the part of the cow and did it very well – an animal that said 'moo' and had horns on its head and milk in back.

The Indians laughed uproariously at our efforts, a good sign. In fact, I was encouraged to do a short pantomime myself, showing them how they should slaughter and eat it.

I hoped they understood and wouldn't go away but wait for us to come back. We could have stayed and waited for the cow but it could still take a good long time before it arrived and, in any case, we should help the boy with it.

I also had a feeling that this first meeting should not last too long. Just as I was withdrawing, walking backwards so that my back would not be turned on the Indians, I stumbled and fell. I must have looked ridiculous, but this time the Indians did not laugh.

Francisco had been having a bad time with the mule which was very nervous. Seldom had that placid beast shown such eagerness to get away from there than at that moment.

We found that the boy, with 'Peace Girl' in tow, hadn't got much beyond the spot where we'd left him. Evidently he had been resting as much as he'd been walking. Nevertheless, we all got under way again – that is, all except the mule which resented any idea of returning to the cornfield so strongly that Francisco had to remain behind with it.

Shouting and hallooing all the way and urging on the heifer, we at length reached the field again. There was no one there!

'They've picked all the corn,' Calderón said, disgusted. Pedro Lopez pointed to a group of footprints. 'The women have been doing the harvesting here,' he said.

It is indeed the women's job to bring in the harvest. They had probably been in the background the whole time, waiting until we left to come out and get on with their work. Now they undoubtedly were on their way home, climbing up to their village on the mountain.

If so, where were the men? We went over to the huts, dragging the cow with us. We sang and blew on the bugle. There was a small plot of grass in front of one of the huts where the cow could browse. Leading it over there, we tied handsome ribbons on its horns and hobbled the poor beast. If the Indians didn't come and get it, I knew we'd have to take it back to the village as I couldn't afford to buy another one. I knew, too, that a jaguar could get it even before the Indians did – if they really had gone home as it appeared.

By that time we were very hungry. We made a campfire in the cornfield and put on an aluminium cooking pot we'd brought along, full of that everlasting soup they make here – *sancocho* – into which you put everything you happen to have at hand.

We wondered as we fixed our meal whether the Indians had misunderstood us or thought we were joking. It was something we had to take into account. But then, it always takes time and patience to make contact with *indios bravos*.

Our heifer had mooed several times. Possibly it felt lonely. But, if any sound could entice these savages out of hiding, that sound could. It certainly had never been heard up there before. Little 'Peace Girl' was, in fact, quite restless. Our one mule, on the other hand, was relatively quiet for once, thinking perhaps that any sound it made might bring back the Indians.

We had just sat down around the soup pot with our bowls and spoons when Calderón grabbed my arm so suddenly that some of my soup slopped over on him. Without a word, he pointed with his thumb.

The Indians had come back! They were hiding in the bushes.

We got up slowly and waved to them. They waved back. I saw seven at first, then more. Suddenly they caught sight of the heifer and stood stock still staring at it.

I called out with wild gesticulations and pointed to the cow, then to the Indians, and tried to explain to them that they could eat it.

They understood. They all flocked around the terrified animal, which tried to break away from them without success. I shall never forget their shouts of glee as they started off with their gift.

Then quite suddenly they stopped and turned back, rushing straight towards us with wild cries and brandishing their weapons. But their grimacing faces were wreathed in smiles and their actions were like children's around a Christmas tree. They threw their arms around us, hugged us ecstatically, and a couple of them gave me

37

their bows and arrows. Now they were pulling at our clothes and pointing up at the mountain, shouting 'Inca, Inca!'

I have since learned that that word means 'go'. At the time, I knew it could hardly have anything to do with the Inca Indians but it was clear, at any rate, that they wanted us to visit their village. Our friendship had been established!

We naturally had to accept the Indians' invitation. The goal of our entire expedition was to get to know them in their own habitat. I was very glad, too, that neither the gendarmes nor Francisco (who had joined us after quieting the mules) were afraid. They thought it would be exciting, which simplified matters considerably.

Nevertheless, it was now late in the day. This time the Indians had the cow to drag along and from there on up I knew we couldn't get very far before nightfall and would have to spend the night in the forest, for I certainly didn't want to do any climbing in the dark. It would be better for us to set out at daybreak.

I explained to the Indians that we wanted to sleep first and start when the sun was up again. I put both palms under one cheek and, with my head on one side, indicated sleep. They understood. Then, pointing to the mud huts and then to us, they gave us to understand that we could follow them early next day. I gathered that they planned to depart immediately – and we were just as thankful because they would be taking the cow off our hands. We had reached the point where they otherwise would have had to take it off in butchered sections.

As the Indians, with 'Peace Girl' resisting every step of the way, disappeared into the forest, their happy cries gradually died away.

As soon as we finished our fairly cold soup, I wrote a few hurried lines to my wife on a page of my notebook, telling her the eventful news and begging her not to worry if we were away three or four days. Then I tore it out and gave it to the boy from the mission. He was overjoyed at being free at last to get away from there, a feeling the mule shared, so it probably wouldn't take them long, I figured, to spread the good news.

The days of silent barter were over. Now we were about to get to know the Indians and their world!

CHAPTER FIVE

I DIDN'T see any reason for mistrusting the Indians. Their invitation could hardly be a trap. For security reasons, they simply wanted to get to know us in their own villages where we four men would be completely in their hands.

Nevertheless, we had to take the usual precautions during the night, so the time was divided into watches and nobody got much sleep.

We were up before dawn and, after having coffee, divided what was left into thermos flasks. I had sent back the aluminium pot with the boy so that we wouldn't have to give it to the Indians. This was not a lack of generosity on my part. It was dictated solely by the fact that it was the only one in Pueblito and we needed it. Maybe, I thought, we could exchange it later for one of the Indians' pottery pots when we got to their village. I knew they made excellent ones.

As it was, we had to take along my camera and film, blankets, exchange presents – hunting knives and axes – a little medicine kit and food supplies. The latter had to be cut to a minimum but I was certain the Indians would provide us with some food, at least. Just the same, the packs were heavier than we had counted on. It couldn't be helped, even though these tropical mountains covered with jungle are the world's worst terrain. We learned that soon enough!

The tracks of the Indians and 'Peace Girl' were very clear. At first the forest was low but very dense, as it had been around the cornfield. There were signs that the cow had been hard to manage and we were glad we were rid of it.

This was the trail the Creoles used to take in the days when they tried to raid the Indian villages. Gradually, the forest changed, the growth became sparser. But instead of being easier we found the tightly grown thickets hard to get through and, in the cracks of the huge blocks of rock which were strewn all over, more bushes were growing.

'This is a bad place,' Calderón told me 'You see that block of stone and bushes? That's where the Indians lie in ambush and that's where one of their arrows killed old Crispin. He—'

I interrupted Calderón by asking him about the trail up the mountainside. I didn't want the gendarmes swapping tales about bloodshed, which would make Francisco's hair stand on end, and their own as well when they really got warmed up.

When I had got all I could out of Calderón about the trail, I changed the subject to discuss our behaviour during our visit with the Indians.

'If they haven't changed their minds,' I said, 'and receive us as friends, we must do more than be friendly in return. We are responsible for the entire population of Pueblito. If we can gain and keep their confidence, everybody will be grateful to us.'

As I spoke, I heard the sound of rushing water and soon we came to a river. Here the trail ended but we had to get across the river somehow. It had a strong current but was not very deep. The water was clear right to the bottom, which gave it a brownish colour as it cut through the green walls of the jungle.

In some trees on the other side we caught glimpses of pretty little grey animals whose ability to jump through the air seemed incredible. They were spider monkeys, the most agile of all the inhabitants of the jungle. Huge, gorgeously plumed Arara parrots flew over us, screaming insults at our intrusion of their forest, and toucans with giant curved beaks, hurriedly flapped away from us, only to return to look us over again as their curiosity overcame their fear. There, in the sunshine, life was burgeoning, while in the jungle shadows, it seemed dead.

We waded across the raging river, the water up to our armpits, holding our guns and packs over our heads. It was really better walking along the river bed, hard as it was, than to scramble out on the opposite bank. We had to watch out for snakes and try to keep from bumping into the enormous ant hills or hitting the low Palosanto trees (which are protected by angry ants). Just the same, no matter what we did, we couldn't escape the attacks of countless little insects.

Once on the other side, we crossed a ravine, balancing on a fallen tree that lay across it, and forged our way through the thick leafy jungle above our heads – only to find ourselves back at the river bank! We must have crossed that river six or seven times – I lost count – but at last we reached the line where the moor-like country began and where the steep climb started. We shouldn't have been able to follow the river any longer anyway as it became still wilder up there, casting itself off ledges in thunderous cascades of white spume to its bed scores of feet below.

The Sierra de Perijá have summits almost 12,000 feet high. Fortunately, we only had to climb to about 3,000 feet as we knew, from having seen them from below, that the Indians had their homes and fields at about that level.

We soon realized that we had undertaken a project more difficult than our most pessimistic counsellors had foreseen. Now we had to hack and force our way somehow through a living barricade of tropical growth. Thorny branches and sharp leaves left burning sores on our arms and legs. We had to drag ourselves up the slopes by grabbing roots or branches which looked firm, since the ground under us was mostly loose moss on which we had a hard time getting a foothold. Insects attacked from every direction and we were so busy with our hands already that the ticks and sand flies got a good grip on our necks and backs without our being able to do anything about them. Swarms of sand flies rained down on us leaving bloody wounds, and the sharp grass we were struggling through left unpleasant sores which we were to discover took a long time to heal.

We crawled more than we climbed or walked. We had to make detours around the Bactrix palms and watch out for the vines as we scrambled through them, just to make sure they *were* vines. Although I am not at all a nervous person, the memory of that red flower, which almost came alive in my hand, hadn't left me. And I couldn't help thinking that the Indians knew an easier way to get to their village. But from all the signs, this was the Indians' own trail. They had a gift for wriggling through anything, I knew, and they could tunnel their way through jungle undergrowth like weasels. As none of us could do that, we were forced to cut a completely new trail for ourselves.

The sweat poured off us in salty streams and we had to sit down and rest fairly often. Once we reached the 3,000-foot level, the forest began to thin out and we came to a little rise covered with bracken ferns as tall as we were.

Now it was easier to climb. The horizon was wider and far below we saw the pale yellow savannas, grey villages and green *curúa* palm plantations. In the distance, too, snow-topped peaks of the blue Sierra Nevadas glittered in the sun.

I was sure now that we couldn't have much farther to go. We began to halloo once more, with what breath was left in us, while Francisco banged a spoon on his aluminium cup. We rested a while, got some more air in our lungs, then shouted again, all together, and we waited . . . listening.

Yes! there came an answer – from very far away it seemed, but when we climbed another knoll to have a better look around, that response suddenly seemed much closer.

In the next moment a half-dozen shingled heads rose up out of some clumps of fern. We hailed them in one voice, although I heard one of my followers draw a big scared breath before he joined in.

With bows and arrows raised in both hands, the Indians were now running towards us. But they were not attacking for, as we were relieved to see, the first thing they did was to hand them over to us and indicate they wanted to exchange them for knives. I figured they must already have quite a store of knives by that time, but thought perhaps they wanted to be prepared for some future emergency. Whatever their motives, our friendship was established by this exchange.

When the Indians had put away all the knives, they immediately picked up our packs and started helping us up the rest of the hill. In another moment we found ourselves standing in the centre of their village.

Their huts were the most primitive I had yet seen. They were more like what we would call wind-breaks – just sloping roofs with-

41

out walls, held up by four posts – identical to those we had seen in the cornfield, which I had thought were only for storage.

We were exceedingly tired. The effects of the suspense as well as the climb were beginning to tell on all of us, and our hosts seemed to appreciate our condition for they literally forced us down on braided rush mats, which they had spread over piles of bracken fern.

As we relaxed, I had a chance to look more closely at these warriors and their women. Squatting on their heels in a semicircle around us, the children peeking out from behind their mothers' heads, they were studying us, too.

On close inspection, the men did not look as fearsome and reserved as they had on first sight. They were mostly young men with frank, childish faces, and the garish painted designs on their faces, instead of being frightening, now made them look rather comical.

The women, too, were young and had lovely figures as well. Nevertheless, I noticed that my followers were greatly embarrassed – the 'civilized' people in this Catholic country are confirmed prudes – for the dress of these 'wild' women seemed to them much too scanty. It consisted of only a brief loin cloth and a short cape over the shoulders. These capes interested me particularly as they seemed identical to those worn by primitive groups in other countries. But these people had no means of communication with any other group. The capes accented the women's nakedness which, in my opinion, was as delightful as their complete lack of false modesty. The women also wore necklaces of black and red seeds and jaguar teeth, a few wearing so many that they covered their breasts.

When the Indians had tired of looking us over, they brought us bowls of a bitter kind of beer, made from corn and almost as thick as porridge, and some cooked yuca roots, served in the leaves of the plant. When we had finished eating, the men picked up our packs once more. It was clear that we were to go on still farther!

Along the way we were drenched by a sudden shower which left us so chilled that our teeth were chattering by the time we saw a fairly large village ahead. I was relieved when we were shown to a hut which we understood we should have to ourselves. As a fire was already burning in front of it, we lost no time in peeling off our wet shirts and pants and laying them out to dry. Every move we made, of course, was watched intently by our hosts – men, women and children alike.

There were older men and women in this village. They kept to the side lines, but they showed us no ill will and were delighted to trade small objects with us. I remember wondering what memories they had of ravaged cornfields and burned villages, of children killed by the white people below. Was the 'savage' perhaps to teach *us* something of Christian forgiveness?

42

Fires were burning outside each hut. The men lit them from torches made of some kind of resin or pitch-soaked cloth wound around the ends of long sticks. In the early evening the women and children went to bed on their rush mats while the men sat around the fires and talked and began to sharpen the knives we had given them on sharp, flat stones in the firelight and the light from the torches.

We felt a little uneasy and couldn't sleep because they carried on with their knife-sharpening the entire night. I was certain there was no implied threat in their work – they probably were glad to have something to do as they kept watch, while at the same time enjoying their new acquisitions. I believe they figured that it just wasn't smart to sleep when your arch enemy was in your house. True, a truce had been 'signed,' but caution is a necessary virtue when dealing with crafty white men who know so much and have so many things to give away, like nuts to monkeys, and those other things that flash and bang when they kill.

I myself was unable to sleep either, but for other reasons. I was so covered with bites, scratches and cuts that I shouldn't have been able to get to sleep even if all the Indians had gone to bed. My shirt was in rags and my whole body ached and burned. Maybe the others had tougher skins than I did but, in any case, we all nearly froze that night.

The day broke clear and peaceful. I could see now that the village lay on a high hog's back behind which, to the east, the blue mountains towered to the sky. Otherwise, we could look out in every direction over the forest-clad slopes which gradually disappeared into a pale grey mist as far as the eye could see. Farthest off the mass of the mighty Sierra Nevada loomed like an immense shadow. Even as I watched, the snowy caps of the highest peak shimmered only for a few moments before dissolving like a mirage.

Suddenly I felt very hungry. The village had come to life with the first daylight. It was still chilly and the women got busy fanning the fires until they flamed up. Some children ran back and forth, playing ball with pieces of fruit tied to strings. As they worked around the fires the women laughed and even flirted with us a little, continually looking up at us with coy, sidelong glances, then quickly looking down again and giggling.

As I listened to their soft speech, it seemed full of flat 'sh' sounds and very different from the machine-gun Spanish I was used to. It occurred to me that, as each word was spoken so slowly and clearly, they were making an effort to help me understand what they were saying. After a while, however, I realized that they always took a lot of time to say what they wanted to say to each other. After all, they had all the time in the world, unlike the 'civilized' Creoles, who chatter like magpies.

43

At that point I knew nothing of their language but I began my lessons right away with my morning coffee. We borrowed a little pottery cooking pot from the women to make our coffee in, and let them taste it. They spat it out, laughing shyly, even though we had taken pains to put in a lot of sugar before boiling it. In no time, they were all laughing at our coffee-cooking as if it were a big joke. Only after a few minutes did I understand why. Indian men never do any cooking. That is women's work. The men are allowed to roast and broil food but, even so, when one of my men wanted to roast an ear of corn and placed it in the hot ashes of a fire, one of the women quickly dragged it out, showing her indignation in every way she knew how. Apparently corn should never come in contact with fire. I made a note of the fact but couldn't help thinking they were missing something good – in fact I felt *something* should be done to their corn. It was not like any other I had eaten anywhere.

We noticed, too, that they shared their food and drink – just one of the many indications I have noted of a primitive communism among the South American Indians which we were to have an opportunity to study more closely on future visits. We already realized that, as their guests, we were going to be spoiled. They pushed corn cakes wrapped in leaves and barbecued birds' legs at us. We tried to reciprocate with food from our knapsacks but not very successfully. The only things they liked were my English biscuits. They would take neither meat nor roasted yuca roots, and let us know it by making ugly grimaces.

We tried to figure it out. My followers regarded it as quite impolite. After all you don't let somebody think the food he's offering you is bad. That was the way they reasoned, at any rate. Only later did I understand that the Indians couldn't eat our food because it was salted. They were among the few people on the earth who had never tasted salt. On the other hand, they used the usual red Indian pepper generously. I also saw them season their food with a mixture of ashes and lemon juice.

There were other things which I expected the Indians to have but which, to my surprise, they lacked completely. I saw no hammocks anywhere. That truly typical Indian bed didn't exist there. Everyone slept on plaited mats laid over soft piles of bracken fern. Nor had they stools to sit on such as neighbouring tribes had made for themselves.

Another thing. I remembered that no dogs had barked at us as we approached the village. And then I recalled that in this part of the continent the pure-bred Indian dogs are dumb and can't bark. Not only that – our Indian friends had no dogs at all. I made a note to bring a dog along on our next visit as a gift to our hosts –

there were so many miserable mongrels in Pueblito. (And we did present them with a dog later, but with unexpected results. On a subsequent visit, the dog had disappeared and we found that they had eaten it.)

By this time, most of the men had set out on hunting expeditions and also, probably, to announce our arrival to their friends. Those who remained worked busily on their arrows. These had pipe-like shafts – a piece of wood and a tip of hardwood or steel. Before the Indians got bits of iron and steel, bone arrowheads were common and I was delighted when, a long time later, I was able to get hold of one of them. I got it from an old man, the only one who still knew how to make them. Now the Indians have plenty of metal, some of it stolen from the white people, and a good deal from various 'peace offerings'.

I got to thinking. These Indians had never associated with white people. How had they learned about working metals? They weren't very good at it but, just the same, some of our knives were fast becoming well-honed arrowheads. They sharpened a knife on a flat stone, hammered the blade with a smaller stone and carried on sharpening and hammering in that fashion, with a seemingly inexhaustible patience. Stone Age techniques applied to the age of metals – a difficult and unbelievably long process, but it worked.

Gradually, and very late in the same day, the point begins to take on the right shape for the head. Finally, a hole is bored in the thick end, it is placed in the shaft and then bound fast with a strong twine which the women spin. The ends of the twine are then braided back along the shaft in various beautiful designs. (The Indians were delighted at my interest in their work – we had got to understand each other so well by that time they could make perfectly clear to me that the designs they wove were those of the backs of various snakes.)

All the Indians in this part of South America of whom I had any knowledge had used poison on their arrows in former times and some of them still did so. These Indians didn't use poison but they liked to use a second or third time arrows which had hit their mark, believing that they would be sure to find their target again the next time. As they are stained with old blood, they readily cause infections, so the Indians may have figured it was unnecessary to bother with poison. Besides, they were all excellent shots.

It was strange to witness a culture such as this – pure Indian in essence but with iron as its principal element. Worked on by these pre-Iron Age people in their own way, iron was hammered cold and sharpened as though it were stone. These 'savages' had replaced their original knives of bamboo shoots with the white man's steel.

They had also learned how to use axes. In fact, they had needed some so badly they had recently stolen a few more. I saw one or two old axes lying around, so battered that hardly more than the hole in the head remained of them.

Only the largest and heaviest arrows are of steel and these are reserved for large, wild animals, including men. The others are often made of soft metal. Small bird arrows sometimes have tin heads, hammered from tin cans the Indians have scrounged from the lower villages.

Their spears were their most prized possessions and therefore the most difficult to acquire for my collection. The head and shaft were joined by a cord which was rolled upon the middle section somewhat like a reel on a fishing rod. When the head caught fast in some animal's flesh, the cord held the wounded beast, preventing it from dashing into the underbrush before the hunter could get to it. Oddly enough, they did not use this system for fishing. The wooden-headed arrows had rows of barbs and I saw bird arrows with a whole cluster of little arrowheads which had the same effect as birdshot when they hit their mark.

I shall not tire the reader with details about arrows. My little band was also interested in them, however, and admired the Indians' patience in their handiwork, but of course their interest did not match mine.

All the Indians had now carefully washed their hands after their noonday meal and gone immediately back to work making more arrows or braiding fans and quivers or making leather cases with covers in which to keep tobacco and knick-knacks.

It is generally believed that the men in a primitive group do the least possible work, leaving most of it for the women. But here, the men took on the heaviest jobs. They cleared the jungle, sowed and planted, built huts, hunted and fished. At home, they were continually busy making bows and arrows, rugs and bags of knotted yarn.

The work of the women in a primitive culture is always tedious. They must harvest and prepare the raw food the men bring in. Grinding corn into meal for bread and boiled dumplings is hard work and takes time.

For clothing, they spun a kind of cotton thread with the help of a simple distaff hung from a rafter, the thread running through a ring fastened in the roof. In one hut, a woman was weaving on an ingenious loom. She was making the material for a man's costume – a sack with holes for head and arms – and a cape, for herself perhaps. The material was strong. It lasts for years despite the wear it gets in the forests where branches and bushes tear at everything. It is also good protection against thorns and insect bites. My ragged

46

shirt and painful scratches were witness enough to the inferior work-manship of the Machine Age.

Along the whole chain of the Andes the Indians have always worn clothes, while those living in the hot lowlands often go naked.

I had to take off my shirt. My back itched so that I was certain it was covered with ticks and when I asked Francisco to have a look, the Indians, not least of all the women, stopped everything they were doing and stared as I pulled it over my head. They wanted to see how a white man looked 'inside'.

Now they had become so accustomed to us they were no longer shy. They crowded around me as I sat there, trying to reach my back. In the end, it was the women who dug off the ticks, not Francisco. And they were skilful workers, apparently used to the job, because you have to pull off the whole insect and not leave the head in the skin as it causes serious inflammation. We usually doped the ticks with alcohol or oil and I was ready to offer a little from our only first aid kit. However the Indian women did the nasty job without it.

After one enterprising girl licked her finger and then touched my body to see if the light colour was real and not painted on, they became braver. Others passed their hands over my shaggy chest, letting out little surprised squeals. Then they pulled up the legs of my pants to see if my legs were white, too. That I also had hair on my legs seemed to fill them with consternation.

The girls – the only ones taking part in this game – had a fine time. They had found a new plaything. I was just a little anxious that they might carry their investigations too far. If they had, it would be I and not they who would have been embarrassed.

Fortunately some men arrived just then, yelling and shouting as they displayed their kill – a monkey and a woodcock. The little heifer 'Peace Girl' had long since been consumed. I had seen its hooves and a few less delicate parts hanging up to dry – the remains of the feast. Meat must be eaten up all at one time, even if you almost burst – that is the custom of all primitive peoples.

As the men approached, they made excited gestures to us indi-cating that we should follow them, apparently to another village. I gathered from their pantomime there would be a feast and singing and dancing.

I had foreseen that we would have to keep on the move during our stay up there. For one thing, the inhabitants of the other vil-lages wanted to see us. They also thought it was safest if we didn't stay too long in any one place. Each village should be able to share in the responsibility in case anything went wrong, of course. Not only that, but each wanted to entertain us in turn.

The Indians are always hospitable when their confidence has

been won and they do everything they can to make a guest comfortable after their fashion. Now I gathered that all the preparations had been made in the next village.

The hunters threw themselves on the ground to rest a little and have a smoke. Out came the clay pipes with wooden stems, and the men were beginning to fill them when I brought out a big bag full of the small home-made cigars which the Creoles smoke, and divided them among the men. They were delighted. Each wanted to try this new kind of smoke. And everybody smoked, men and women, too. The children were also given a puff, even those who couldn't yet walk.

'Smart kids,' said Francisco, as he watched them. In his village no one was allowed to use tobacco before he was married. How customs vary and what strange things shock us!

No one smoked a whole cigar by himself, I noticed. The Indians were so polite they handed a half-smoked cigar to the next one, just as they passed their pipes around. As soon as I laid aside my cigar, an Indian girl grabbed it up and stuck the wet stump into her mouth, then passed it to her neighbour. Fortunately, she was healthy-looking and very charming. Anyway, in the wilds, one is not so sanitation-conscious and a lot of our 'civilized' worries seem a little silly.

We now drank up the last of the sour corn beer. I found that it didn't matter to me at all that one of the girls had chewed the mash and then spat it into the bowl I was drinking from. The beer was refreshing just the same. It had not had time to ferment so it wasn't intoxicating, for which I was grateful. The Indians were all gay, giggling and teasing each other. Probably they were showing their relief at finding that their white enemies wanted to make peace with them.

After a bit, we all got up and began climbing once more. The high ferns soon gave way to more forest and the Indians were very helpful. They carried our packs, cut back bushes and branches in our path and held out their hands to help us up.

My followers weren't very happy about handing over their packs at first, but I reassured them. I was convinced that the Indians were sincere in wanting to be polite and helpful. As it turned out, we never lost a single item of our personal belongings during all our visits with them which, incidentally, is generally true of all independent, 'uncivilized' peoples.

When we arrived at the next village, which was much bigger than the one we had left – there were twenty huts – we saw that it was set on a height from which the forest had been cut back. The inhabitants crowded forward to meet us. They were very gay and noisy and patted us all. Their faces were brilliantly painted and from their antics I wondered at first if perhaps their beer had fermented. But it wasn't ripe yet and their childish gaiety was entirely sober.

The women approached carrying calabash bowls of pale violet-coloured corn 'soup'. Their corn is not yellow but has many-coloured kernels, with red predominating. The 'soup' was served from a huge wooden cask shaped like a canoe, which stood in the middle of the village. There were a good many foreign bodies in the brew but our hostesses thoughtfully fished them out with their fingers before handing us our bowls.

Two incidents occurred here. First, Francisco got a shock and then I got one.

Good old Francisco couldn't help showing the Indians how to use an old pair of scissors of which he was the proud possessor. He clipped a piece from his shirt, which was just as torn as mine, and made a bandage of the cloth for a cut on his leg which was bleeding. The Indians were fascinated with the scissors, to them a completely new tool.

Just then, a little girl asked Francisco in sign language to let her borrow the scissors. Francisco always had a hard time resisting a pretty girl's smiles and teasing so he handed them over, even though he never let anyone else touch them. The girl tested them on a rag she found, but they didn't work very well. The scissors were dull and she hadn't learned the knack of using them. A man came over to help her and succeeded so much better than she that he decided to keep them. He handed Francisco a basket in exchange and was about to leave with his prize, obviously believing they had been offered as an exchange gift.

Francisco became furious and dashed up, demanding his property back in Spanish as well as his own version of several Indian languages. The man didn't understand what was going on until Francisco grabbed the scissors from his hand and threw the basket in the Indian's face. The latter retreated, looking very angry.

I hurriedly told Francisco to let the Indian have the scissors and promised to give him a new pair when we got home. As I was talking, I saw Francisco suddenly go pale. The Indian had returned and was coming straight towards him, a bow in one hand and arrows in the other. Looking grim, he drew the drawstring and shot an arrow right at Francisco's feet. My friend jumped a foot and a half into the air, thinking his last moment on earth had come. In no time he handed over the scissors and just as quickly received the bow and arrows in return.

The Indian had only played a joke on Francisco, I learned, with a sigh of relief. I have often noticed among other tribes how they like to tease each other – aiming carefully and snapping a bowstring without releasing the arrow, then laughing their heads off as they watch their 'victim' run. I knew, too, that often when Indians visited others, they would shoot an arrow into the ground right at the foot of their guest, in an original sort of greeting. But I was not sure how our new friends might react to conduct they did not understand.

Later I saw Francisco's cherished treasure. It was no longer a pair of scissors. Its new owner had taken it apart and was using both pieces as bores to make holes in his arrowheads.

It is difficult for people not accustomed to them to shoot with the flat, straight bows the Motilon Indians use. Francisco was a good shot with most kinds of bows. In his tribe they were merely toys, however, just as they are at home. But he didn't get anywhere with this bow. The Indians laughed as he tried to draw it taut. To be fair to Francisco, I have to confess that I later took some of the Motilon bows to other Indians, who are known as excellent shots, but they couldn't do anything with them either. In the Motilons' hands, nevertheless, a big-game arrow shot at close range can go right through a man.

The second episode occurred while I was trying to learn something about the language. The Indians understood perfectly what I wanted and tried to help in every way. It amused them immensely when I tried to pronounce words after them. After a good many misunderstandings, it wasn't long before I caught on to several things, but what I thought meant 'What is this called?' they understood to mean 'What is this used for?' Sometimes, the answers were so lengthy that I had to start over again until I got the idea across.

Everybody helped, enjoying the proceedings hugely. They made jokes and roared with laughter when I missed the point. The lessons certainly weren't very serious and several times I was the butt of their teasing. One interesting sidelight to me, however, was that there didn't seem to be any vulgar words in their vocabulary and, when we named all the parts of the human body, there was no self-conscious snickering. They apparently believed in calling things by their right names.

The women here, too, soon began to examine my skin, evidently having got the idea from the women in the first village. But as they pointed out various sections of my anatomy and told me what they were called, they also found the little holster and pistol in it which I carried and which had escaped them up to that point.

There was nothing for it but that I take it out and show it to them. But I did so with some misgivings, as carrying a concealed weapon might easily be misinterpreted.

They knew immediately what it was. 'Pong, pong!' they yelled. Then they made defensive gestures which said, 'Don't shoot!' Their ability to express themselves to someone who didn't know a word of their language was indeed remarkable in its simplicity. But they were still play-acting, I was glad to note, and remained just as happy and child-like as before, not taking seriously the discovery of my gun.

I drew some pictures showing them that I had it to shoot monkeys and birds with and they seemed to understand. It wasn't difficult for me to choose such fictitious game because at that very moment the monkey and the birds were being grilled over a big fire on a spit-like frame made of hardwood called *barbacoa*. This is the same wood used by Indians in the North American South-west, the ones who originated the present-day barbecue.

The sight of the monkey, small and thin as an undernourished war orphan, lying stretched over the coals, brought back the same cannibalistic visions I had experienced at El Jobo's ruins around the steaming kettle out of which the monkey's hands had waved.

According to legend, these Indians had been rugged cannibals. But neither then nor later was I able to find any truth in statements I had heard that they usually ate their dead enemies. On the other hand, they did admit that a neighbouring tribe – and they emphasized that it was not theirs – sometimes ate one of their older citizens when they were completely out of food. Nevertheless, the Motilon Indians do belong to the Carib tribe or Caribans, whose name is the root of the word 'cannibal,' meaning those who eat human flesh.

The day passed quickly and that evening there was to be a feast. Again I was grateful that the corn beer had not had time to get very strong. No one could foresee what might happen if these people got even a little drunk. I had had some experience with drunken Indians before and these were genuine wild warriors, after all.

When under the influence of liquor, the men always fight. I was already clear on that point as most of them had long scars on their heads. When I asked how they got them, the men showed us how they acted, reeling and snarling at each other until finally they brought their bows down on each other's heads. As these were made of the heavy Bactrix palm and had sharp edges, they made serious cuts which could put a quick end to a warrior's career.

But I also noted their pride in these wounds, similar to that taken by German students in the old days in the sabre scars on their cheeks. The Indians shook their heads in sympathy because I didn't have any scars on my head – they evidently thought I should have some but I secretly hoped they'd forget all about it. Fortunately, the Indians got neither drunk nor into the mood for fighting that night.

Both men and women gathered around the central clearing where

the beer cask stood. Then two men appeared carrying what looked like a couple of big axes with long, heavy handles. To my great surprise, the men raised the axe blades to their mouths and began to play on them. The blades were mouthpieces for a kind of flute and were blackened with pitch. The deep sounds came from the hollow wooden handles. The musicians also danced as they played, taking long strides, then turning quickly back again.

All of us, after having been lined up in a row, danced too. I was dressed for the occasion in an Indian cape I had just acquired and my hosts had carefully painted my face and chest. We slid bows over one shoulder, holding them with our hands while we danced forward and back, forward and back, singing, 'Nay, Nay, May, May, May, May, Na, Na.'

Sometimes the women lined up behind us and, during a pause, they put on a kind of solo exhibition. There were pan-pipes which were passed from one to the other, each woman blowing a few notes on it as she did some dance steps. Francisco was quick to learn the Motilons' dances, which were very simple, and he also tried their flutes. He was very musical and confided to me that the Indians couldn't play well at all. It appeared that they had the same opinion of his musicianship.

Several of the older ones happily joined in the dancing but one old man half-lay a little to one side of the fire, braiding a fan. He was very sick and had a frightful cough. From time to time he inhaled the smoke of a plant which he believed would help his chest, but it seemed to me that the smoke must irritate his throat still more. I went over and sat down with him. His name was Quiycio and he was making the fan for my daughter. The Indians all knew by that time that I had a little girl and that my wife had stayed behind down in the village.

The old man was so sick that he would soon die – both he and the other Indians made that fact clear. I knew that I shouldn't see him again when I came back the following year, as I hoped to do. And, as it turned out, it was much longer than that before I did get back.

Long before the next visit, however, evil befell these happy people – the first to have made contact with white men. Luckily neither they nor I knew it then as we danced in the soft, warm night by the light of the fires and torches. I gave old Quiycio some opium and that was one night he was able to sleep without coughing.

The following day we were to go on, a good idea for several reasons. I wanted to see as many villages as possible and it still wasn't wise to remain too long in one place with the natives of these wild mountains.

The women stayed behind this time. The men picked up their baskets, which they carried on their backs after placing the wide band attached to each across their foreheads. I had seen the women do the same.

Many of the Indian women were very well built and had a certain charm, and we had already discovered that the men were jealous. It was prudent, I reminded my followers, to watch their behaviour; some of the girls were real flirts. The men understood the risk, fortunately, and in their own interests were very polite, patiently resisting every advance and turning away from some very real temptations.

When you are out climbing with Indians you never know when you will arrive at your destination. You can't be fussy even if they waste four or five hours along the way. If they saw the tracks of a buck or a wild pig, they had to follow it. One scrambled up a tree to tease a monkey down, another stood and stared at the top of a huge old tree. Sniffing the air, he then began to climb to the top of it after a cache of wild honey. We soon saw him high above us, his arm half-way inside the trunk and surrounded by a swarm of angry bees. But there was no danger. For some reason, South American bees seem to be the only insects on the whole continent which do not sting.

The Indian came down after a while and offered us sweet-smelling honey, which he served in a little bowl he made of some leaves. It had a delicate aromatic flavour.

Nevertheless, our whole company was broken up, what with tracking animals, hunting and collecting honey. Hunting is difficult in this area as it is so easy for animals to hide and get away. You have to be patient, a good woodsman and scout, able to move quickly and silently in the jungle. The Indians are all these things and it was fascinating to watch them. To facilitate their exploits, they had built shelters here and there in the trees, like big bird nests, from which they trapped birds and monkeys. Farther on, we came upon similar low cupola-shaped hunting huts on the ground.

The boys from the village had come along with us and were much in evidence. One of them sat behind a curtain of heavy vines, waiting for a huge ground rat to come out of its hole. Others had camouflaged themselves with leafy boughs and were hunting small birds. They were very skilful in handling their small bows and their arrows always hit their mark.

When our little band was collected once more, with no other treasure but honey, the boys remained behind, later to go home with their catch to their mothers who would help them roast whatever it happened to be.

Before we reached the next village, we passed another cornfield where the women had just finished harvesting the basketsful of ears which they were swinging up on their backs when we caught sight of them. They walked on, bending under their burdens, not paying any attention to us.

We were warmly greeted in this village as well. They were expecting us. Several of the women were already busy grinding corn and they continued the job all night by torchlight. The men, too, stayed awake all night. Only the children slept, stretched out on their mats, completely oblivious to the lights and murmur of voices.

The Indians had a good supply of corn. They had large fields because, like the majority of South America's native people, their livelihood depended on agriculture. Hunting and fishing were only side lines. They move about more than most farmers do planting their fields on different temperature levels of the mountainsides so that the harvest will fall at different times during the year. They also seemed to have some understanding of letting fields lie fallow and 'rest' a season or two. Most Indian corn grows well in the mountains but the so-called sweet corn (Mandioca) which they called *yuca*, thrives best in the damp lowlands.

A woman was preparing a dish from *yuca* roots and I stopped to watch. She crushed the roots between two stones, then packed down the meal in a calabash bowl with water, finally surrounding the thin bowl with red hot stones. The contents quickly came to a boil. After a few minutes, she removed the bowl and set it to cool. Later, when she invited me to taste it I found that it didn't taste like much of anything but was undoubtedly a good source of starch.

By this time our supply of exchange gifts was completely finished. Extra shirts and such things were all gone and we had left only what we stood in plus my camera equipment and, of course, the little collection of valuable curios I had acquired. Nevertheless, we still had so many packs that it would take several men to carry them – much more than we could handle by ourselves.

The Indians had been so kind in helping us that I hoped they would be willing to go along with us to the cornfield where we had first met. Now we must go back and, when I told them so, they solemnly nodded. And they did go back with us the whole way to the cornfield, carrying our packs for us and lending a hand every step of the way!

The climb down was more difficult, if that were possible, than getting up there had been. But at length we reached the old cornfield where, not so long ago, we had felt chills running up our backbones when we had caught our first sight of the painted faces of these 'savages' staring at us out of the dark forest.

We were still putting our packs of collectors' items under the old shelters around the fields to protect them until we could come back

54

and pick them up when our Indian hosts and guides took off, shouting and waving their farewells. We all waved back and as I did, tired as I was, I could not help wishing that what we call 'civilization' would spare these happy, very charming people. And in some respects, as I discovered on my later visits, my wish was fulfilled.

CHAPTER SIX

ALTHOUGH the gendarmes preferred to remain overnight – they weren't the least afraid of the Indians any longer – I wanted to get along even if it meant coming home after dark. Francisco went with me.

We arrived just as the sun was going down. I went straight to our little house and called out while still some distance away. As it was on the outskirts I didn't have to go through the village first to get to it. No one answered me!

I walked faster but, even before I got to it, I knew the house was empty.

My heart was somewhere in my throat. What had happened?

Looking around quickly, I spotted the old woman in the next house just as she leaned from a window, a long *calilla* cigar in her mouth.

'A-ha. Don Gustavo! Welcome back. Eh, your family will be happy you're home,' she called to me. 'They've moved. Come here you little brat,' she then snarled at a small child. 'Get along now with Don Gustavo and show him where they are living.'

Calling out and with the child walking ahead of me, Esther saw me first and ran to greet me. Yes, we had moved and she had a story to tell me, all right!

'One night while you were up there with the Indians,' she began, 'we had a terrible tropical storm – thunder, rain, everything. That little palm-roofed mud cottage was just about to blow away.' She stopped to catch her breath as we walked along, arm in arm.

'A corner of the roof fell in and the rain poured in so fast the walls started to crumble on that side. And if that wasn't enough, we felt some earthquake shocks,' she blurted out.

'I had taken Sif into the hammock with me and covered us both with the raincoat. When I heard Beatrice and that child of hers, calling out and crying in their house, I went over there. Our floor was a lake but, fortunately, even though her roof was leaking everywhere, the walls held.'

She stopped to catch her breath and was able to laugh over the whole thing when I told her, 'Now we know why our guest house had stood empty until we arrived.' I was grateful things hadn't been worse.

My wife then told me about the new place she had found but added: 'The first night we slept there it was so hot I put the tent bed right by the window. In the middle of the night I woke quickly when I heard heavy breathing. Guess what it was?' she laughed. When I looked at her not knowing what to expect next she relieved my worst fears. 'The warm muzzle of a cow which was contemplating eating my hair! It does look a good deal like straw, I'll admit. Oh, for some good soap! But when the cow saw my face, she was more scared than I was. Maybe's she's still running.'

Esther stopped laughing and looked at me seriously. 'Next time you go to visit those Indians,' she announced, 'I'm going with you!' I didn't answer right away, but I knew she usually did exactly what she wanted.

After I cleaned up, I went over to the monks' house, where the greater part of the village's inhabitants had already gathered to hear an account of our visit. In one corner I found Francisco holding forth and displaying a gift for fantasy I had not credited him with.

Both the monks and the mayor wanted me to get the Indians to come down to Pueblito, but it didn't interest me very much. In fact, it could be quite a risky experiment, but I promised to see what I could do.

As things developed, I was to spend more of my time from then on with the Indians than in Pueblito. My men and I liked the Indians and also preferred the cooler air up there in the mountains. Also, I no longer had any qualms about taking Esther along. The visit had to be a short one though, because of the baby. She was weaned by then but still needed her mother's care. The nuns agreed to look after her.

CHAPTER SEVEN

THEIR delight knew no bounds when the Indians met a white woman for the first time. She could do things with them which I had not been able to – going with them to the cornfields, collecting wild herbs with them and studying their ways of doing things, something it was impossible for us men to do. Needless to say, it was decidedly undiplomatic for a man to show the slightest interest in the womenfolk of an Indian village.

The Indians felt they knew us so well by that time that they began to invent games. One which they noticed I enjoyed, too (my part was very comfortable) worked like this: Someone called my name as loud as he could. No answer. The Indians said to each other the equivalent of 'Gustavo far away.'

The next time they called, I answered very faintly. They would look at each other: 'Aha, Gustavo *is* far away.' When they called the third time, I shouted in a thundering voice: 'No, Gustavo is here!'

They always howled with laughter over this simple game and we had to play it over and over again.

It was about this time that they discovered that Calderón's front teeth were false ones. Like most people in the lowlands, he had lost almost all of his teeth but he was very proud of his plates. The Indians had certainly observed his displaceable set of teeth on pre-vious occasions but now they felt we were such close friends that they wanted explanations about absolutely everything. So Calderón had to show them how his teeth were put in, both uppers and lowers – they didn't fit him very well, I noticed. It wasn't long, how-ever, before he tired of the Indians' inquisitiveness. In one gesture he took the whole set out of his mouth.

The Indians gasped with astonishment and even more so when he returned them to his mouth and they saw that his teeth worked just as before. They made us understand that they thought the idea was a practical one although the Indians, for their part, had excel-lent teeth.

Next, they got the idea that my wife and I could take out our teeth, too. When we told them we couldn't, the Indians carefully pulled at them until they were convinced that they would remain fast in our jaws. However, as a result of their experiments, I noticed that Calderón had assumed increased importance in the Indians' eyes because of his unique appurtenances.

There are many tales about the impressions false teeth or a glass eye have made on primitive people, who regard these as tokens of witchcraft or magic. I was interested to see that 'our' Indians had much more practical views about such things. They seemed to think that Calderón was a lucky fellow, really.

When I talked to the Indians about coming down to Pueblito with us, they were extremely pleased and demonstrated their plea-sure in every way they knew how. After all, a white woman had dared to come up to visit them. Why shouldn't they make a return visit to the white people's village? It was agreed.

Quite a crowd of men, women and children started out with us, but the climb down naturally took some time. In fact, we spent the night at the cornfield where our first peace overtures had been made. Once there, I sent Francisco on ahead to tell the monks what to expect next day.

The group which finally approached the village with us was

considerably smaller than that with which we had started down the mountain. Several of the Indians had disappeared along the way. Others, more cautious, remained behind in the cornfield.

So it was that Esther and I entered Pueblito followed by about twenty yelling and whooping Indians, fearsome-looking, to be sure, but at that moment behaving very much like a class of children given an unexpected holiday from school.

We were met *en masse* by Pueblito's citizens. The people did not exactly throw flowers in our path but the Indians were nevertheless showered with tobacco leaves and cigars, which they certainly appreciated a great deal more.

As we walked along, several Creole ladies joined the parade and hastily pulled old cotton dresses over the heads of some of the Indian women to cover up their 'shameful' nakedness. The Indians, completely ignorant of the high purpose which motivated these gifts, danced around a while in their new attire, showing off like little pigeons. Then, tired of their play, they tore up the dresses and made bundles of rags for future use as diapers, perhaps, or bandages or mats.

A meal of cornmeal mush with unrefined sugar on it was waiting for the guests. The mayor made a speech, which seemed to please him a lot more than anyone else, then the guests took off with a simple finality which left something to be said for a serious review of our more boring civilized adieux.

In less than an hour they had seen all of Pueblito's sights worth seeing. And I had to agree that there were many more interesting things to see in their own villages.

One of the Indians, however, whom we called Toshibo and who had rather attached himself to me, wanted to stay overnight with us, so I agreed. I wasn't sure that he had understood that it was all right, though, as he went off hunting in the afternoon. But he came back later, lugging a huge tortoise he had captured.

I had not let anyone know he was staying at our house as I wanted to avoid having a crowd of curious people hanging around all night. Toshibo crept in softly that evening and we made him at home.

Before he lay down on the straw mat I had placed outside our bedroom door, he handed me an axe, a knife, a couple of handkerchiefs and a few other objects he had collected during the day. I took them, understanding that he wanted me to take care of them for him because he was, after all, in an 'enemy' camp.

Next morning, Toshibo called me at daybreak, got his belongings from me, and took off for the mountains. I stood in the doorway watching him, the tortoise tied to his back, its legs wriggling helplessly in the air.

On my next trip, I experimented with using Toshibo as a messenger, but something happened then which I had not counted on – my wife's consternation when she went to change Sif one morning and found a war-painted Indian sitting on the floor playing with the baby on the straw mat. She managed to control herself and watched him for a few moments as he carefully fingered the child, then held up a small toy, played with it himself and handed it over very reluctantly when Sif demanded it loudly – in fact, at the top of her lungs. The crying did not frighten him from his mission, however, for when my wife greeted him, he said my name and handed over the dirty bit of paper on which I had written my message, all the while sitting with his bow and arrow held firmly on the floor with one foot, as every warrior of his tribe had been taught to do from time immemorial.

He stayed only a moment after eating a good meal and taking along a few presents for both his wives. He was married to sisters, which occurs now and then among the Motilons. His visit had proved an important point, at any rate – it was an assurance that the Indians considered that a state of peace existed between them and the people of Pueblito. The little cow, 'Peace Girl', had not been sacrificed in vain!

CHAPTER EIGHT

THE rainy season was fast approaching. It would make further trips up the mountains impossible for a couple of months. Other considerations also made us begin to think about getting back to Sweden. One complication was that there was a war. We didn't know much about it as news trickled rather slowly through the jungle. It was 1915 and we understood that fighting had been going on in Europe for about a year.

A second problem was that we had no passports – such things hadn't been necessary in the uncomplicated world we had left before the war. But before we started packing up for the trip home, we wanted to make a try, at least, to reach one or two more of those groups of Indians nearest us who still had not attained friendly relations with white people. Primarily these were the Casacará and Socomba people we'd been warned about.

We had discovered that the Socombas' villages were the easiest to get to and were near a village called Becerril, on the plain below us. Besides, we needed to have some of those village people with us if we were to succeed in another peace expedition.

Our Motilon friends didn't think much of the idea. They warned us that the Socomba were dangerous and shot at anything they saw.

They called them *Yucuri* (we found later that the Socomba called themselves *Yuco*), and told us they were cannibals. To illustrate their point, so that we would be sure to understand, they caught a few of their children who were playing around, and pretended to eat them right under our eyes.

The Socomba or Yucos were supposed to live along the Maraca River which passes through Becerril. And, from what I was able to learn from our Indian friends, these were tribes whom white people didn't even know existed.

There were, of course, many Indian settlements in those mountains. But were they of the same tribe and could they understand each other? As no one could answer my questions, I was more determined than ever to find out.

Even today I might add, however, we aren't certain. They killed each other off to be sure, but had they also intermarried or had other contacts with each other? Most important, would they attack white people 'on principle' before giving them a chance to explain their invasion of these silent, mysterious mountains?

The only way to get the answers was to find out for ourselves. But 'our' Indians had told us something else that set my imagination on fire. They said that their fathers used to go to a 'big place' towards the east – which meant that it had to be in Venezuela – called Manastara. It was the first time we had heard the name and I couldn't find it on the map either.

It occurred to me that the Indians might lead us there but they said they couldn't go there any more. Apparently their fathers had got into trouble with other tribes over there and they were now *non grata*. However, they gave us vivid picture descriptions of Manastara, showing us how huge the 'city' was and how it was surrounded by water.

I knew right away that we had to go there, crossing this unknown chain of mountains from one country to the other. What adventure! But could we really do it? Not right then, at any rate. So much was certain. And if 'our' Indians couldn't come with us, I didn't see how we could do it at all. One thing was clear. We had to come back, see our Indian friends again, and try once more to persuade them to help us to achieve our dream.

At that moment, our financial situation would let us make only a few more limited forays. We decided to go to Becerril and get to know the Socombas.

The expedition was quickly outfitted – the two gendarmes, Francisco and Beatrice and only one pack mule were to go along this time.

The trail was very beautiful. The belt of forest along the rivers and the open grassy savannas, where here and there clumps of

60

curua palms shot out of the fertile soil, made wonderful contrasts. One would expect to find herds of wild animals grazing there or see broad ranches and plantations. But we saw no living thing – man or beast – except for the screaming little monkeys darting about the treetops and the flame-coloured parrots who screeched their protests against our intrusion of their paradise. Indian raids had decimated the population in the entire area. The survivors had fled.

When we reached the Sicarare River we called a halt and went to work on our meagre food stores. I sent out the gendarmes after the meal to see if they could find any traces of Indians. It was just about here that the bishop's expedition to the Casacarás had once camped and, even though I knew these Indians lived too high up in the mountains for us to get to them, I thought they might somehow have got word of our approach. But as the gendarmes found no signs that any Indians had been around there for some time, we collected our gear and went on.

Several people had warned us about the belt of forest which covered Monte Espina – the spiny jungle. But we got through it with remarkably little trouble. It was just getting dark when we reached the first human habitation we had seen – a cattle ranch called Latio. There were still a couple of miles left before we could reach Becerril and, as we didn't much want to get there after dark, we gratefully accepted the invitation of the elderly lady who owned the ranch to spend the night at Latio.

She was quite a character. We learned that she had stuck it out there all those years despite threats of Indian raids. They had killed one or two animals but otherwise had left her alone.

We asked if she hadn't been nervous at all during the time she had lived there.

'Well, once in a while,' she told us, in her high, ladylike voice, which she couldn't have used to another living soul for almost the same length of time. 'But,' she said, philosophically, 'you learn to get used to 'most anything, you know.'

Next morning, after thanking her and leaving a few of our precious supplies in return for her hospitality, we started off once more and reached Becerril just before noon.

It was a terrible place – a clutter of miserable mud huts where a handful of mulattoes eked out a bare existence, though it was difficult to see how they managed even that. There was nothing to eat, neither root vegetables, corn nor meat. All we could find were tobacco and coffee. I had to send back one of the boys to Latio for some cheese while another rode south to the neighbouring village of Jagua, where he managed to get hold of some *yuca* roots. After that, we lived on *yuca* and cheese, which got a bit tiresome after a few days.

Meanwhile, the mayor had sent for two guides, old grey-bearded woodsmen who, if one was to believe their stories, were covered with scars from their battles with the Indians. They told us that they'd be glad to go along with us – the pay was all right with them, too, I gathered – but only on condition that we took more people along with us. If we weren't a bigger party, they insisted, the Indians would be tempted to attack us.

I told them that, as far as I was concerned, the whole village could come along, even though a quick mental reckoning warned me that our few remaining funds would be wiped out if they did. As it turned out, I didn't have a thing to worry about on that score.

Early next morning, the whole village was aroused by beating drums – that oldest of ways to call the clan together. The mayor's secretary then read aloud a formal decree stating that, with the permission of state and church authorities, an expedition to the Socomba Indians was authorized and would volunteers please step forward.

There was no great rush from the ranks, to say the least. Although a few men came over to talk about it with me, none of them signed up. On the other hand, just as in Pueblito, the people were very much interested in hidden treasures and the rich gold and silver ore they'd heard should be buried up there in the mountains, and they were eager to learn more.

As I have already noted, I did know of one such treasure, some-where along here, according to two Spanish historians who had carefully documented their information. As the story might arouse some interest in our expedition, I resolved to tell the people of Becerril about it:

'Right here in 1530,' I began, 'the hard-bitten old robber whom the Spaniards called Alfinger (his real name was German, Ehinger), was laying siege to this area and plundering the whole valley. He had stolen masses of gold bracelets and necklaces from the Indians and he always won battles against them, chasing them before him with his cavalry as they retreated in disorder. The Indians were afraid of horses,' I reminded them, 'and didn't dare stand up against such cavalry attacks.

'As soon as he conquered one Indian tribe, he made the chief hand over all his weapons. Then he made them give him every-thing they had made of gold. The Indians didn't mind that so much – they preferred iron, really – but they were angry when he set fire to all their bows and arrows and clubs.

'Finally,' I continued, 'old Alfinger had so much gold that he couldn't drag it along with him. So he decided to send it on ahead over to Venezuela where he had his headquarters.'

I paused in my story and noticed a growing interest among my listeners, who nodded vigorously, urging me to go on.

'Well, about twenty men volunteered to take the treasure over the mountains,' I told them. 'They were tired of the heat and the bloody battles, they said, but they really intended to get away and divide up the loot among themselves.

'Off they went with a whole line of Indian bearers ahead of them, chained together with rings around their necks. If any one of them collapsed under his burden, the Spaniards simply cut off his head.' I heard gasps flutter across my audience. 'It was quicker than stopping the whole caravan to release the bearer from his iron collar,' I explained.

'What the Spaniards hadn't counted on was the kind of ground they'd have to go through – these woods and jungle-covered mountains. You see, Alfinger had come down from the coast in the north and had only to cross the lowlands. But all of you here know how hard it is to get through these forests. On top of that, they couldn't find anything to eat.

'First they were soaked in sweat in the steaming jungle, then about six thousand feet up they nearly froze to death and their breath came in short gasps.' A few of the older guides nodded knowingly, as if they remembered.

'But,' I continued, 'the Spaniards went on, even though their food was all gone by that time. The forest was so wet they couldn't make a fire to get warm and they were so exhausted they could scarcely stand up. But it was too late to turn back. They knew what lay behind them all right. The only thing they could do was go on if they didn't want to die right there on the spot.

'In order to go on, though, there was one thing they had to do,' I told them and waited for some reaction. But my audience was already way ahead of me. 'Yes,' I said, 'they couldn't carry the gold any farther. So they decided to bury the treasure where they stood. They chose a place at the foot of a giant *ceiba* tree, so tall they were sure they could find it again. But it was as though they had buried their hearts with it, they were so reluctant to leave the spot.

'Struggling on, they were starved to the point where they killed the Indian bearers who had managed to survive that far, and ate them. Then they couldn't agree on which direction to take, got separated and eventually died – all but one, a soldier named Martin. Some friendly Indians found Martin and took him to live with them.

'Some years later, when Alfinger and his men finally came through that way, they were frightened by a war-painted savage who halted them suddenly, aiming an arrow directly at Alfinger's heart. But imagine their surprise when he hailed them in Spanish! 'Me, I'm

Martin!" he called out and I'll wager they had a hard time believing him.

'He'd become just like the Indians – had a wife and children up there in the mountains. But he got permission from the Indians to go along with Alfinger, after he was promised some of the gold if he helped the Spaniards find it.

'With a Spanish officer and sixty men,' I told my listeners, whose patience and interest encouraged me a good deal, 'Martin set out to keep his promise. But, after all kinds of hardships and wandering around, he still couldn't find the right tree. By that time the whole band was so sick and exhausted that everybody climbed back down the mountain to Alfinger's headquarters and Martin, who was homesick for his wife and family, went back to his Indian friends.'

I wanted a breather and a short smoke but my listeners wouldn't let me stop. Apparently I'd built up more suspense than I'd reckoned with. I stretched myself, then continued.

'Well, another Spanish troop came through there some time later and took Martin along with them as a kind of hostage but also because they said they didn't think it was right for a white man to live with Indians. They really hoped he'd remember where that tree was, I imagine. Once, Martin escaped from them. But they finally captured him and sent him so far away he never found his way back to his family again.'

It was quiet for a few moments. Then one of the old guides spoke up: 'That's just what I figured,' he said. 'It isn't just Indians this learned *hombre* is after, *amigos*. He knows where that gold is!'

I hurriedly explained, as the murmur of concurring voices got louder that, before we could even think about buried treasure, we had to make friends with the Indians.

Several men in the crowd agreed and the clamour was getting livelier every minute.

Taking advantage of the temper of the crowd, the mayor then put in his two cents' worth and finally, after a lot of argument, seven men actually agreed to go along with us. We decided to get started the very next morning before they had a chance to change their minds.

That evening, when things had calmed down a little, an older man whom we had met before at the lean-to (where for lack of anything better we had had to make our headquarters) came up to me, a bottle in his hand. Behind him trailed a sullen-faced youngish woman.

The old man explained that he was embarrassed that a foreign lady should be going out to meet the Indians when no local woman dared or wanted to make the trip.

'They aren't used to walking any distance,' he told us. 'But I have something here which is just what will make her strong enough to accompany your wife. I bought it at a real pharmacy,' he put in, 'and if this girl drinks it all she'll be strong enough to go,' he said, a little anxiously, it seemed. 'What do you think, Señor?'

I took the bottle from him and smelled the contents. It was cod-liver oil!

The girl was the type common enough in such villages. She had never walked farther than to the stream to get water. I had such a hard time to keep from laughing that I hurriedly told the old man that this medicine took a long time to work and that it would be better if the girl waited to join us on a later trip if she felt strong enough by then.

With remarkable speed the girl turned and started off for home, the heels of her ragged slippers slapping her dirty bare feet and her long skirts stirring up little clouds of dust behind her. Her whole bearing showed her relief in having escaped the forest and the Indians.

The man lingered on a few moments, however, but as he, too, turned away, shaking his head, I heard him say, 'I wonder what kind of tonic that foreign lady takes that makes her so strong!'

I thought to myself that a little get-up-and-go wouldn't hurt most of the people in that village. It could have been quite a flourishing town if they had bothered to make peace with the Indians. As it was, it was falling to pieces, a sort of open grave they'd all bury themselves in sooner or later.

CHAPTER NINE

I HAD hoped that the men would be willing to go along unarmed but they said they didn't dare leave their guns behind. In that case, I had to let the gendarmes take theirs as well.

The trail led through the forest – what trail didn't? – but it was fairly well cleared. Just the same, time and again we had to wade across a river. A continuous rain had soaked us through right at the outset of our little expedition. The river was cold, the air hot and heavy.

In all their forays into the Sierra de Perijá, white men have always followed the rivers. Of necessity they must set up camp on a river bank and it is often easier to walk along a river bed than to force your way through the undergrowth along its banks.

We got off to a late start but nowhere along the way did we see a trace of Indians.

'Tomorrow!' said the guides.

We spent the night on the river bank after the men built five shelters out of palm leaves, which took them only a half-hour to complete. These leaves can be as watertight as a tent but the speed with which ours had been constructed was perhaps responsible for the fact that it leaked considerably over just about every spot on which we tried to put down our sleeping bags.

While we were eating our *yuca* soup flavoured with salted cheese, one of the guides told us that the previous year, in exactly the same spot, fifty-six armed men had set up a fishing camp. At certain times of the year, the catch here was excellent he said, and this was one of them. I found myself dreaming more about eating a fresh fish than listening to the story the man was telling, until I heard him say, 'Just after the fishermen had spread out along the river bank, arrows started whizzing over their heads and then one of the men fell flat on his face in the river, dead!'

A hush had fallen and all eyes followed his hand as he pointed – 'Right there!' The spot was about two feet from where we were sitting.

'Another one got it in the leg, over there!' the man said, in what I thought was a rather studied tone of voice. But he went on: 'When we got collected, we went over the place, every bush and tree, our guns ready. But we could only find traces of two or maybe three Indians. No more.'

'There, you see?' one of the gendarmes interrupted. 'It doesn't make any difference how many we are.'

This conversation was decidedly unfortunate, I decided. Several of the men were already casting furtive glances behind them and I was convinced they would grab their guns at the slightest rustle or movement. I found myself thinking that this could be a decidedly dangerous peace expedition.

A few of the men sat up all night around the campfire, which in itself was a wise precaution. The others, however, seemed to be having bad dreams, for they mumbled and cried out in their sleep now and again. Needless to say, I, too, was one of those who remained on guard.

It was still raining. We tried to use the palm leaves as umbrellas but they didn't help much. As our packs were reduced to the barest necessities – the men wanted to be free to run fast if they had to – we didn't even have a change of clothing.

When we came to our second camp site, I noticed that the men were more particular in building the shelters, however, and I was probably right in thinking that their last experience had taught them something. They seemed to like the place, too. Here, they said, you could settle down and fish and raise cocoa trees. Such trees

66

thrive in a warm, damp climate and no one could ever deny that these forests filled those requirements.

I reminded them once more that they could only realize such ambitions if the Indians were peaceful. But they were so keen on the idea that they wanted me to name the future colony right then and there. It must be a holy name, they insisted, so I gave them our Swedish patron, St Birgitta, whom they called Santa Brigida. It seemed to satisfy them although the thought crossed my mind that our friend the bishop would doubtless claim the place for Bridget, that saintly lady from Ireland, if he ever heard about it.

As things turned out, it didn't matter. No colony was ever established and the Indians themselves are gone. Another fate awaited them.

Our camp was really quite comfortable. The palmleaf huts, like big beehives, stood in a semicircle, their entrances all facing the camp fire in the centre. We hung our lanterns directly behind three of them. The Indians would not dare come within range of the light, the men assured us.

As one of the guides had shot a big fish with a bow and arrow, our supper that night was a decided improvement on our usual *yuca* soup. We had no plates. We fished out the vegetables and whatever else was in the pot with our fingers. My wife and I did have our own spoons, though. The men drank their soup out of cupped leaves.

We had to sleep on the ground even though there were as many millipedes as ants crawling around. But, rolled up in our damp blankets, we were fairly well protected.

The next day, the march began exactly as before but this time, after a short time, one of the guides held up his hand suddenly and we all came to a halt. Grunts – a terrific racket – then a herd of wild pigs charged through the forest, leaving a putrid stench in their wake.

Fortunately, the men had enough self-control to keep from shooting one of them – it was certainly hard to see all that fresh pork disappear into the jungle, I had to admit – but the sound of a shot was not advisable at that point if we were to succeed in convincing any Indians lurking around of our peaceful intentions.

Now we began to see signs of Indian life. Slabs had been cut off the trunks of several black palms, the wood they use for bows and arrowheads. They had evidently hacked at some of the thinner palm trunks with stones, then broken them off with their hands. Finally we came upon footprints – fairly fresh ones, too. As it was still raining and tracks quickly wash away, they must have been made very recently.

Suddenly ahead of us we saw three camp huts of the usual type. I decided it was time for us to announce our presence. So the gendarmes and I took up our old cry of 'Yacano, Yacano!' as lustily as we could.

The men from Becerril, however, remained absolutely silent. What was more, they were hiding behind tree trunks and bushes. I had to tell them to come out of hiding or the Indians might think it was an ambush.

'Oh, no,' they whispered in tremulous voices. 'It's the Indians who are lying in ambush. We aren't budging an inch from here. Oh, no Señor! You may believe we mean what we say.'

My wife and I decided not to waste time arguing with them so we both went on ahead with the presents in our hands, yelling 'Yacano!' at the top of our lungs. After us came the gendarmes, without their guns. But when we reached the huts, they were empty.

After looking around, the gendarmes built a little lean-to of palm leaves opposite the huts and carefully hung up all our exchange gifts inside it.

There was nothing for it this time but to go back. I had to admit that we just didn't have the right men with us for an expedition of this sort. But I did plan to come back, at least, to see if the Indians had been there and taken our gifts.

My wife was riding on ahead. She had the best mule and always liked to set the pace for the caravan. It also took some time to straighten out the packs on the other mules. So I stayed behind to give the men a hand, which gave her still more of a head start. Of course, she knew as well as I did that no one should travel alone in that area without an armed escort. But she liked to listen to the forest, she told me – to the woodcock's cooing and the screaming and chattering of the monkeys as they played in the tops of the trees.

Suddenly, far ahead of us and looking as though they had sprung from the earth itself, stood a crowd of Indians – painted faces, bows and arrows, everything – right in her path!

Were they the Socomba we were looking for? No, she thought, they couldn't be, but they might very well be Cascarás. Not that it made much difference what they were called. None of them looked particularly 'tame'.

'I asked myself what I should do,' she said after it was all over. 'But I got no answer.'

Then it came to her, that wonderful word, 'Yacano!' She called it out over and over and the Indians understood!

They were very much puzzled, nevertheless, to hear a word in their own language spoken by a white woman on a mule in the middle of their forest. They began to jump up and down, calling 'Yacano' back at her and a lot more words she didn't understand.

'If only I had something to give them,' she thought. But all the gifts were hanging at that moment in a palm shelter which seemed very far away just then.

Suddenly she found a safety pin, one of those big blanket pins, bright and new. She held it up and motioned the man, who seemed to be the leader, to come and take it. As he did so, slowly, her mule bucked and whinnied but she held on and somehow managed to show the man how to use the pin, first pinning it to her shirt, then opening and shutting it as he watched her every move.

Handing it over, then, she told him to pin it to his cape. After a couple of tries it worked and soon all the Indians had flocked around him, watching carefully as he pinned and unpinned his shiny prize.

Looking up at my wife, he took off his braided headband and stretched it out to her as best he could with all the others still taking turns at opening and closing the safety pin.

Now they were fingering her hair, with great care and curiosity for naturally they had never seen blonde hair before. They also stared into her eyes – blue eyes were so strange. Finally they pointed to her pistol holster and made signs telling her not to shoot. She managed to get the idea across to them that she carried it with her only to shoot parrots, which amused them greatly but also increased her first impulse to turn the mule around and trot back to where she hoped we were still waiting.

At that point, she told me later, the most natural thing to do seemed to be to take them along with her. So she gave them a sign to follow her and, after a little discussion among themselves, they did so.

When the men and I looked up and saw my wife approaching (quite cockily, too!) surrounded by a horde of painted Indians, we stopped everything we were doing, dumbfounded. I hurriedly managed to find a few more strings of beads, knives and other odds and ends and when I handed them over, the Indians were delighted.

After that was done, they went along with us all the way to the Sicarare River, walking beside the mules, that happily, reacted less violently than I had expected.

My wife had been right. These Indians belonged to the Casacará tribe and, thanks to her, we could tell the people of Pueblito that they, too, were 'tame'.

CHAPTER TEN

AFTER a couple of weeks back in Pueblito, where we wound up our affairs, we returned to Becerril. But this time we did not ask the help of any of those cowardly men. Now we could find our own way. Taking only the gendarmes with us, we set out one morning for the three huts.

Our gifts hadn't been touched! Although we searched high and low through that forest, yelled our heads off and blew on the trumpet, not a single Indian answered us. Had they left the place? No. They'd been there. We could tell by the tracks, the marks on the trees and, I was almost going to say, the faint smell, which I was beginning to recognize.

Discouraged, we headed our mules back down the mountain and packed our things once more. Only many years later did we learn that the Socomba we had been searching for never made friends with the white people. They couldn't. But the story of what did happen to those brave people must wait.

For many reasons we simply had to get back to the coast. It was a long way to Sweden and we knew it was going to be difficult because of the war in progress. We had already learned that without passports we wouldn't be able to get anywhere at all, and we were told we could get them only in New York or Rio de Janeiro and it might take time.

We were on our way to the coast when we got word that an epidemic of measles had broken out in Pueblito, the village of which, in spite of everything, we had grown so fond.

I didn't realize at first what the news meant and remember thinking only that we were fortunate that our little Sif had not caught it. But in these mountains, epidemics were so rare that, when they struck, people fled from village to village to escape the sickness as though it were the pest, thereby spreading it in no time over the whole countryside and to those who had built up no resistance to the germ.

The tragedy was that measles also attacked our new Indian friends who caught it from some whites and carried it back with them to their mountains. From letters we received from the monks, we learned that, in the course of only those few weeks, all but about one-tenth of the Milagru Indians in the Motilon mountains above Pueblito had died.

Maybe it would have been better for those happy people if we had never succeeded in bringing them into contact with civilization. We were very depressed as we continued on our way down to the coast.

We also had word from the very cordial border inspector, Londoño, who told us that ever since we'd talked over our plans, he had been thinking of ways to get to meet the Socombas. He didn't see any reason, he wrote, why, when we came back next time, the government couldn't assign the whole gendarme force to such an expedition – especially if he could get some of the Casacarás to go along as guides.

He reported that a small band of gendarmes had already been in one Indian village where the people seemed to understand the language of the Motilons. But they had been separated from the central villages of the tribe for so long that they were very different in many ways. For one thing, Londoño said in his letter, they didn't understand anything about exchanging gifts and refused to trade with anyone. After three weeks of trying to get some kind of contact with them, Londoño wrote, he and his men had been forced to retreat, completely exhausted. As for himself, he was still sick and didn't expect to get out of bed for several days more.

His letter caught up with us in Colón, Panama, on board a Swedish steamer which was to take us to Brazil. There we got our passports and another ship to Norway. It managed to escape the German U-boats, creep around England without being stopped and boarded by the British and, after two months at sea, we were able to land our Indian collection, the baby on top of them, on the dock in Oslo.

At home in Sweden next day, we immediately became involved in what was now to us an almost foreign way of life. And I knew I had left thoughts and longings behind, high in the mysterious Andes. I knew, too, that we had to go back. Go back we did, but not so soon as we had hoped.

BOOK TWO

CHAPTER ONE

ESTHER and I were once again in our beloved South America after five years of planning, and this time we had a photographer with us, a Norwegian, Ottar Gladtvet. We planned to visit our Motilon friends first and get some good pictures of them and decided once again to make our headquarters at Valledupar

We arrived at a swift river which careers so fast between its high banks that we had to cross it in a canoe. Once we were on the other side, the frail little craft had to make several trips to bring over all our packs. After hitching the mules together with lines secured to some trees, the animals were then urged into the river which they swam across, protesting with noisy brays every minute of the way.

As we were gathering our things together again, we saw a cloud of dust billowing towards us. At first we couldn't distinguish anything but gradually I saw that it was a little welcoming committee riding down from Valledupar to meet us – one of those nice old-fashioned customs which people around there held fast to. They would ride out to welcome travellers and escort them part of the way on their departure, too, waving them off and wishing them Godspeed.

I had telegraphed ahead announcing the approximate day of our arrival because there was no hotel in the town and I wanted to be sure we had a place to live. And here they came – remembering us after all the time which had passed since our first expedition!

We found that the well-to-do Creoles now lived in the brick houses. In what might be called the 'suburbs' were the mud huts, often roofed with palm leaves, where the Negroes and mulattoes lived.

A few of the houses were really quite charming with brilliantly flowered patios framed by white pillars and moss-covered tile roofs. These hung low over the outer walls, shading the walks off which the doors opened. More often, however, plants and vines had been left in unkempt snarls and more than one patio was cluttered with cartons, rubbish and not a few chamber pots.

The walls were plain and the furnishings of spartan simplicity – cedar chairs covered with jaguar or cowhide, open shelves, here and there a camp bed but more often only iron hooks in the walls from which to hang hammocks.

Chickens and dogs, pigs and sheep wandered through the streets just as the naked children of the Negro servants, all former slaves. The kitchens were exceedingly primitive. In most cases, food was cooked over a fire built on the earthen floor in pots set on three stones, just as the Indians do. In a few homes you could find a hearth built of brick and clay, but without any chimney.

The streets were unpaved; when it rained they became small rivers, but there were high, narrow sidewalks on each side. On rainy days, small boys earned a few tips by wading into the streets with chairs over which people could step across to the other side.

The entrance to the backyards of most houses was through the main room, *la sala* – a real 'living' room, one might say, and usually the dining-room as well. You were not supposed to be surprised if a stranger walked right through your house after having tied up his horse in your backyard. Everyone rode. Even to cross the plaza, one got on a horse and rode across it. In fact, some of the shops were built so that a rider could make his purchases while on horseback right at the counter. For riding around the town and its environs, one rode only horses and always with a lead mare (a good one brought a very high price). Only for long trips could one be seen on a mule, while donkeys were the mounts of the poorest people and the children. However, it was not unusual to see small boys riding sheep around the plaza. Once, too, I saw a Negro riding an ox, a custom brought with them from Africa when the Spaniards imported the Negroes as slaves.

As for bathrooms – they were scarce. You could get a quick shower by standing in the middle of the floor and scooping water over yourself from a cistern in what served as a kitchen, but most of the villagers bathed in the river, the women managing somehow to wash under long bathrobes.

Water was always a problem. Every morning you could see a long line of women walking back from the river carrying crocks of water on their heads, happily smoking their thin little cigars, all the while gesticulating and cursing the small boys riding donkeys alongside them. The curses were usually well deserved for the boys liked to ride so close to the women that the kegs of water strapped to each side of the donkeys would bump one of them and, happy chance, maybe upset her balance, toppling a water crock to the ground with a crash.

The street scene could be lively indeed. It often happened that the peace was disturbed by a whole herd of cattle being driven through and, what with the lowing and bellowing of the animals and shouting of the herders, you could scarcely hear yourself think. It was a good idea to get out of their way and even seek temporary shelter until the dust had settled again.

The food was uninviting, even in the homes of those fairly well off. With our morning coffee we had toasted cornbread or toasted unripened *platanos,* a kind of banana which has to be cooked before it can be eaten. That hard, and hard-to-digest, fruit was a little better if dipped in shredded salt cheese. Sometimes we had to be content with salt cheese and unrefined sugar which was sold in big bricks. Their high quality *panela,* on the other hand, was a delicious sweetmeat. In fact, they preserved all kinds of fruits, coconut and even potatoes in a sugar and water syrup. Milk was cooked down with sugar to a sweet caramel consistency to make *dulce de leche.* Cut into squares, *dulce* was served most often when company came and was always accompanied by a glass of water. But we had to decline the water; it came from the river and hadn't been boiled.

Dried meat played a big role in planning any menu. When it was fresh, it was cut into long thick slices, salted and hung out in the sun to dry. Ready after a few days – dry as leather – it had to be boiled, hammered with a mallet and then fried to taste like anything. Most often it was put into the soup pot just as it was, which gave the soup a somewhat unpleasant flavour. If you aren't used to this meat it can give you a stomach ache for several days. But I was reminded again of the wisdom of the old lady at Latio who had remarked, 'One can get used to anything.'

Among the wealthier citizens, rice was served quite often but it was very expensive. Also, as olive oil was prohibitively costly, our hosts used bacon fat on it. After such a meal you were conscious that you had eaten heartily . . . though against most dietary rules

It seemed to us that the majority of the people here never got enough to eat, but the poorer people seemed to be content with soup made of vegetable roots with a little fat or salt pork in it. The old ladies in the town told my wife that in the old days things were much worse because they didn't even have the dried meat, except on holidays. The vegetable-root soup was flavoured then, as now, with an old meat bone which hung over the smoke from the fire. It was called *el hueso gustador,* the flavour-bone, and was loaned from house to house.

In this part of the world you had to do without bread, milk, butter, potatoes and a good many other things which 'northerners' are used to. But something they had which we did not was coffee – the way it should be – black, strong and boiled with sugar. Chocolate used to be their national drink but today it is coffee, and with good reason. Even in the simplest hovel it tasted wonderful.

We had to get used to several customs. The women often ate together without the men and meals were served at very odd times of day. Because of the heat, we had to keep our dining-room doors open and very often a little group would gather outside and watch us at dinner. At other times they would collect outside the wooden-barred windows. There was so little entertainment in the town that our meals became a local spectacle.

We were particularly interested in the customs which still existed here from the first colonial period and the days of slavery.

The early Spanish conquests had resulted in severe population losses among the Indians, especially the warriors. The surviving Indian women, unable to support themselves, came down to the settlements where they became housekeepers to their conquerors. As most of the latter had left their women at home in Spain and the Indian women no longer had their own men to beget their children and protect their honour, a Creole generation was born.

In later years, when the Spaniards imported Negro slaves, the Creole men, who were still regarded as second-class citizens, took Negro mistresses, bringing a new strain to a new culture.

Apparently there was still a female majority in this area for my wife and I knew of few well-to-do Creole gentlemen who did not have one or more mistresses, each of whom was taking care of one of his properties as well. A young man of good Creole stock usually had several children by women in the village before he was married. As soon as he was established in his own home, his children were then moved in, too, as helpers around the place. They lived in their own quarters with one or more of their mothers as chaperones.

Nor was it at all unusual for the man of the house to have several offspring with his newly employed maidservants. The kinder, handsomer and richer he was, of course, the greater his status as an employer and citizen. This patriarchal custom, useful as it was in solving the servant problem, was also a decided advantage in increasing the population.

As a gentleman, he never denied the paternity of his children and regarded it as his duty to care for them, no matter how many they were. We knew of a plantation owner who had over one hundred children and when the time came to count his grandchildren, he had to collect them in the patio as there were too many to get into his house at one time!

These children were not accorded the same legal status as legitimate children, however. When a Creole gentleman became governor here, he appointed his legitimate relatives to high offices in the government while his 'half-relatives' were made sheriffs or firemen. But he never forgot them nor left them out altogether.

Quite frequently a man would introduce himself to us saying 'I'm Jack Doe, the natural son of so-and-so.' In fact, among these people, weddings were a rarity in this part of the world.

From an historical point of view, it was extremely interesting to see how many old customs had been retained down here.

75

The first time my wife and I had come to Valledupar, for instance, we had little Sif with us. Everyone understood that she was my wife's first child – Mrs Bolinder was scarcely more than a child herself. But I was already 25 and that it should be my first child, too, was more than they could understand. They told me so quite openly.

At that time I had not fully understood that the father of the house was expected to have children by the maids, as a matter of course. The girl working for us was a very handsomely built mulatto whose mother had done everything she could to get her the job in our house. It didn't bother me too much at first when she fluttered her eyelids at me or accidentally touched my hand or shoulder. I had noticed that all the girls around there flirted with the men but apparently with no satisfaction for their pains.

I did start to wonder, however, when she asked me one day to help her get water from a well in a rather lonely spot. I knew she was used to carrying enormous jugs of water on her head without any help. When I told her so, I noticed she didn't like it. I also refused several other obvious invitations, quite oblivious, at the time, to the tradition I was breaking.

Finally she became so furious with me that she went home and brought back her mother to complain to my wife about my behaviour. The mother was beside herself at this insult to her daughter's charms.

'It's written right in the Old Testament,' the mother bawled at me in Spanish. 'You should be proud that I chose you to take care of my daughter and the child you should give her. This is the girl's first job and I was very careful choosing it even though, I must say, you aren't as well off as foreigners usually are!'

By the time my wife and I got the full impact of her indictment of my character, the mother was finishing a tirade in which she announced she was taking her girl home with her 'Pronto!' and would find a better job where she'd be made more welcome.

After they had gone, my wife and I had a good laugh, mostly at our own ignorance. But she also cautioned me in mock seriousness about doing any further research on that particular custom.

As I have said before, there were few amusements in Valledupar. There were cock fights now and then – it was more fun to watch the spectators, I thought, than to watch the cocks. The people went completely wild when they weren't sitting tensely on the edges of the benches. They bet high and a loser could often be quite disagreeable, threatening all kinds of tortures to those he claimed had fixed the fight.

Once in a while there was a dance, too – usually a subscription affair – in someone's house. The town's string orchestra, which was a good one, played *pazillos*, tangos, *pasodobles* and similar local dances for the young girls and their beaux. The married women didn't dance. And watching through open windows and doors were the 'men in the street' who seldom missed anything that was going on.

On Christmas Eve there was a big cock fight and dance before the midnight mass. Then, when the first cracked tones of the church bell called the people to the service, they began to gather, bringing with them their house pets – dogs, monkeys, piglets, turkeys, goats and sheep – to be blessed. But the barking, squealing, grunting and cackling that went on did not disturb the progress of the mass in the least as the town's brass band drowned every other sound with dance music, the only kind the musicians could play.

Since then – almost forty years have gone by now – the priests have drawn the line at the animals and have set a time limit on the band's contributions to the service. The men of the village now squire their women to the church. However, as soon as the band's part in the programme is finished, the men manage to slip out of the church, join their musical friends and go around the town serenading the ladies who stayed at home that evening.

After the mass, we went with the others to sample the huge meals which were spread in several houses around the plaza where everyone was welcome. Colour and sound mingled with odour and heat on this strange celebration of the Christ Child's birthday. In the back streets, the simpler folk, too, were celebrating in their way, dancing with lighted candles in their hands to the sensuous rhythms of African drums.

That this was a high holiday was evident from the women's dresses, styled as they had been for many generations. They wore bright blouses and wide, starched skirts, while no man could be seen without a jacket. To go about in shirt sleeves on such an occasion was a degrading thing for a true *caballero*. In fact, in some towns on the coast the police took charge of every man not properly attired on feast days.

We were always received as friends in Valledupar's homes and the people were very kind in overlooking the *faux pas* we seemed constantly to make. For example, although the food and drink were laid out on long tables in many houses for all to see, we discovered that visitors were expected to pass them by, with many thanks, and not partake unless they had previous invitations. Those who did were expected to share with all the rest, standing or sitting about the tables, everything they selected from the bowls and flat dishes so that no person should be jealous of another. It was certainly a generous and friendly custom but one could go home a bit hungry.

FROM Valledupar, the three of us, Esther, Gladtvet the photographer, and I went south through sections of the country where there were few villages and where the settlers and trappers had a hard life. Many times we spent the night in the shacks of these simple Creole people, almost all of whom were the descendants of slaves.

It is not hard to know when you are approaching a ranch as the mules' ears begin to twitch and they go a little faster, knowing that food and water are waiting ahead. I had noticed those unmistakable signs as we were crossing a dry patch of grassland and just before some starved-looking dogs came running towards us, barking savagely.

We stopped and waited until the rancher came to our rescue, shouting at the dogs, 'You're supposed to keep off jaguars, you stupid beasts, not travelling strangers!'

He and his whole family had the darkest skins we had seen for some time. They invited us into their ranch house with all customary courtesy and a little added politeness, too, for we were foreigners as well as strangers. For our part, we answered all the usual questions about our health, our destination, our families and a score of other subjects in the polite phrases which are such a large part of the language of etiquette there.

The 'ranch house' was simply a palmleaf roof held up by four poles. It had no walls but several hammocks hung from the poles. There were also a few stools and the usual primitive kitchen utensils – wooden mortars to make corn meal and clay pots for cooking. From one of the latter, standing on three stones over a fire, arose that wonderful aroma of coffee. We were thankful once more that this is the drink of welcome for we were both exceedingly tired and thirsty.

Trying to carve an existence out of this land can be discouraging and these people usually lived close to the edge of poverty. Nevertheless, their hospitality is genuine and they share their corn and *yuca* soup with one and all. They offer everything they have to the traveller, which sometimes means their hammocks too. In any case, there is no question of privacy. For one meal, they will kill a chicken, perhaps, or bring out a bit of dried meat as a special offering and a bit of luxury for themselves at the same time.

Gladtvet and I hung our hammocks as high as we could in order to avoid colliding with the chickens and pigs on the earthen floor.

Both man and beast are scraggly in this countryside and this family's clothes were worn ragged. The babies crawled about naked on the filthy floor. But these people have patience. They don't complain though their work gets precious few results. Nor, unfortunately, have they developed and grown spiritually. No longer slaves as their ancestors were, they have nevertheless remained like them. Serving the land now, freed from slavery, to be sure, they are otherwise little changed in their thinking. They do things the only way they have ever known them to be done and it is a hard way.

Just keeping the jungle back from the door is a lifetime's work. To clear their fields is always fraught with risks, not the least of them the poisonous snakes which can snuff out a life after only a few moments of lonely agony.

The housework is tedious and exhausting. Every utensil has to be made by hand before corn can be ground or coffee boiled. Even the heavy salt they use must be crushed between stones and sifted through grass strainers before a little can be added to the soup.

In reality these dark-skinned Creole pioneers had a much harder time making a living than the Indians did. They lived alone and not together in villages where the work could be organized and divided up, the harvest distributed and shared.

All the Creole farmer had besides his corn and *yuca* fields was a small pasture for his only donkey and maybe a cow. A traveller's animals could spend the night there, too, for a small fee.

Sickness also must be given continuous battle. The Creoles seemed more susceptible than others to malaria, which is endemic in that section, and almost everyone suffered from tropical anaemia. This obviously contributed to lowering their ability to work and it left them so weakened that they picked up practically every other germ making the rounds.

When the first settlers came to South America from Europe they found a completely new life lacking everything they knew or recognized. Nothing they were used to growing survived in that climate. For this reason they were soon forced to raise the Indians' crops by Indian methods. The strange thing to us was that they didn't use even the ploughs their ancestors had used. Perhaps they had forgotten, if they had ever known, how to invent, improve and develop new ways – in short, how to progress, as man must do to survive. On the other hand, perhaps the daily battle against the jungle took all the strength they could muster to keep it from defeating them.

We said goodbye to our hosts next morning and, shortly after having our coffee, set out for our second visit to the Motilon Indians.

BOOK THREE

CHAPTER ONE

WE had been through, back and across all the Indian trails on the Goajira peninsula. I had renewed my acquaintance with the natives of the tropical, snow-peaked Sierra Nevada – natives who still believed in magic. We had even come upon some of their wilder relatives, the Chimila, at the base of the mountains where the forests were thickest. We had taken pictures every inch of the way and were much pleased with the results.

Now we were about to start out towards our real goal – the Motilon Indians. It seemed a matter of course to us that we should see them again and get pictures this time.

It was no surprise that, exactly as before, our resources were at low ebb. As a result, this second expedition was even less pretentious than the first, if that were possible. We couldn't even afford a guide this time so Gladtvet and I decided to take over the reconnoitring ourselves. We took along only one pack donkey. Gladtvet rode another, while I ambled along on my mule.

We had a lot of gear with us – it seems inevitable no matter how small any expedition is. Getting across the wild Cesár River was a nuisance and, as a result, night fell before we got to the next Creole village where we could stay. We got along all right in the darkness just the same, and the evening chill was pleasant, making the going easier. The donkeys, too, seemed to like it and we were going along at a good pace when we suddenly came to a bridge.

Who could dream there would be a bridge there? The trail was no wider than a cow path. All my experience told me that bridges were unheard of in this part of the country. But there it was – three tree trunks trimmed smooth on their outer sides.

Our flashlight wasn't working so we had to light our way with bunches of grass we set a match to. On close inspection the bridge looked strong enough, even though it was fairly narrow, but now we were faced with another problem. Our donkeys came from the Goajira plains and knew nothing whatever about either water or bridges. They refused absolutely to set foot on the tree trunk bridge. There was nothing for it but to force them across.

I went ahead with my mule and Gladtvet started the pack donkey across behind me. In the middle, the pack donkey suddenly shied, stumbled and splash! There it lay in the stream with our cameras, film and everything else we owned!

The animal lay quite still on its side as Gladtvet started to retrieve our packs. After a lot of hard work in the darkness, he managed to haul out one after the other, handing each to me while I tried to manage my mule with the other hand. Everything was dripping with water and mud but Gladtvet reported that, as the river bottom was so soft, the donkey wasn't hurt.

Nevertheless, friendly persuasion left it completely disinterested. It continued to lie there. There was nothing for it but to be as tough as its former owner and give it a good kick. That was the language the donkey understood and in less than sixty seconds it had clambered to its feet and scrambled out on the bank.

We were in a bad humour – wet and muddy – as we led the animals along in the dark. But it wasn't long before we heard voices and the squeaking of machinery. Directly ahead we saw a sugar mill.

The men were working on the primitive contraption all night as it was harvest time. They were very friendly and offered to put us up for the rest of the night. Next morning, they also helped us mend the damaged saddle we had left on the riverbank and rescue the rest of our belongings from the river.

We said goodbye then and started off on the trail which was to take us through several Creole villages that day and the next. But we were getting nearer the Motilon Indians' mountain fastnesses. I knew that 'our' Indians no longer lived around Pueblito. They moved often but we had to get to Pueblito before we could learn where they had resettled. We had got as far as El Jobo by that time, just as on my first trip with my wife, but we were still a good bit north of our destination.

I planned to start out one day later than the photographer since his donkey was slower than my mule. However, as I also had some unexpected trouble with my saddle, I was delayed still further. For that reason Gladtvet was first to arrive at a primitive ranch house where, thinking I might have got ahead of him somehow, he asked if anyone had seen me.

The owner of the place, a Creole, was very much surprised to hear my name. He had known me from my first visit but had no idea I had come back. When I did turn up at last, he greeted me so warmly that I was a little suspicious. Reputations are built quickly by word of mouth down here and these people had had five years to build up the 'foreign visitor' who, I found, had gained a considerable personal fortune in the telling.

The owner's name was Tomas Rafael and he was a rascal though probably not a crook. He told me that a handful of Milagru

Indians who had survived the measles had joined another group and were living in the mountain jungle right above his ranch, a place called Tocaima. When I had returned to Sweden five years before, they still hadn't made peace with the whites but now, I was assured, they had buried the hatchet. As proof, Tomas waved proudly toward his ranch house which he had dared build right in their back yard. He suggested we stay with him a few days, then he'd go along and show us the way up the mountainside. I was pleased at the suggestion even though our host was not exactly reliable.

His 'ranch house', like so many others, consisted of a roof and no walls near a newly planted cornfield and small pasture. At any rate, we had a roof over our heads, which was all we needed. This time I hadn't bothered to bring a tent.

I thought we should stay only one night but it turned out that our host had other ideas. He said we should rest several days before setting out and seemed over-solicitous of our welfare. I found the man an awful bore and wanted to get on.

'Why should we wait?' I asked Tomas. 'Is it so far away or is it too strenuous?'

'Not really,' he confessed after some hesitation. 'You can ride most of the way in a few hours, even though the climb after that is pretty rough. But why all the hurry, Señores?' he added plaintively.

It became apparent why he was so reluctant for us to leave. Gladtvet was very handy at carving and carpentry and, while waiting for me to get there, he had made some useful articles for Tomas's primitive household. The man didn't want to let this chance go by to add to his furnishings and I had to admit he had a point there.

But we had to get on just the same. If we wanted to get pictures of the Indians above us we had no time to waste. Down there it is never wise to wait for mañana.

I told Tomas quite sharply that we intended to start off next morning and he was so surprised that he couldn't think of any more arguments against it. Very reluctantly therefore, he began to make the necessary preparations and next morning we actually found ourselves fed, packed and on our way.

It was a hard ride. There was no trail, the forest seemed denser than usual and it was late in the afternoon before we reached the foot of the mountain where the climb was to start. But, as it was too late to consider beginning it then, we decided to put up in some Indian lean-tos we found after a miserable time surveying the area.

Early the next day, after leaving the mules in the care of a boy Tomas had dragged out from some neighbouring ranch, we started the climb.

The mountainside seemed almost perpendicular and presented what looked like a solid green wall of jungle. Hacking our way through, we hauled ourselves up painfully, grasping at roots and bushes as best we could, our packs seeming all the time to be dragging us back the few steps we gained. Thorns and nettle-like bushes cut our hands and legs. Stinging insects attacked like little bombers from every direction, delighted at finding such juicy landings. We had to keep a continual weather-eye for snakes, poisonous ants and millepedes and at several points I found myself thinking of some old engraving I had once seen of demons in hell.

It was a long day and it was almost done by the time we at last saw the bee-hive shaped huts of an Indian village clustered on a little promontory above us. Mustering what breath we had left, we started to halloo and call out, just as the Indians themselves announce their approach to neighbouring villages.

Receiving no answer, we dragged ourselves up the last few yards only to find the whole village deserted. We were too tired to care much at that point. Later, I learned that a young girl had died there suddenly and that the Indians had felt impelled to move on in order to escape the evil spirit which had claimed her. I found myself secretly hoping that it was not a measles spirit.

Our guide had also had enough by that time, but he was scared too, and wanted to turn back. We wouldn't let him. We had to spend the night there as it was already dark, and I told him so. I may have imagined his disgusted look at the back of my neck. I probably did.

As soon as the sun was up we were ready to move. I found a trail, after some searching around, which looked as though it had been used quite recently. After a final cup of coffee, we followed the trail up a steep hillside. But at least the terrain was easier going now that we were out of the jungle at last. On the other hand, the sun was blazing down on our backs and we were almost blinded by sweat.

Suddenly, just as everything happens in the mountain jungles of South America, the trail ended at the brink of a look-out point. The view was magnificent but I was in no mood to look at it for very long. It was definitely the end of the trail and there was nothing for it but to turn back and find the right one.

After quite a search, Gladtvet called to me and I saw some fresh marks on some trees leading farther up the mountain. Following it, we came upon a half-harvested cornfield and knew we wouldn't starve, at least. The Indians were not far away now. They couldn't be. But I also knew they wouldn't mind if we helped ourselves. All travellers are allowed to take what they need of whatever is available, and are expected to replace it if they can. Such communal sharing had been developed by the great Incas into one of the world's first socialist states.

We had found the Indians at last. I could tell from several signs – the marks I knew so well by that time. Once more we began shouting at the top of our voices and, in no time, we were answered by a terrific commotion and a crowd of Indians rushed at us from behind clumps of ferns, yelling and banging on anything that would make a noise. It was a really joyous welcome and, prancing around us, they led us up to their camp.

Everything had gone well so far. It was easy to look friendly – these Indians were friendliness itself – so far. But now we had to be careful and very diplomatic.

When we reached the village, the women spread big bracken ferns for us to sit on, then brought us roasted nuts, corn balls, boiled pumpkin and bowls of corn beer. We were hungry and we ate a lot.

As I munched the nuts, I noticed that these Indian women wore the same simple dress of their tribe that I remembered – the loin cloth, the cape over their shoulders, the ropes of necklaces and nothing more.

Once rested and finished with our corn beer, we paid for our meal with some knives, glass beads and a sack of empty tin cans (which I had remembered they prized very highly but which I was relieved to have finished hauling on my back up the mountains). The Indians were delighted.

There was to be a dance that night, we learned, and the Indians helped Gladtvet and me to get ready for it. As our faces had to be painted, the women brought some red fruit in a bowl and mashed it until colour ran out. Then three nursing mothers took turns milking their breasts over the bowl – a few drops from each breast was enough – while the others mixed the colour. When they painted the designs on our faces it was smooth as cream and, fortunately, quite easy to remove.

I had already spotted the leader of the group, an older man who appeared to know magic from the odd symbols hung around him. As it was important to be in his good graces, I made a point of trading the best items I had with me for his spears. And his wives got the blue glass beads – a colour I had found they and many other Indians preferred.

He was married to two sisters, I learned. A suitor has to work quite hard to win a bride and he saves a lot of time and effort by taking two girls from the same family.

It was one of the witch doctor's wives who was now painting my face – an apparent gesture of respect for she had let fall several extra drops of her milk into the colour pot. She was applying the paint to one side of my face while her husband did the other side.

Behind his back, Tomas Rafael saw his chance to flirt with the younger wife. Although he was only teasing her, he was tickling and patting her in fairly ticklish places, which amused her immensely. Although she did not resent his attentions, I had few doubts as to what her husband would think about it and none at all as to what he might do about it.

As the Indians didn't understand Spanish, I was able to tell off the fool Tomas, reminding him that the Indians had just killed a white man for less – they had got it into their heads that he had his eye on one of their women and that was the end of him. Swift and sure, an arrow found its mark and he probably never had time to wonder why.

The dance was beginning, exactly like the one I remember so well – the same humming song, the same weird music piped on flutes – made of human bones this time. That was the only difference.

The following day we got some very good pictures but the witch doctor's temper was getting short, I noticed. Possibly the others had seen the little flirtation of the day before and had told him about it. He wouldn't have anything to do with picture-taking and refused to pose. He didn't seem to like the camera or tripod or anything about the whole process. And I had to admit that our gear looked a lot more frightening than his magic paraphernalia.

It is not wise to have an unfriendly medicine man for an enemy so I decided that we should go down to the deserted village that same afternoon and continue our travels next day from there. For a couple of long hunting knives, two Indians agreed to go along with us and help carry our packs to the lower level.

We had just said goodbye and given away a few farewell tokens of friendship when Tomas got another crazy idea into his head. Gladtvet had thrown away a length of blank film which an Indian girl had picked up and wound around her neck. Suddenly Tomas snatched it from around her throat, put a match to it and then swung the sputtering, blazing streamer around his head in the air.

The Indians stopped dead in their tracks for an instant, then retreated as the old man rushed towards us brandishing his knife.

This was a bad moment. It was all too clear that he thought the burning film was some kind of white witchcraft or a mysterious pest-bearer. He had mistrusted the camera and film all along. Now he was proved right!

The other Indians had collected by that time and were coming towards us with bows and arrows fixed. The women also were sneaking away to hide – a bad sign.

I tried in every way I could to quiet the old man as he was bearing down on Tomas who, for his part, was pale with fear. I thought fast and quickly found another knife in my knapsack and a few more beads.

Fortunately it was the best knife of the lot and had a beautiful, shiny sheath as well, which the old man inspected carefully. It was certainly the finest he had seen, at any rate, for I had assumed the role of chief peddler down there by that time. When at length he took the beads and hung them around the necks of his two wives, I began to breathe more easily.

As well as I could I explained to the old fellow that the gifts were compensation for my guide's behaviour. When he still hesitated, I dug up some more 'compensation' and handed it out to the Indian men and the few women who had remained with them. Even so we didn't dare turn our backs on them although several of the Indians were laughing among themselves again as they inspected their presents. Then the old chief, having finished carefully examining his newest knife and the necklaces, gave a sign and the Indians gradually withdrew and went back to whatever they had been doing before the excitement began.

We, in turn, began our retreat, walking backwards quite a few steps, all the while keeping an eye on the medicine man in case he should lose his temper again.

The recent events made me decide not to spend the night in the deserted village after all but to continue our trek all night. The village was already some distance behind us when Gladtvet and I nearly stumbled over two of our packs – the ones the Indians had been carrying. They were lying right in our path and there wasn't a bearer in sight.

We halted and looked around us quickly to make sure. But the forest was as impenetrable as a black velvet curtain. Had word of our adventure managed to reach our bearers from the village somehow? Were they lying in wait for us behind that velvet curtain, silent arrows aimed at our backs?

For several minutes we didn't dare move. Even with revolvers, the white man draws the shortest straw in this kind of encounter, chiefly because a pistol shot could trigger trouble not only for us but for the entire surrounding population.

We jumped a couple of feet at least when a peal of laughter broke the deathly stillness of the forest. The two Indian bearers were lying in wait for us all right but this was their little joke. They crawled out of the bushes and came running over to us like schoolboys caught in an April Fool's prank.

Even though they knew nothing about what had happened in their village, I wanted to get out of that section as speedily as possible. Indians prefer not to kill strangers in their own villages but what happens to them anywhere else doesn't bother them in the least and they had plenty of time to track us through the mountain jungle and put a quick end to our expedition then and there.

We would have broken a world's record, if there had been one, in getting down that mountain. When we found our mules at last, the boy we'd left to guard them had disappeared but we couldn't waste time worrying about him either. We mounted and started back across the savanna to deposit a somewhat chastened Tomas Rafael at his ranch house. After some coffee, we took our leave of him, relieved in the realization that it was probably the last time we would ever see him again. Gladtvet and I were once again on our way to Pueblito.

CHAPTER TWO

WE were heartily welcomed by Father Camilo who was then in charge of the mission. He immediately approved my plan to go to Maraca, arranged to get a mule driver for us and recommended that I get in touch with a trusted guide in Becerril named Lazaro Montecristo, whom he had used himself on several missions to the Indians.

I found Pueblito as unattractive as ever and hastened to finish our business and get out of it. The guide who was to take us to Maraca was a one-eyed Negro, but it soon became apparent that he was smarter than many others I have known who had the use of both their eyes.

We were riding south across the lowlands at the mountain's foot but it seemed to me that the trip was much longer than it had been five years before. It was monotonous now whereas, that first time, it had been exciting. Now all the treacherous Indians were gone. We just rode and rode across the same savannas, along the same rivers with their same jungle-covered banks. Savanna – forest – savanna – forest. It was so boring that we even welcomed our arrival at the Monte Epinas forest where we had to cut our way through some nasty, spiny undergrowth.

Whereas before no one had dared settle in this region, we now found a few ranches here and there on our way to Becerril. Replies to my inquiries about the Socomba Indians, whom we had had no luck in contacting on my first trip, were disappointing. They hadn't been heard from since then at all. The people said they thought the Indians had all been wiped out in the measles epidemic which had taken so many farther to the north. It was only much later that I learned what had really happened to them.

We rode beyond the town and spent the night in the open country. It was cooler there and didn't smell of civilization. It had been arranged that Montecristo would join us a little later. As I wanted to get over the Maraca River next day, I knew it would be easier if we could get the hike across the savanna over with before the sun's heat got too strong, so we set out before dawn.

We timed the trip pretty well in fact for, sooner than I had hoped, we found ourselves entering the forest – that 3,000-metre high jungle forest which covered the mountainside and above which lived the Indians we wanted to meet.

The trail wound through heavy vines, crept between giant bushes and under fallen trees. It hid itself along the edges of cliffs and led us across smooth rocks, making the heavily laden donkeys stumble and almost fall at times, unable to get a proper foothold.

When we reached the river at last, we found a bit of sandy beach where we could set up camp. As I had not brought a tent this time, it meant that we should have to sleep on the sand – it was too late by that time to start building a shelter – but it was a cool and very beautiful spot and it didn't look like rain anyway.

What I had noticed, however, were the jaguar footprints in the sand. This was probably where they came down to drink, and that meant we should have to tether the animals very close to us if we didn't want trouble. On the other hand, with their keen senses, they were good 'watch dogs'. Watching them now placidly munching the corn we'd brought along, we prepared to settle down for the night.

As we lay in our sleeping bags looking up at the sparkling night sky, Gladtvet and I talked a while after the one-eyed one had solemnly announced, '*No hay plaga.*' He was assuring me that after a careful search he had found no 'plagues' around – no ants or termites, no scorpions, millepedes or sand fleas – good news it was and practically a utopian condition for that part of the world.

It made me think, though. I had to warn Gladtvet constantly against going barefoot. He hadn't yet had enough experience in the South American jungle to know how dangerous it was to take your boots off.

This was a good chance to remind him of all the biting, stinging devilish bugs and creeping things he should watch out for.

'If it isn't snakes,' I told him, 'it will be flying bloodsuckers or yellow-fever mosquitoes.'

He refused to look alarmed in the least.

'Walk on that sand barefoot,' I told him, warming up to my subject, 'and you'll pick up little sand flies that lay their eggs under the skin. They make your feet swell up so you can't get your boots on and you can hardly walk. In fact,' I added as threateningly as I could, 'if you get those damn bugs in your feet, I'll just leave you behind to rot in the jungle.'

Pretending to be frightened at that prospect, he promised to take more care. I proceeded to follow up my advantage and warned him about drinking unboiled water. 'A few parasites in your guts and it's tropical anaemia for you my boy,' I said, 'to say nothing of any of a hundred other varieties of dying quickly down here.' And I listed a few of the more unpleasant ones – slithering millepedes, scorpions, jaguars – the memory of those tracks we'd seen came to both of us at the same moment. I decided to drop that subject and returned to the world of bugs.

'There's one kind of fly,' I explained, 'a big one they call *nuche* here, which lays its eggs under the skin when it bites you. After a while, big boils develop out of which the larvae crawl all over you – between your fingers, behind your ears, under your arms.'

Gladtvet, looking a little nervous now, furtively held out his hand and looked at it carefully before putting it back under his blanket.

'I once knew a diplomat in Bogotá,' I continued, 'who was bitten by one of those flies – its real name is *Desmatodia hominis* – and he had to wear gloves for a couple of weeks. Then, there's a kind of bee here which attacks all kinds of food and, amazingly enough, even likes salt. Then, as soon as the fever mosquitoes go to bed after their night's work,' I continued, 'the day shift of sand flies takes over . . .'

Gladtvet had had enough. He covered his head and groaned, 'Stop, stop! I won't be able to sleep a minute tonight. I'm itching all over.'

I laughed. We were good friends and apparently I had got some important fact across to him at last. He was already well acquainted with the small white ants that love anything sweet or oily. They had got into his bags in the fairly clean hotel where we stayed on the coast. Nobody can understand how they manage to get into a tightly closed bag, then into a piece of chocolate in tinfoil or a jar of cold cream, but they can. They are also partial to starched shirts.

In the jungle the ants are black and bigger. You can't for the life of you see how they can get into your clothing and shoes hanging from the middle of a tent but they do – and so do the scorpions. You have to shake out everything hard before putting it on. There wasn't any DDT or citronella oil in those days and I've always wanted to shake the hands of the men who invented them.

It was not unusual then for a sleeper to wake up and find himself and all his bedding swarming with ants. The only thing to do when it happened was to dive into the nearest water. It hadn't happened to me but it was close, once. We had made very simple camping arrangements on a wooded slope where we couldn't put up our tent.

My camp bed stood on the open ground. Before getting into it, I looked around carefully with my flashlight to see if there were any ants around. There were – a whole parade of them, each about a quarter of an inch long, marching straight up one of the criss-cross legs of the bed. Then, unaccountably, they continued following the leader down the other leg and back to the floor. A crazy idea – they were evidently stupid as well as a damn nuisance. Just the same, I didn't sleep much that night, wondering when their leader might change course up over the covers and down my neck. After that I always set the legs of my camp bed in tin cans filled with water and kerosene whenever I had the chance. Ants were one reason hammocks were so popular down here, I discovered, but they weren't always antproof either.

This was the land of ants! All kinds – big, small, all colours – infested trees as well as the earth. Some built nests which hung from branches – often purposely, it seemed, at just head level in the middle of your path. Others gathered in the crevasses of palm tree trunks, sucking their sap and, in return, protecting the tree from other attackers.

The bites of some of these ants are very painful. One of them is called '24' (veintequatro) because the pain lasts exactly that many hours. I was once bitten by one of that breed and can confirm that it is correctly named. In some tribes, boys let themselves be bitten by these ants to prove their manhood, not only to show that they can stand pain but as a cleansing rite. It occurred to me that, as a result of this custom, the Indians in effect had immunized themselves to these bites. I did know, however, that this rite was part of the preparation for marriage and that they also took some of these ants along with them when they went hunting.

Just push aside a bush and ants rain down on your head and neck. They crawl all over your body under your clothes, nipping you wherever it suits them but usually in places you can't reach without undressing.

Our one-eyed guide interjected at this point, 'The worst are the driver ants. There's no stopping them on their march over anything that stands in their way. Only thing to do is run and get a lot of water between you and them. But you know,' he added, 'some people say they've seen them cross water, too.'

I admitted that if I had to choose I'd pick them as the most frightening insects in the whole lot. Stories of their exploits are seldom exaggerated. They swarm in a living black river which flows through and over and around anything they come to. When the danger signal sounds, men and animals flee before them and whole villages are evacuated.

'I saw such a village once,' I told my companions. 'It was in Africa and after these carnivorous bugs had gone through it was clean as a dried bone – not even a mite of garbage or a rag was left.'

Termites are not ants but they are another plague in South America. I had seen termite hills out on the plains which I had at first thought were man-made monuments to fallen heroes. As is well known, they eat anything that isn't made of glass or metal and some people swear they have now learned how to bore into tin cans. Termites are night workers and don't like the daylight but, when they're working on something particularly delicious, they make a cover to keep out the daylight and continue their skulduggery until, if it happens to be a house, a man could push it off its foundations with one hand.

I told my companions about the time I forgot to hang up my boots one night. 'When I picked them up off the floor next morning,' I said, 'the uppers were completely severed from the soles and some of them were eaten too. The same thing happened with wooden boxes – anything standing on an earthen or clay floor could be wrecked in a single night.'

Then there was that old English consul down on the coast. He was a good friend of my family, and my wife and I visited him whenever we could. He had a large library and the shelves were carefully protected with glass doors, but he hadn't done much reading down there – probably too hot. At any rate, it was several years since he had touched a book when he opened the bookcase one day and the whole row of book backs fell bang on the floor at his feet. The books were gone – completely devoured by termites!

'A huge tree can suddenly tremble and totter over on a man as he moves through the forest – the bare shell of its bark being the only thing holding it up,' I added.

To get even with me, Gladtvet stirred sleepily and remarked, 'It's those disgusting beetles I hate most. The ones that stink to high heaven. Why they're almost as big as turtles!'

'You only find them in houses,' I told him. 'Out here there aren't any.'

'Well, I don't miss them. And, incidentally,' said Gladtvet, 'I wish you'd shut up. I'm seeing little bugs and big bugs and flying bugs and sticky bugs. Let's get some sleep.'

Our guide agreed with him enthusiastically and I could hear him mumbling some quick prayers to himself before he dozed off.

We didn't have to keep watch at least, as the mules would warn us of any danger. I was so tired anyway that I didn't much care if a jaguar or two sniffed around or not that night. Maybe they did.

We broke camp at dawn and saddled the animals. It was quite bothersome crossing the river – we had to cross it nine times in all as it wound and unwound its way through the jungle. The animals weren't used to water and at each new crossing they were as stubborn and stupid as at the last one. I could understand their nervousness over slipping on the smooth round stones of the river bed but I couldn't do much about it.

Fortunately, Montecristo had caught up with us at that point and gave us his expert assistance. He was a quiet, self-assured man, used to his job. We had now come to the foot of the mountain where the climb was to begin and we needed him. Time after time we had to dismount, hack a passageway through the tangle of lianas or mend a part of the trail with stones before it would bear our weight. In some places, we wondered if we'd get the animals beyond that point – they scrambled and stumbled and several times fell down altogether in a sweaty, smelly heap of donkey, mule, saddles, and cluttered packs.

At two junctions, I told Montecristo I didn't believe the beasts could make it. But each time he quietly assured me they could and that we would need them to cross the high valley above us where the Indians lived.

After a fairly miserable night nursing our sores, we set out the following morning and soon found ourselves, still intact, at the foot of a breathlessly high hill covered with man-high dry grass. The mules and donkeys panted as they zigzagged up the steep slope but they made it, just as Montecristo had promised they would.

At length – and it really was – we reached the summit. Before us stretched a broad plain which seemed to reach off the edge of the plateau straight into the sky. With what breath was still left in us we began to shout and yell to announce our approach.

In what seemed the next instant, Indians appeared from every direction. I saw the same wild, dark-skinned painted faces, got the same faint smell. Oddly enough, the donkeys didn't wiggle an ear. Probably nothing that could happen now would bother them after what they had been through.

The Indians were friendly! Somehow, even if they hadn't been I think at that point I should have sat down and not cared much what happened.

I had thought from the first, however, that there was something odd about these Indians. It was only on second inspection that I realized what it was – they were as small as children, yet were fully developed adults!

Gladtvet and I are fairly tall European types but even alongside the two Creoles these Indians seemed unbelievably small. They seemed amazed to see giants walking around in their valley, but they controlled their curiosity with a certain careful respect. I was as astounded as they were. There were certain tribes of Indians I knew who were relatively short in stature but these were no taller than Pygmies! The women looked exactly like little circus dwarfs and none of the men was much over four feet in height. They were all thin and the older men had remarkable beards. Pure Indians, as everyone knew, had very little hair anywhere on their bodies.

The dwarf is not a true Pygmy, it should be remembered, but is the abnormal offspring of normal-size parents and is usually sterile. The Pygmy is fertile, well-proportioned and reproduces its own pocket edition of mankind as we know it. However, although Pygmies were known to exist in Africa, Asia and some parts of the South Pacific, this was the first time that any white man or native had seen a tribe of Pygmies in South America!

There were many stories down here of 'little people', who were said to live in the forests, coming out at night to steal food in the fields. But when scientists had looked closely into such reports they found that either monkeys or imagination or both had been responsible.

Here I stood, feeling very much as any scientist must feel when he has made a discovery – it takes him some time to get used to it himself.

These little people had no memories of ever having fought with white people – with the Indians, yes. They had fought them off and on for years. But they had had no unhappy experiences with Creoles or whites. They knew nothing as yet of the darker sides of 'civilization'. They knew only that there were knives and axes down there, tin cans and cloth. But they never went down their mountainside to get them. On our arrival they learned about trading for the first time in their lives – and liked it.

As these Indians had seen no white people except a couple of monks and Montecristo, who was a really 'nice guy', they apparently took it for granted that Gladtvet and I could hardly be worse. As a result, we were greeted with unreserved warmth and kindliness.

Our blond hair fascinated them, as it did all Indians, and several of them stood on tiptoe to look up into our blue eyes. Gladtvet's corn-coloured shock of hair – he badly needed a hair cut at that point – impressed them especially. They smiled as they stroked it, then nodded smiling at each other as Gladtvet, too, smiled at their childish pleasure in his hair.

The women, I noticed, were not as handsomely built even in miniature as their full-grown sisters farther north. They wore the same short capes and a handkerchief-size apron, but few necklaces. They lived in the same small huts as the Indians we had visited and only here and there were there any odd or individualistic details to give us a hint of a particular Pygmy culture.

It was easy to trade with these little people, and I found that even when our supplies ran out, our credit with them was good. They trusted us implicitly.

It was a pleasure to photograph these people. They helped us in every way they knew, posing at the slightest opportunity and smiling into the lens as Gladtvet took roll after roll of film – of the miniature boys playing 'Indian', of the men sitting around their fires smoking their odd little pipes, of the women bathing in the shallow stream or sitting on the bank splashing water over themselves with scoops of hollowed calabash.

It interested me that they never removed their little aprons even while washing themselves. Whether this was a concession to feminine modesty for our benefit or not I couldn't make out. Even so, to Montecristo they were still indecently immodest and he gave two of the girls his only extra shirts to hide their shame – a genuine sacrifice for him but one which apparently satisfied his stuffy soul.

They tried on the shirts to please him – they almost touched the ground and made the girls look as though they were walking around in pillowcases – but they refused to dance or have their pictures taken in them, and I didn't blame them. I am afraid they had seen me trying hard to keep from laughing at their fashion modelling but they understood, at least, that I wouldn't hold it against them if they removed Montecristo's gifts. They proceeded to do so, hanging them over their shoulders and tying the sleeves around their necks.

Our hosts didn't mind our photographing them in groups, as I have said – lined up in two rows, dancing their simple back-and-forth steps, or even eating around a campfire. But it was harder to get individuals to pose for us. We had to tease them, laugh, and do all the things old-fashioned photographers used to do to keep a child's attention in order to get any portraits at all.

While we were seated one evening, drinking corn beer in the familiar circle, which is so friendly and affords protection for all at the same time, one of the Pygmy men left, returning shortly with a package which he placed between us. I had seen such packages hanging under the palm roofs of huts in several Indian villages but had no idea what was in them.

As these Pygmies understood the Motilon Indians' language, I decided it was time to find out about the packages. The answer was simpler and more startling than I had anticipated. Each package, they told me, contained the bones of a relative and whenever one felt lonely for the loved one who had passed away, he went over to the hut, got his package and placed it beside him so that he and his mother or father or a grandparent, perhaps, could be together again for a little while.

I was already acquainted with the practical acceptance of death by all these tribes. But to find this expression of filial affection was a refreshing insight into the supposedly savage minds of these little people.

The preparation of the bone packages is quite simple. First, the corpse is stretched on a rack under the little roofed hut, open on all sides, and covered with dry grass and leaves. When nothing is left but the bones, the men go to the hut and collect them all carefully – as carefully as they can that is in their condition, after the wild feasting and dancing which precedes each job of bone collecting.

Once collected and neatly sewed up in heavy cloth or woven matting, the package of bones is tied to the back of a surviving relative who proceeds to dance with it the rest of the night. The dead one thus takes part once again in the feasting and corn-beer celebrations he knew so well and probably had been missing.

The discovery of the secret of the bone packages pleased me greatly as, in my studies up to that point, I had found nothing comparable to it in any other culture. The procedure afforded two funeral feasts – one on the immediate departure of a member of the tribe and the second on this reincarnation in the bone, if not in the flesh.

Human bones were the flutes at the death dances, of course, but in addition, the women carried magic sticks covered with strange symbols carefully burned into their shafts. When the corpse was laid out, a clutch of such magic sticks was tied together and also hung in the drying hut. I gathered that the story of the deceased's life was told in these crude etchings, but I could never confirm it or decipher them. I was fortunate in obtaining such a bundle of magic sticks but the Pygmies naturally declined my request for the bone package which went with them.

We were always on the look-out for examples of the art work of each group of Indians we met, and the work of the Pygmies was particularly fascinating as everything, of course, was made in miniature. I was delighted when I saw a small loom in one hut on which the weaver had a half-finished headband he was working on, the simple but colourful design quickly taking shape under his deft hands.

The Indians do not like to trade anything which is not finished, which makes such things all the more valuable, of course. I was determined to have it. After a little bribery, I was able to make a deal with the weaver for his loom and the unfinished work on it, and he promised to deliver it to our hut that evening. He didn't show up with the loom until the next day, however, and when he set it down we saw that the headband was finished! He must have worked on it all night and the whole day. I had, of course, to hide my disappointment.

The Indians, these little ones among them, lived a good life up there. Crops were plentiful and didn't require too much work. There was plenty of time to hunt and fish, on the side, in the lower valleys. They had no need to hurry and had a hard time understanding why we were so eager to get on our way. After all, we hadn't lived with them for a full month even! We, too, were reluctant to leave their cool, beautiful mountains, whose thousand shades of green blended into a dark blue like mighty waves, then paled in mist until our eyes could no longer follow their wake south. We loved the Andes, the backbone of this mysteriously lovely continent. And, as always, when we turned our gaze eastward to Venezuela, I knew we had to come back.

The Pygmies had told us more about the Manastara, the people in the land on the other side of the mountains. They confirmed that there was a big Indian village there, built in the middle of a lake. To enter the village you had to know the password, they told us in hushed voices. But they didn't dare guide us there. The Manastara Indians didn't like them any better than they liked white people, we were warned.

But all such talk only served to pique my curiosity and my resolve to return and make the trip somehow. Now, however, we had work to do in the lowlands.

'We'll be back,' we called out to the little people as we started off again. Montecristo was already quite far ahead while Gladtvet and I and the one-eyed one trudged down the steep trail behind the heavily laden pack animals. It seemed that long after we could no longer see them I could hear their high, piping halloos as these amazing little people called after us.

CHAPTER THREE

IN Becerril we hired an extra pair of donkeys but still had no inclination to spend the night in that miserable place. However, we were stupid – I should say rather that I was stupid – to decide to make camp on the other side of the Monte Espina as we had barely got to the edge of it by dusk that evening. I wasn't too concerned as we had always got through it fairly easily. Our one-eyed guide was dead set against trying it at night, though. But I was stubborn. We simply had to get through and not waste any more time, I insisted.

Once inside the 'spiny forest' everything dissolved into thick, stifling blackness. As the donkeys and mules could manage in the

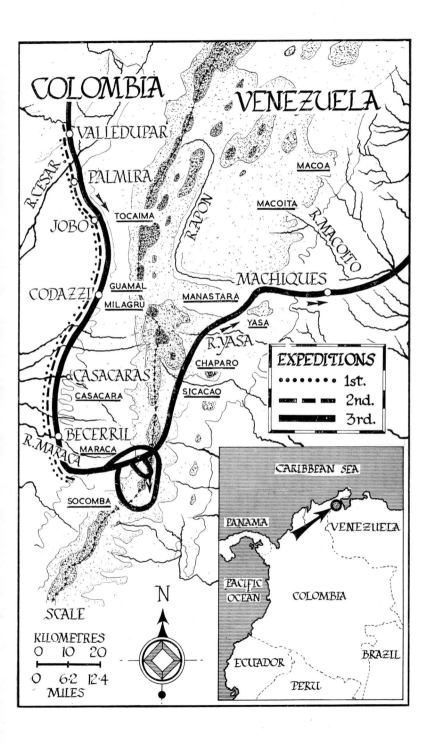

COLOMBIA

VENEZUELA

R.CESAR

VALLEDUPAR

PALMIRA

MACOA

MACOITA

TOCAIMA

R.APON

R.MACOITO

JOBO

CODAZZI

GUAMAL

MILAGRU

MANASTARA

MACHIQUES

YASA

R.YASA

CHAPARO

SICACAO

CASACARAS

CASACARA

EXPEDITIONS

• • • • • • • • 1st.
— — — — — 2nd.
▬▬▬▬▬ 3rd.

BECERRIL

R.MARACA

MARACA

SOCOMBA

CARIBBEAN SEA

PANAMA

VENEZUELA

PACIFIC
OCEAN

COLOMBIA

SCALE

KILOMETRES

0   10   20

0   6·2   12·4
MILES

N

ECUADOR

BRAZIL

PERU

A young mother and her child

An Indian showed us his skill

A typical street in a Creole village

Our pack mules set off across the savannas

Fording a river in the jungle

Maraca village set high in a mountain clearing

A young girl grinds corn for porridge and beer

Women, decorated for feast in Guamal, and a small boy

Esther Bolinder and Mariana, the young "second" wife

*The "dentist" at work. The tooth is knocked out with
the help of a stick and a stone*

Some of our men and Indian guides prepare "sancocho" soup

The unexplored Andes lying between us and Venezuela

Indian women, faces painted and smoking pipes

Even the little Indian boys like to smoke

Warriors of the Colombian mountain jungle

Two full grown Pygmy women offer Esther Bolinder some sour caviar from bags made of leaves

Fernandez shows Nasio how to brush his hair

Two girls of Sicacao who had never seen white people before

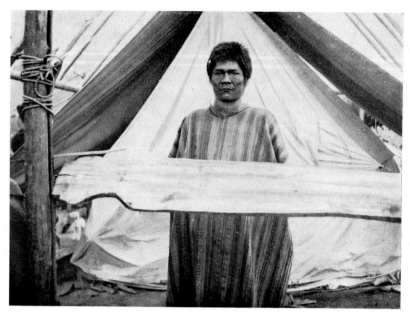

The Indians' fetisch, a long painted board, with picture writing

Esther Bolinder in the Valley of the Dead, stops at the hut full of "bone packages"

*The author and
two Pygmy Indians*

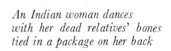

*An Indian woman dances
with her dead relatives' bones
tied in a package on her back*

The morning bath in the stream

dark better than men we let them have their heads and tried to ride as best we could.

Suddenly the mules stopped dead but we could hear the donkeys clopping and crashing off in the dark somewhere ahead. When we dismounted to see what the trouble was, we found that a huge tree had fallen over the trail. It was high enough off the ground for the donkeys to get under but not the mules with the packs, even though we had dismounted. As we couldn't very well unstrap everything from the beasts' backs, it meant we had to hack our way through some of the most cruel undergrowth we had encountered up to that point – all the way up one side of the tree, around the crown and back down the other side, to get back on the trail again.

We managed to get going again, but almost immediately bumped into another tree, like the first, bang across our path. By the time we had cleared that one, we were too worn out to care much when we discovered that the donkeys, of course, had disappeared.

The jungle seemed alive. It was as if millions of dripping sticky spiny arms were closing in to draw the last drop of life blood out of us. Gladtvet bore up remarkably well. In fact, he graduated from the jungle tenderfoot class that night. Our shirts were in ribbons and only the drying blood from our cuts kept what was left of them sticking to our bodies.

Gradually the dawn shed more and more light on our sorry caravan. We were out of the Monte Espina now, and it was flat enough on the broad savanna stretching ahead of us for the mules to trot along at a good pace. We had to find the donkeys before we could clean up and make some coffee, so again we let our steeds have their heads.

Yes, there they were, our little grey donkeys, their packs apparently intact and without a scratch on their tough little hides. But they were also enjoying their unusual freedom exceedingly and it took an exasperatingly long time to collect them and tether them all safely – all, that is, except that of our guide, which led him a merry chase and, as it turned out, a most welcome one.

The little beast had got the scent of human habitation and made a bee-line for it – water and food were uppermost in his thoughts as well as ours, so we followed its lead as best we could. It brought us to a small wayside rest house and chapel which the monks used when they came along this way. There was no one about, but there was water and – yes – there were hooks in the walls for our hammocks! We lost little time getting them up and for two wonderful hours we slept, with the Virgin Mary and Infant Jesus watching over us from a crackled old painting on the hot adobe wall.

My second visit to the Indians was at an end – a remarkable visit because I was the first white man to meet this Pygmy tribe in the mysterious mountains of Colombia. We knew that there were emeralds and platinum in those mountains but, for me, the friendship of the dwarf Indians we had discovered was worth a mountain full of riches. The scientific world questioned the veracity of our discovery of these curious little people until we published Gladtvet's photographs – a good friend who certainly earned his spurs or whatever it is a jungle-exploring photographer earns.

My scientific papers on the South American Pygmies caused a stir when we got home. But there were still the unknown Manastaras who lived on an island and to whom none of the Indians we had so far encountered dared lead us; and there were still the elusive Socombas, whose fate I was determined to discover.

But altogether, it meant simply one thing – we had to come back and cross over the giant Andes to find the answers. That another sixteen years were to pass before we fulfilled this promise to ourselves was fortunate from many points of view. But during all the intervening years, when my work took me to the interior of Africa, I would often close my eyes and remember the cool mountain night when we all danced in the light of sputtering pitch torches to the eerie music of a human tibia flute, while diminutive relatives took the bones of their loved ones out for a little fun and frolic.

Maybe this culture, too, would succumb to civilization. It was 1920, after all. We learned when we got back to the coast that the League of Nations had been officially constituted; America's Herbert Hoover was organizing relief for the starving Russian people; and our Swedish Queen Victoria had just died. Nevertheless, I looked at the bundle of magic sticks standing in a corner of my hot hotel room and knew I had not been dreaming.

BOOK FOUR

CHAPTER ONE

IT was good to be back again in this part of the world we knew
so well and had missed so much. Sixteen years had intervened; it
was 1936 now and my wife and I looked forward to noting all the
changes we were certain must have taken place meanwhile.

We left the ship one July day at Colombia's busy port, Barranquilla. Then and there we noticed that it had grown from a dusty,
sloppy little town into a prosperous city. As soon as I had bought
some supplies, we took off by plane for Santa Marta, which the
people down here call 'Banana Town', and from there took a
memorable motor-boat trip in exceptionally bad weather – so bad,
in fact, that the boat sank almost immediately after it had deposited
us in Rio Hacha, a small town farther down the east coast.

We had chosen this way of getting back to our old haunts in the
Andes because we had been told that an automobile road from
there to Valledupar was almost completed. This meant that we
wouldn't have to ride all the way on muleback and could
save a lot of time at the start of this, our third expedition.

Roads were being built in every direction, we discovered, and
new houses were sprouting up alongside them. Fernandez, our good
old friend from the gendarme corps, was with us again by courtesy
of the government. We considered it a great favour but we found
that he did too, as he much preferred going along on our rambling
adventures to working at daily routine service.

I tried without success to hire a small truck and I had begun to
think we would have to rely on those trusty mules again when the
foreman of the highway gang happened to drive up in his pickup
truck. We were completely overwhelmed when he assured us that
not only could we borrow it for as long as we liked, but offered us
a dusty but sturdy-looking car into the bargain.

Losing no time, we thanked him and roared off ahead of Fernandez driving the truck in the direction of the mysterious mountains
we were so impatient to see once again.

The road went through the valley between the Sierra Nevada de
Santa Marta, following the old trail we had taken so long ago.
Although it crossed the backs of a few of the lower mountains,
from which the views were stupendous, for the most part the road

99

skirted the cut-back jungle and passed through the lowlands and the rather boring patches of the lower plains.

Suddenly (the unexpected, quick surprises here had not changed in the least!) a band of men holding revolvers dashed into the road ahead of us, signalling our driver to stop. He braked the car gradually, apparently not as perturbed at the interruption as I should have been. But I saw, too, that he quickly buttoned his jacket right up to the neck. We soon understood why.

The men ahead were customs inspectors and not highway robbers . . . by profession, at least. I was relieved, even though our driver didn't seem to share our pleasure. He had on a new silk shirt and wasn't keen on paying duty on it. Silk brought a high price on the black market. Meeting the small Dutch traders in the bay, the pearl fishers exchanged bolts of silk for a few not too good pearls almost every night. It was a common sight to see pretty women with voluminous skirts get off the buses in a small town. When they took the bus again, after a short visit somewhere they were decidedly more slender in the hips.

A monk I knew told me about the time he was asked to take a package to a parishioner's friend in another town. Suspecting nothing, he did. When the customs men inspected his package, as well as those of the other passengers on the bus, however, his face grew very red as quantities of silky ladies' underclothes were held up for all to see. He told me he could still hear the crowd laughing whenever he thought about it.

I was prepared to open all our bags and knapsacks, although it would have taken considerable time. But the men approached our car smiling and waving their arms in magnificent gestures, showing it was unnecessary. I was puzzled until I looked again and saw that they were all brothers in a family from Valledupar. Twenty-one years earlier when our daughter, Sif, was born, their mother and father had stood with us at the little church altar as her godparents when she was baptized. As another of their sons was now governor of the province, the whole family held various posts of importance. As a result, we were greeted as spiritual members of their family whenever we met with customs inspectors, police chiefs, or mayors in every community in the region.

I was exceedingly pleased to do away with an inspection, not that we were smuggling exactly, but I, too, had bought some silk shirts in Barranquilla where they were so cheap.

After another half-day's drive, the highway came to an end at the Cesár River. As there was still no bridge across it we had to leave our truck and car for the drivers to take back to their owner and put our gear into a canoe pulled up on the bank. Once we were across, the canoe had to make several trips to bring everything over.

But everything went well, and the car for which we had telegraphed ahead finally rattled up and took us on our way to Valledupar.

Modernization had made big inroads in the old town. Already there were several refrigerators and we could get ice water. There was even cold beer now, which the town's German dentist told us represented the greatest advance in civilization in this part of the world in the past four hundred years. I found I almost agreed with him.

We learned that a small electric plant was being built and they were even talking of putting in water pipes, though the latter improvement was not considered very urgent as every well-to-do house kept numerous small boys who had nothing to do but run errands and bring water from the river.

Garbage collection, on the other hand, was a revolutionary innovation. It had been instituted by the newly appointed health commissioner who had come to the town from a more prosperous community. A two-wheeled cart – also a new departure for the town – went around once a day to collect the garbage. Not everyone saw any need for it, however, and the driver was often taunted and laughed at.

'I haven't got time to collect garbage for you,' an old woman shouted at the poor man one day, after removing the long cigar from her mouth. 'My yard's big enough to hold the stuff. Leave it alone!'

We were wakened several times at night by the sound of rifle shots. The police, we learned, were out shooting pigs, since it was now against the law to let swine and chickens run loose in the streets. The police enjoyed the hunt immensely while the pig owners did not. But it was certainly a sensible law and a long-needed one.

Some other marked improvements were not particularly welcomed by the populace, which regarded them as expensive, newfangled notions. Home owners were now required to build outside toilets and no new building permits were issued which did not include these quaint outhouses. Our friend, the mayor, reported that the health inspectors had managed to get them built but that it was another thing to make the people use them exclusively. Nevertheless, he took considerable pride in his 'new deal' in Valledupar, and was tireless in showing us every improvement he had sponsored.

But there was still no law against noise, we noticed on our first night there. Whenever anyone felt like having a party, he hired a musician and invited his friends in. After they were warmed in the glow of several bottles of rum, the whole group started a round of the streets, singing, shouting, playing, periodically soothing their hoarse throats with more rum and dancing with more and more gusto until they dropped. The police never bothered the revellers, however, feeling that people should have some fun once in a while. We agreed, and fell in love with Valledupar all over again.

No hotel had yet been built, we discovered on that first night. They didn't need one, really. Travellers were welcome to hang their hammocks in anyone's house – the arrival of a traveller was an excuse for a good meal, good talk about happenings in the outside world, a good smoke over a glass of rum and a cup of coffee, often a brief romance and always a sound sleep before setting forth again next day.

We rented a house in the town because we planned to come back several times between trips into the mountains. Now, however, we wanted to get on the trail as soon as possible and planned to set off early the next day.

Meanwhile we had made the most of our time in town by renewing old acquaintances, paying several calls and receiving old friends who came to visit. The familiar little group of citizens gathered outside our door, which always stood open during the day. People we scarcely knew greeted us with friendly embraces and often quite effusive speeches. I doubt there was anyone in Valledupar who didn't know we had come back. We couldn't possibly remember them all, of course. There was the old man who beamed at my wife: 'Don't you remember me, Señora? I sold you a dozen eggs the last time you were here.' And it was the same at every shop and street corner.

The last time we were here! Sixteen years had gone by since then but they didn't seem to mean so much in Valledupar. When we called on the governor's mother, Rosa Castro de Monsalvo, she didn't seem a great deal older than on the day she had stood as godmother for little Sif. As her 'co-madre' the proud little old lady regarded herself as a member of our family and we of hers, as much so as if we were blood relations. And she kissed the photograph of her godchild which we had brought her in the most touching way before setting it in a place of honour where everyone could see it.

Of all the changes in the town, the new buses seemed to us to spoil most of its old-world atmosphere. They made a honking swing up one street and down another before each departure, the driver yelling out 'All aboard' for whatever destination he was bound. It was impossible to miss a bus in Valledupar. So much was certain.

As no bus went to Pueblito as yet, we decided to rent a car and finally found an extraordinary contraption for a considerable fee. The body was made of wood, a lot of it home-carpentered. The top was split across the middle and the fenders were tied up with rope to keep them from hitting the wheels. One headlight was gone and the other was so crooked that its faint beam didn't even hit the road. As for the motor, it was held together by a complicated network of wire and cord, these repairs made by an owner as much an optimist as he was a bad mechanic. It was a miracle that the thing ran at all, but it did!

Sputtering and choking, the car rattled along the stony road and the rutted trail through the forest, which was barely wide enough for it to get through. Once we thought we'd lost the top for good when a big tree branch got wedged in the crack. With some help from my wife, who anchored one of the braces which seemed to be its only point of contact with the rest of the car, it held together.

Pretty shaken up, we at last chugged into Pueblito. Although it was on the map now and was named Codazzi (after the cartographer who had mapped the area before he died there) everyone still called it the 'Little Town'.

We scarcely recognized the monastery. The monks had built themselves a new brick cloister with running water, a bath, and even a radio set. We received a warm welcome at the monastery and enjoyed a wonderful evening catching up on events since our last visit.

A good deal had happened, we discovered. The Capucine Brothers had continued their peace missions and some of the Indians had become 'tame' enough to wander through the village without creating undue excitement. A few had even picked up a little Spanish. But, in general, they still kept pretty much to their mountains.

Now there were two tribes living above Pueblito, the monks told us, who were constantly fighting between themselves. Hoping to arbitrate their differences, the monks had invited men from both tribes down to the monastery to draw up a truce.

Things were going fairly well when, for some reason, their anger flared up suddenly and a pitched battle began, with arrows zinging through the cloister as more Indians vaulted the low walls into the gardens and chased each other from pillar to bush. The oldest monk, who had been conducting the peace talks, made a dash for his cell, closed the door and locked himself in. He had bad nerves, we were told, and it took several hours of earnest entreaties on the part of his brothers – who had meanwhile succeeded in restoring order – to get him to come out again.

We learned, too, that the place where the Indians now lived had been given a name – Guamal. We wanted to go up there as soon as we could because, despite the passing years, few modern improvements had reached Pueblito. It was the same miserably hot and smelly place we remembered so well. Farm animals still wandered loose through the streets and, even though the sultry nights made one gasp for air, we had to keep our bedroom window closed. At least they had got in some window glass since we were last in the village, and we were grateful.

WE were once again on our way to visit the Indians. Our guide, at the head of our caravan, knew the way by heart. Fernandez rode behind us, guiding the pack mules up the steep and so-well-remembered mountainside. We knew that the Motilon Indians moved fairly often and were uncertain whether we would soon be greeting old friends or if we were about to make new acquaintances.

The trail seemed just as narrow and slippery as ever but the mules knew the way. The monks had recently built themselves a palm-roofed adobe retreat near our first cornfield, where they spent a large part of the hot months when Pueblito became intolerable, and the mules had made the trip a hundred times.

When we had climbed between 2,300 and 2,400 feet above the lowlands, we found ourselves on an open hillside from which the view was magnificent. Far below us lay the broad savannas, striped across with ribbons of rivers and punctuated by little ranch houses and occasional villages.

Micael began to unpack our supplies while Fernandez started supper. Micael was very light-skinned for these parts and, perhaps for this reason, he was especially popular with the darker-skinned daughters of the villages in the area. It would be an exaggeration to say that he was good looking. He was a good worker, though, always smiling across his yellow stumps of teeth – nearly all Creoles had bad teeth, we'd noticed – and he never complained about a thing. On the other hand, he was completely oblivious of his appearance. He always wore the same ragged broad-brimmed hat, a pair of striped pants which had long since seen better days and a dirty cotton T-shirt. But the Indians loved him and we never regretted that we had taken him on to join our expedition. With his jokes and hearty laugh, Micael made the going a lot easier.

By the time our belongings were sorted out for the night, supper was ready but, while we loved Fernandez for many things, cooking was not one of them. He was the artist, always experimenting with new recipes which seldom turned out as he had planned. The food was edible, though, and we were decidedly more gourmands than gourmets that evening after our day's climb.

We had no sooner begun to eat than a downpour forced us to retreat into the monks' shelter. The roof there leaked practically everywhere and, before we could stretch our tents under it and set up our camp beds, the floor was about an inch deep in water. But not even the damp kept us from sleeping that night, and at least it was cool.

Next morning we woke to find the sun streaming across our beds and when we went out the sky was as blue and clear as the Caribbean itself. After a quick breakfast, we took off again towards the Indians' village.

At first the trail wound up the hillside, but after a couple of hours the steep slopes began and we were soon puffing our way up almost perpendicular cliffsides. We thought we had managed pretty well considering we were not yet in training, but if anyone had told us that for the next three weeks we should be doing nothing else but climbing those beastly cliffs, we would quite possibly have settled right where we were until we had caught enough breath and energy to climb back down where we came from.

It didn't take more than two hours, however, to reach the first Indian village – a cluster of shelters – roofs with no walls. All but one, that is. In the one hut which had walls, we found an old Indian who called himself Juan, and he remembered us from sixteen years back! As he had since learned quite a lot of Spanish, he buttonholed me and began to tell me everything that had happened while we had been away.

After solemnly exhibiting the old pair of trousers he now wore as evidence of his civilized state, he lit a cigar and told me the story.

'Yes, Señor,' he began, 'we Motilons finally made peace with the wild white people. Now the white people are tame,' he assured me as his wife set out braided mats for Esther and me to rest on.

Soon other Indians gathered around us and Juan introduced them, solemnly, one after the other.

'The last time you were here,' Juan went on, as though it had been only a few weeks before, 'I didn't know any Spanish and could not greet you as I would have liked. My tongue couldn't give me the Spanish words. But now we can talk together, Señor. Yes,' he repeated, smiling, 'we can talk now.'

Whatever the changes we had noticed, nothing had been done to improve the flavour of the corn beer which the Indians brought out almost before we had had time to realize that we were sitting on a tenuous borderline between the savage and the civilized.

It was fascinating in itself but was even more interesting because the element of surprise was never farther away than an accidental motion or sudden misunderstanding. Although Juan spoke good Spanish and now looked like any other town citizen, I had to remind myself that I was not speaking to a man reared in the Spanish-speaking culture whose way of thinking I understood. Juan remained pure Indian in his thinking and his reactions. The main advantage was that I could now penetrate deeper and try to understand how 'primitive' the so-called primitive really is.

With the beer we were served the usual cornmeal balls which, this time, were mixed with little pieces of monkey meat, the skin and hair still on them. It was never wise to refuse any Indian food, I knew, so my wife and I managed, with a little sleight-of-hand, to dispose of them without hurting our hosts' feelings. Fernandez, on the other hand, did not fare so well. He let himself be challenged by the Indians to drink two huge bowls of corn beer and force down a cornmeal-monkey-ball with each. As a result he had to wake me in the middle of the night for a dose of mustard and water.

It was the first maize season here and the Indian women were busy night and day grinding it. I discovered some hens running about, pecking up spilled kernels as fast as they fell. This was something new, for the Indians had had no pets or poultry the last time I was there. When the chief gave us a hen for our supper I was delighted. But I was equally curious to learn why the Indians still ate neither chickens nor eggs. The hen was a pet – no real sacrifice for them and a blessing for us. I was glad, incidentally, to see that my wife was helping Fernandez prepare the poor bird and save what was left of it for our *sancocho* later.

As I had anticipated, we did not get much sleep that night. The village was lighted with resin-dipped torches which smoked and smelled badly. While the women ground the maize – not a very quiet job in itself – the men sang and talked, lying around the fire braiding mats, their bows and arrows at hand alongside them.

In general, I observed, the Indians had guarded their own customs well. Nor had they, in any way that I could see, discarded their own code of morals or become morally weakened through their contacts with white people. This was very encouraging, although perhaps not as strange as I thought at first, when I realized that very few whites ever bothered to venture up these tremendous heights and that the Indians probably sent only a select few to fraternize below. This was not a matter of mass assimilation of new and different *mores* at all. None had taken place and my wife and I found ourselves wondering whether, in those fifteen-odd years, the Indians had had a good look at civilization and preferred their own way of life.

We could leave our exchange gifts quite safely in our shelter and know they would not be disturbed – Indians do not steal from their friends. Even in their expeditions to white settlements for iron and steel scrap they took no more than they needed and left everything else alone.

I was amazed that in all these years these Indians had not acquired any firearms. They were just as interested in them as children but no longer as afraid as I remembered they had been on our previous trips. A good part of one morning was taken up with demonstrating our rifles and two revolvers – my wife still carried her little pearl-handled Browning.

Then Fernandez gave an exhibition of his marksmanship one evening. He was a good shot and the Indians were delighted, but the little demonstration almost had a tragic ending. One shot went wild when someone bumped his arm and almost struck an Indian named Carcamo. The old warrior was badly frightened as the bullet sang past his right ear. He made a lunge towards Fernandez but Juan stepped quickly between them and, talking very fast, explained to the other Indian that, if he *had* been killed by the bullet, we would have carried his body down the mountainside to the monks. There the monks would arrange the same wonderful funeral for him which they had often seen down in Pueblito, Juan explained. He'd have everything, including a solemn procession with candles and bells and the monks would all stand around his bier and pray for him all night. It would be very beautiful and sad – everyone would be crying, Juan told him. By that time, Carcamo looked genuinely disappointed that he hadn't been killed after all.

Once on the subject, Juan went on to tell us about the monks. I had already gathered that they were not as popular as they used to be with the Indians, but had no idea why. We were sitting around the fire now, having happily passed the little crisis with Carcamo.

It turned out that the monks had been very lavish with their gifts in former times and the Indians had taken the gifts for granted. Today, the monks were facing difficulties in getting sufficient funds for their work and had practically stopped all peace offerings. Their reasoning had been all wrong from the start, of course, as they did not exchange gifts but let the Indians get used to accepting charity, thereby undermining the sense of pride which Indians guard so jealously. As a result, the Indians resented the stoppage of the largesse without understanding the reasons for it. From this experience, the Indians logically included all whites in their resentment over what they felt to be their stinginess and superior attitudes.

With us, at least, they did a rush business since we wanted as many spears, bows, arrows, and quivers as we could trade from them. They gladly handed over quantities of their craftsmanship for the comparatively inexpensive manufactured articles we had brought with us. It was easy for them to make more bows and arrows and baskets, after all.

The Indians also told us time and again how much they liked us and showed it in every way they could think of, from a shy little pat on my wife's shoulder to an extra thick layer of bracken for our beds and juicy broiled birds' legs. For the most part, however, I felt that this friendship did not go much deeper than a good business relationship. I wanted to strengthen it, to get to feel that I could really count on a genuine friendship pact which would be mutual. We should need it if we were to get through the wilder regions on our way across the Andes.

With this in mind we took every opportunity to visit individuals in their huts. It was difficult to remain inside any of them for very long at a time, however, as they were infested with fleas. Millions of fleas managed to survive our efforts to exterminate them.

I decided to move back to the monks' shelter; even though the roof leaked, it was relatively free of the pests. The Indians nodded when I told them, and indicated that they would return our visit in a couple of days.

Sure enough, they all arrived early one morning as we were finishing our coffee. What was more, a group of Indians from another village also chose that day to visit us. The situation was a little delicate as the two villages were rivals and their citizens often settled their differences in pitched battle. That was bad enough, but for us to be in the centre of such a scrap was distinctly unhealthy. The Indians we had just visited now regarded us with very proprietary feelings and themselves as a kind of 'chosen people' as we had come to them first. Any trouble now would possibly ruin our plans if, indeed, we survived to make any.

I was relieved to notice that the Indians had apparently decided to be on their good behaviour. One group of about ten settled down around our cookhouse. The other gathered outside the shelter itself. Fernandez put the biggest kettle we had on the fire and made a really good soup for the crowd. While waiting for it, we did a huge trading business which seriously depleted our barter stocks and left us with quantities of Indian handiwork to pack and drag with us somehow.

The Indians from the neighbouring village left the same evening, apparently satisfied that the reports they had heard about us were true and that we meant them no harm. The others spent the night, climbing back home next morning.

CHAPTER THREE

FROM what I had learned from both tribes, I realized that none of them knew anything about conditions in the interior. If we were to get across the mountains we would have to do better than we were doing in finding trustworthy guides.

I suddenly recalled our Pygmy friends and was convinced in that moment that they were the ones we needed. They knew the people living in the remotest parts of the northern Andes and they knew the terrain. This time we also had good men with us – Fernandez, Micael, and the older Montecristo, who had taken me to the Maracas and knew several Indian dialects.

Montecristo was an unusual man. In appearance he reminded me a great deal of Roald Amundsen, the famed Norwegian explorer. He was a quiet, modest man, but he knew what he wanted and got it with a gift for diplomacy which earned him the respect of Indian and white alike. He was delighted to have another chance to join us as he had not visited the Maracas – our Pygmy friends – for a long time.

He told me he had heard that the trail which we had once cleared was all grown over and said it would be a tough job getting through a large part of that forest again. Just the same, I hoped that, once we reached Becerril, we would get more detailed information about current conditions in the Sierra de Perijá.

Because I so well remembered what a miserable place Becerril was, as a precaution I sent ahead a whole donkey caravan of food and other supplies. The caravan was on its way as we would follow next morning. Although donkeys were still a much better means of transportation than a truck would have been, there are a number of things which can happen en route to upset your plans. Sometimes, of course, only one of them will occur but oftenest all of them do. A donkey will get tired and have to rest. The load may shift and have to be completely repacked and strapped on again. Something may frighten the beasts and they will either refuse to budge at all or scramble off in different directions.

I had a few forebodings, I confess, as I watched the beasts amble off towards Becerril with their donkeymen. The trail across the savannas presented few difficulties, but the swampy, spiny Monte Espina still lay between them and the town.

We managed to get organized early the next day, but I told everyone that we had to ride at a good pace if we were to get through that spiny forest ourselves before nightfall. I was determined never again to try it at night. My mule was acting up so badly that Fernandez suggested we switch animals. I took his horse and he got on the mule, which seemed to understand right away that it couldn't get away with any more nonsense with a master gendarme aboard.

I galloped ahead to catch up with my wife and the others – it didn't matter that Fernandez lagged behind a bit. By the time we had reached the edge of the forest, however, he still hadn't caught up. We decided to start through anyway, as it was fast getting dark.

On the other side I pulled up and we waited. As there still was no sign of Fernandez, we could do nothing but continue on to Becerril. Arriving there about eight in the evening I was very glad to see that Micael had stacked all our packs and boxes neatly in the middle of the cold clay-walled room he had rented for us. After cleaning up, we went out into the street and were quickly surrounded by the curious villagers come to look us over.

By that time I was a little anxious. Fernandez had not yet arrived, but there was nothing I could do about it. Reluctantly we went to bed.

The sun was hardly up when the lost one woke us and began to relate his adventures over the hot coffee he had made for us.

Shortly after we had left him, Fernandez reported, he had to get off the mule to tighten its cinch, but he had forgotten to tether the beast before doing so and it had lost no time in trotting off to freedom, leaving Fernandez standing there. When a mule wants to go fast it can, and Fernandez knew it would be hopeless to try to catch it. He therefore set out on foot to follow us and keep our rendezvous in Becerril. That he managed to get safely through that spiny jungle remains a mystery to me.

'Oh, I got out all right,' he assured me, as I could see perfectly well for myself. 'But I was pretty tired when I got to the clearing so I lay down to get some rest. It was terrible, horrible, Señor! Big clouds of mosquitoes – you couldn't see through them – dived down and attacked me. I made a fire to smoke them off but it didn't help at all until I got a bright idea.'

Fernandez's idea was indeed not without its better points. He had taken off his sweaty socks and put them on the fire and the smudge was effective until they were consumed. After that, he said he wasn't sure what to do as he didn't want to burn up his uniform, which was all he had with him.

'It was when I woke up I was angry, Señor,' Fernandez ended his report. 'A little farther – not ten minutes more – and I came to an adobe shelter where I could have spent the night in peace!'

I gave him a pair of my socks and sympathized as best I could. However, I found it difficult to hide my feelings. One of our best mules was gone and with it an expensive saddle, a fine Swedish camera, and several other things I hated to lose.

On seeing that I was rather downcast, Fernandez had just resigned himself to going back to search for the animal when he saw a small boy approaching, leading a mule. Emerging from the dust cloud, Fernandez recognized the mule! Saddle and pack were apparently intact but now there was also a passenger astride the weary beast.

The boy told me and my wife that he had caught the mule on the other side of the Monte Espina, had recognized my saddle by its trappings, and had made his way through that jungle by himself just to bring it to me. Moreover, the passenger – wearing an enormous straw hat and holding a half-dead chicken across her lap

– was none other than our old cook, Beatrice! She had stopped the boy on the way, learned that we had returned and insisted on coming along to welcome us back. The chicken was the only gift she could put her hands on quickly, she said, as my wife and I greeted her with real emotion – though sixteen years had done little to improve her appearance.

That night we had one of the best meals we had eaten in many long weeks – a hearty welcome celebration. The people in Becerril weren't so bad either, we found ourselves thinking. Everyone was so friendly and kind, I regretted my former criticism of them.

Beatrice absolutely refused to eat with us, nevertheless, and she was just as adamant about going along on any expedition to the Indians. And as things turned out, it was just as well.

Becerril was unbearably hot and we longed to get up into the cool mountains. It was comparatively easy to hire mules but not so easy to get their owners to catch them first. The animals browsed freely on the broad savannas, and their owners were apt to accept our money, then wave grandly towards the savanna, telling us to take our pick. A whole afternoon was spent chasing donkeys but Fernandez and Micael at last rounded up some strong, healthy beasts and tethered them securely to each other until we were ready to start off.

With us this time were three young fellows we had hired to help hack our way through the heavy underbrush. The trails were all grown over since our last visit and I saw right away that we weren't going to progress as fast as I had hoped.

We nevertheless made a rather impressive appearance at the take-off – my wife, Fernandez and I, Micael, the men to clear the trail. But that was not all. Two negro boys on mules brought up the rear leading a scrawny cow between them. I was not sure whether I would give it to the Indians as another 'peace offering' or not. In any case, it assured us of some fresh meat and I now had quite a retinue to feed. Besides, this was the best way to take meat where we were going. By making the trip 'on the hoof' we were spared the trouble of salting and packing the meat as well as saving the space in the donkeys' load.

As we trotted out into the bright savanna at the foot of the mountains which swooped up over our heads, we experienced a wonderful sense of relief. We always felt happiest when we were on our way to meet adventure and always resented a little the delays caused by details, which had to be attended to, of course, before we could set out for anywhere.

Riding along through the palm groves, we were enjoying life in general when some little female donkeys trotted over towards us and began flirting with new friends and claiming old ones among their more sedate brothers in our caravan. Their antics and whinnied greetings were amusing but they succeeded in no time in disrupting the morale of all our caravan animals. Several of our donkeys forgot their duties completely, broke their tethers and cantered after their temptresses, braying and kicking up their heels as best they could with their heavy loads.

We lost another good hour rounding them up again and hitching them to each other. When at last we reached the narrow trail, I was relieved; it was so narrow that such escapades were out of the question.

After we had climbed fairly high up into the forest-covered lower hills, we came once again to the cool Maraca River, dashing over its stony bed. Its waters were so clear we could see every stone but it was also too shallow for any fishing. The fish I had been looking forward to preferred the dark, quiet pools close to the jungle's edge. This was the fourth time we had crossed it, counting our previous visit. Now we had just time to get over it before setting up camp for the night.

In the dark forest on the other side, when my wife and I stood close to a tree and looked straight up its trunk, through its leaves hundreds of feet above us we could see patches of brilliant sapphire sky, seemingly all of a piece with the shadowy rocks of the Indians, fastnesses up there.

'Think, if we could just climb this tree,' Esther said, 'we could step right off at the top and be there.'

It did look that way. Instead we both knew it would be a couple of days at least before we would be standing on those rocks.

Our chief problem now was with the cow, which disliked mountain-climbing as much as it did water. The men dragged and pushed the poor beast (which had already lost several pounds along the way) every step.

That night we pitched our tents as carefully as we could between the huge ant-hills in the forest. It was too dry for the fever mosquitoes to be out, a fortunate thing for us because the leaf-cutter ants cut down all our mosquito nets that night as soon as it got dark. We managed to get some sleep in spite of sessions of scratching and slapping and oiling ourselves. This time we had some insect repellents with us but I could not refrain from thinking that the scientists should have tested them on South American insects – ants, ticks, fleas, and all the host of creepy-crawlies here instead of on their less voracious Swedish relatives.

Next day we faced a tiring, rugged climb. The almost perpendicular cliff slopes were treacherous and the winding trail slippery. Almost as bad were the abrupt little descents we had to make over sharp, loose stones before gathering our strength for another steep climb. It would have been impossible to have kept a trail cleared in this part of the mountains. The lianas ran wild, and thorny branches reached out at us from above as well as from both sides. We had to dismount several times and walk; and sure-footed as they were, the donkeys often fell. In fact, it was here that one of them was so badly injured that I had to shoot it and load its packs on my horse, but in spite of everything, we managed to reach the first Indian huts that evening.

A group of Maracas – the little people – was waiting to greet us – they had naturally heard our approach, for no one can be very quiet hacking his way through a jungle. The Indians had had time to do a fresh paint job on their faces but they were not wearing their ceremonial dress, I noticed.

I had never known them to have more than one change of clothing, if their simple garments could be so dignified by the name. And it mattered little that they tried to wash them. The water in this area is so hard it is hopeless to try to get anything clean even with soap, which the Indians, of course, did not have.

We had become fond of these unwashed little people but it was still difficult to get used to their smell. It permeated the air around them and their dirty clothing, particularly as these Indians were very demonstrative. They patted us affectionately and several threw their arms around us at the slightest provocation.

While we rested, we had to undergo another thorough examination as they crowded around, taking turns wetting their fingers in their mouths, then trying to rub the white colour off our skins. All this while, it took some strength of character to avoid showing the slightest distaste in our faces.

I was relieved when the group broke up for the evening meal and even more so when several Indian men offered to clear the trail for us to the next village. They set off before dawn next morning, a machete in one hand, a bow and brace of arrows in the other.

The news of our arrival certainly moved faster than we did – I shall never understand *how* it travelled – and little groups of Indians (or perhaps I should say, groups of little Indians) came running to greet us all along the way. They looked savage enough but their greetings were hearty and very noisy. Not much out of the ordinary happened in their villages and the sight of white people, even after all these years, was still an event for most of them. It was not only our odd colour which puzzled them, of course. The men liked to stand next to me or Fernandez, who was about my height, and measure themselves. Their heads seldom reached my elbow and the women were even shorter.

Running on ahead, they slashed down vines and hacked off tree branches with swift, clean strokes, but the trail they cleared was not really high enough for us to pass through without either dismounting or lying prostrate on our saddles. Our legs were protected with cowhide chaps and we wore leather gloves, but by the time we reached a broad plain in a beautiful highland valley, our clothes looked as though we had been attacked by wild animals.

Here were two large villages and we were greeted with much ceremony and shown to a spot where I understood, from their signs, that we could set up our tents. I decided to decline the offer, nevertheless, and settle temporarily a good distance from the hot, open field. And I met with no dissent among my followers, for the remains of an Indian, who had been killed by a jaguar, were lying in state there to dry out, contaminating the whole area in the progress. The smell was revolting enough but the corpse, under its grass shroud, was alive with maggots and flies and beetles of every description.

After a short tour of inspection, the men found an excellent camping spot in the forest at the edge of the clearing, protected on two sides by small streams about a hundred yards apart. We had all the help we needed in setting up our tents there on what amounted to a little island. The Indians' curiosity slowed things down somewhat as each item had to be carefully inspected and its function demonstrated before being installed – tent poles, stakes, lanterns, camp beds, blanket rolls, tarpaulin – everything.

While their friendliness was genuine enough, the Indians knew very well that their work would be paid for. My wife had already set up shop and was doing a brisk trade at our simple 'post exchange', after straightening out the first misunderstandings. She had had to make it clear that one knife was worth three large spears or six small ones, and so on down quite a long list. I was interested to see that should one Indian think another had got a better bargain than he, there still was no apparent jealousy or ill feeling between them.

Our rather cramped camping grounds were soon swarming with Indians – men, women and children. Several of them started campfires and gave every indication of intending to move in with us. There was quite a heavy turnover, however. New groups of Indians from quite far away kept replacing those who had seen their fill of our odd ways and departed. That we slept in separate beds under blankets was only one of our more obvious idiosyncrasies, in their eyes. Toothbrushing fascinated them no end and, given more time, I believe my wife would have made toothbrush drill a new Indian game.

On the second day I decided that it would be safe to send back the boys who had been taking care of the cow and our trail-blazers with them. That left only Montecristo, Micael and Fernandez to help us, but I felt now that I could count on the Maracas. We had no reason to doubt their friendship any longer and I had been able to confirm for my companions my own faith in their complete honesty.

The Maracas could easily have stolen almost anything they wanted. We had to leave our cooking pots, plates and eating utensils on open shelves night and day, and they set high store by such things. But we never missed so much as a bent spoon.

Caution was none the less recommended. Despite their diminutive size, I had been informed that these people had a reputation throughout the region for being extremely warlike. And as I watched them, I was reminded of jaguar kittens. They could play and purr one minute and snarl and bristle the next, without any apparent provocation. That my informants had been correct was left in no doubt by the story we heard one night sitting around the fire. Because Montecristo knew their dialect fairly well, we were able at last to learn, that night, the fate of the Socomba Indians for whom we had been searching from the very beginning.

As I have said, we were sitting around the fire. Fernandez and Micael had helped the Indians roast the cow, which had made the supreme sacrifice that evening, and we had had an excellent meal of veal steak and corn bread. The Indians were still gnawing on the remains – nothing went to waste, not the heart, ears or even intestines. An old Pygmy was mouthing small slices of burned hide in his toothless gums, apparently finding it delicious.

As I put the translated story together, it developed that one night the Maracas had held a council of war and decided to put an end to the Socomba whom they had long hated. Taking them unaware, these little people had managed to kill every man, woman and child, with the exception of one little boy whom they took prisoner.

When Montecristo pointed him out to me, sitting on the ground by the fire, it confirmed what I had noticed from the start. His profile was more sharply drawn, his forehead higher and, although not yet fully grown, his build was normal.

Here he was – the last Socomba Indian in the world, now living as an indentured servant to his Pygmy master. He was required to work for him but, as slavery is unknown to Indian cultures, he was allowed to keep everything he made as well as the harvest from the patch of cornfield which had been allotted to him. His captors had also selected a wife for him and it didn't seem to us that he was too badly off considering the fate of his tribe.

We didn't get much sleep that night. Even though the Indians were relatively quiet, a thunderstorm attacked the mountains with cannon-like explosions that shook the earth. Lightning like the flash of dynamite blasts lit up the forests and valley below. Even the Indians seemed worried. A group of older ones gathered stealthily and began a ritual – 'blowing away the storm'. With rhythmic motions they alternately puffed out their cheeks, blew hard in the direction of the storm centre and then, lifting their arms straight in the air, pushed back the wind and the rain in spasmodic, frantic gestures.

The fact is that after a few minutes of this anti-storm dance, the weather actually cleared for a while and the thunderheads went rumbling after each other on down the valley. The rain did not ease up, however, and we felt sorry for the Indians who were lying on their mats under the sky with no protection, but it scarcely seemed to bother them. Next morning they found some dry wood, kindled their fires and danced themselves dry, laughing like children during the whole drying-out process.

Little by little we learned the Indians' names and found that several had now adopted the Spanish names recommended by Montecristo. In addition, we discovered that the wife took her husband's name with what I supposed was the feminine suffix. Monaro's wife was called Monarongsanú; Erepaximo's wife was Erepaxmanú. But when I asked one young man what his wife's name was, he told me he would have to ask her. When she replied that she had no name, her husband laughed and said he would give her one. I never found out what name he selected but, with time, we managed to learn most of them.

Many of these Pygmies went around with pets they had tamed. Most were small birds which perched on their heads or shoulders and were never put in cages. Some Indians were followed by tame ground rats which nibbled food from their owners' mouths; and several Indian women kept baby animals to help keep their babies warm and which they nursed at their breasts with their own young.

Walking along the forest path one morning, my wife met a little woman who wore her pet monkey like a boa. Another monkey got so fresh, darting around the camp and stealing bits of food from those gathered around the fire, that one man threw a javelin at it. He just missed it – purposely, I believe, because at twenty feet he could easily have pinned it to the ground. The javelin had the desired effect, at any rate, for the monkey scampered up a tall tree in a terrible temper and remained there screaming all kinds of insults at the people below.

I found an orphaned baby deer in the woods next day and took it back to the camp. It became tame in no time but the woman quarrelled noisily over which one should have the privilege of nursing it. Only when one of our men gave the women a small puppy to nurse too, did the squabbling stop.

We left the deer behind when we left the village, knowing that only after it had died a natural death would the Pygmies eat it. And then, only the old men would be permitted to eat the head, for it was believed that young people would get sick and die if they should eat such meat.

Some of the Indians who came to visit us were from the encampments we had passed on our way up to the Pygmies' mountain. Others came from the largest of all the villages which lay to the east, at the other end of the valley. They were not especially friendly with our Pygmies and, although hostilities did not actually break out, they didn't have a single good word for each other. When the visitors invited us and the Pygmies to a feast, therefore, I was somewhat reluctant to accept. We wanted above everything to avoid being mixed up in any feuds. It was doubtful that we would be in actual danger, but any trouble at all might put an end to all our plans then and there. Friendly relations were indispensable if we were to get across these mountains to Venezuela.

The Indians living nearest our camp had collected various articles of Indian crafts for us and occupied themselves with showing off to the visitors from the far end of the valley – in a comic pantomime. One of them lay stretched out in the gorgeous new hammock one of the women had woven for my wife. He had on one of my old hats and was languidly giving orders to one of his wives. She hurried back and forth bringing him refills of water in an old flowered enamel shaving mug as he lazily patted a small dog beside him.

My wife and I had a hard time keeping back our laughter – the parody on civilized living, such as we, perhaps, symbolized to him, was masterful, although I must say, I could not remember ever having to ask my wife for a drink of water. The effect on the visiting Indians was no less amusing; but as their envy was becoming more pronounced every minute, I felt it was time to step in and claim my hat. I turned over two cigars to get it back and made sure the chief visitor got his, too, before going back to our tent.

After talking it over we decided not to go to the party. The corn beer had fermented early and no one could be certain what might happen.

As things turned out, our Indians started off fairly late in the evening. Half-way to their destination, they met others coming back who told them the beer was finished, so they all came home except for old Monaro who, as president of the Elders, had felt impelled for diplomatic reasons to represent his village at the feast.

Much later in the evening, Monaro, too, returned, crying bitterly. He was very drunk but we managed to get the story out of him. It seems the other Indians had talked the entire time about his son who had died following a similar beer festival. They had warned Monaro that he would end up the same way and it broke his heart, he told us, to have that sad event brought up again. In fact, he said, he had been impelled to get back at his tormentors by shooting a brace of arrows into the crowd. Fortunately he had been restrained before any damage was done and sent off to find his way back alone through the forest.

Monaro had managed remarkably well, considering the condition he was in, and had made his way straight to our tent to pour out his trouble. There he sat, cross-legged on the floor, weeping for his son although the boy had died a good many years back. Monaro's face, carefully painted for the party with fine red spots and black stripes, was smeared now by his tears. After he finally nodded off to sleep, his wives came and carried him home.

Although the Indians in this village had missed one feast day, they saw no reason for not having another. Next day we noticed that preparations were under way for a big affair with dancing and music. A large smörgasbord started the whole thing off. Spread out for all to share were broiled and raw fat white larvae, resting on leaf plates, and a special kind of caviar, which had been kept several months to judge by its smell.

As the moon came up, the dance began. The men were lined up in one row, the women in a row behind them. Singing their own music softly at the start, they began to sway, first to the left, then to the right. We thought we knew individuals well enough by that time to be able to tell just which ones would begin the stamping to set the rhythm. Yes, Esther guessed correctly that it would be Miro and his wife, the village's uncrowned beauty queen. She was indeed prettier than the other women but she was so short and dumpy that any other claims to beauty she may have had were not obvious to our eyes.

It seemed they must tire after three hours of chanting, swaying, and shouting, but their enthusiasm only increased until, with a final chorus of war whoops, the men shot a hail of arrows into the ground and the party broke up.

The elders watching from the sidelines nodded to each other as if to say: 'A fine feast. Yes, a splendid feast!' But although I asked everyone I thought would know, I never discovered what Miro and his wife contributed to the general welfare except always to be on hand whenever there was a feast. He always kept a sharp eye on his wife, however, watching her like a cat, and no other Indian dared approach her for he was quick with an arrow. Miro also admired my wife and asked me once where he could get a white woman like mine. During the dance, in fact, he was showing off for Esther's benefit to such a degree that she thought it wiser to go to see what had happened to little Mirtu.

The child, scarcely able to walk, had toddled into the dance, a bow and arrow in one hand and a lighted cigar in his tiny mouth.

We were concerned lest Mirtu be trampled in the mêlée. But he was rescued in time by his aunt who hustled him back to his mother, protesting every bit of the way. He was furious at being treated like a child and several times tried unsuccessfully to shoot his aunt. Once back with his mother, however, he threw down his little weapons and, after taking the cigar out of his mouth, snuggled into his mother's lap and was soon feeding contentedly at her breast. Now, we said to each other, we have seen everything!

The following day I had a talk with our hosts. Knowing their language fairly well by that time was a great help in getting precise information about conditions in the mountains to the east. And what I learned filled us with high expectations.

Our Maraca Pygmies were relatively good friends, they said, with the Sicacao tribe, although they did not meet often. Every detail, added to what we already knew, made me certain they were talking about the Indians in Venezuela! Modern geographical boundaries, of course, did not concern the Indians in the least if, in fact, they even knew of their existence. We faced only one set-back at the moment – we couldn't make a move until the dry season between December and March.

However, we needed the time in between to build up our food stores and replenish our stocks of gifts and other supplies. I therefore decided to build a small house with the Indians' help while my men began work on shortening the trail to the lowlands so it would not be such a difficult task getting stocks up to our new head-quarters.

Work on the house was in full swing when he had another set-back. I had the misfortune to come down with malaria. In the first days of the attack, I lay flat on my back with a temperature of 105° – at night in the tent and during the day under a nearby tree, as the tent was then like an oven. A week of atebrin treatment quelled the fever and just in time time, too, for the rainy season had set in in full force. The Indians did not try to blow away those rain storms – experience had made them resigned.

As I needed some further treatment, we decided to go back down to the coast and perhaps make some side trips to the Indian villages in the northern section of the Sierra Nevada, where these amazing people still believed in magic, and (more practically) where the rains were not so troublesome. I also hoped to find a few sturdy bearers there for, strong as they were, our Pygmy friends could not, of course, tackle a grown man's job.

As we felt we should make a goodbye call in the large neighbour-ing village, Montecristo saddled two mules – one for my wife and one for himself. I could not go along, not yet being able to stand on my feet for very long at a time. I watched them from my hammock, which the Pygmies had covered with a huge umbrella of leaves, as they started off towards the valley one wet, green morning.

CHAPTER FOUR

I SHALL try to put down my wife's report of her visit as she told it to me. First, there was the ride through the fabulously beautiful valley itself – green hills folded into new valleys through a silver shimmer of rain and always there were the stately jungle-clad mountains forming a majestic backdrop. Of all the places we had ever been, she said (and I was to confirm this later when I saw it for myself) this was where she would like to live forever.

The village was alive with grownups and children who greeted her and Montecristo as heartily as they knew how. Perhaps her gifts had something to do with the reception accorded her, but Esther doubted it. It was when she was handing out lumps of sugar that she saw a pitifully thin, naked little boy looking on longingly from the edge of the crowd. The child apparently didn't dare come forward to take any sugar with the others dancing and squealing around her. He seemed not to belong to the others. No one paid him any attention as he stood looking on with big, black pleading eyes.

When my wife asked the chief about him she learned that he was fatherless and that his mother had left him to fend for himself. Esther called the boy to her but it was some time before he at last sidled over to her, carefully keeping out of the way of the others. He was badly undernourished and his little body was covered with ashes, possibly because he had lain in the remains of some campfire to get warm. She was amazed to see that the child's head was shaven like a monk's and it became more and more apparent to her that the others had shaved this little scapegoat to tease him. He grabbed the bit of sugar my wife gave him but as he sucked at it eagerly he didn't take his pleading eyes off her for a moment. She, in turn, saw that his thin body was covered with deep scars.

Esther was amazed to see such wanton evidence of cruelty to a child as this boy presented because the Indians are known to be especially fond of children. She determined to get to the bottom of it. And this was what she learned:

The boy's father, Narichinachimo, had been extremely wild and cruel. He had killed twelve Indians – not in battle but just when he was in a bad temper. His last escapade was to shoot four of the village's leaders when they were off guard. That was too much and one of the tribe – the half-grown son of one of the victims – finished him off with one well-placed arrow, to the relief of the rest of the population.

This revelation of the existence of murder and justice in an Indian tribe was astounding enough but the sequel was even more so.

The mother went off immediately with another man and left the boy to his own resources. Now no one would have anything to do with him. In fact, it appeared they all thought he would be happier dead. The reasons for this attitude were almost too simple. The Indians believed that the son of any man naturally is a replica of the father. In this philosophy, the mother is compared to the earth which receives the seed and brings it forth. But the sower of the seed is the one responsible for what is brought forth and it is therefore obvious to the Indians that the male child shall be like the male parent.

As a result, in this case, the boy's own mother, even if she had been so inclined, would not have dared to take care of him for she would thereby become responsible for bringing up another murderer. While this elementary reasoning was interesting in itself, I was particularly fascinated to learn that these primitive people had worked out their own theories of heredity. Whatever the reasoning of the elders, the poor child had to get along as best he could by scrounging scraps of food and eating earth when he had to.

My wife was so concerned about the child that she asked the chief if she could take care of him. The chief was delighted to get the boy off his hands. Esther was accorded guardianship for the price of one handkerchief, and so it was that we acquired a foster child – a scrawny, pathetic youngster not more than six years old!

We now had a real little savage sharing our home – or rather, tent. But he seemed devoted to us and even to Fernandez who, with his warm-hearted good nature, took to the child immediately.

At first it was a little difficult to feed our new child. He preferred banana peels and odd vegetable roots – he had obviously never tasted anything else – and he insisted on roasting scraps of animal hide over the fire until he finally understood that we really meant it when we offered him meat. He refused for a long time to try crackers, cheese, soup or other foods which he had never tasted, but he watched us with interest when we ate them. Also, he could not get salted meat down, but this he had in common with all Indians to whom salt was unknown.

We decided to name him Atanasio after our good friend the bishop, who had long since died but who had conducted so many friendly expeditions to the Indians. But when our adopted son, with a child's gift for simplification, shortened his name to Nasio, he was so called from that time on.

We had now definitely decided to make our autumn head-quarters in a section of the tropical alps of the Sierra Nevada. At six thousand feet the climate was healthy and just what Nasio and I needed. There was a village of friendly Indians in the area and the monks' mission station was nearby. To get there we had to cross the land of the white man and Nasio saw some very strange animals for the first time – horses, cows and donkeys – which looked danger-ous to him but which he gradually discovered would not attack him. However, he became almost hysterical when an apparition, clanking and spitting fire, roared down the road straight at him. He was so frightened of the truck which passed us that he bit Fer-nandez in the arm and remained trembling behind his big friend. At that point I felt rather helpless. How, after all, do you explain a gasoline-driven truck to a six-year-old savage? After that, every time Nasio heard a truck or car coming he would scamper off and hide from the 'devil wagon'.

He was much happier when we arrived at our destination in the mountains. The Indians of the Sierra Nevada are as different from his little people as it is possible for Indians to be – peaceful, stable and dependable. Nasio immediately took to them as if he were one of them and, while he could not understand a word of their language, would listen to all conversations in rapt attention.

We lived in a clay hut up there and, while it was extremely primi-tive, we did have a small fireplace where Nasio liked to warm his hands and feet. After we taught him how to use matches, he built his own fire outside the hut and never ceased copying everything else we did. He was particularly fascinated by the little kerosene stove on which my wife cooked our meals and in no time learned how to clean and light it. Although we did not allow him to light it himself, he was delighted when Esther gave him a rag and let him polish it. He always was eager to help and do his part.

The first time we gave Nasio a glass of water he drew back and refused to touch it. Colourless water in a transparent container must have seemed magical to him. But only a few days later, he was help-ing wash and dry the glasses, holding each one up to the light, as he had seen Esther do, to make sure it was clean.

Fernandez, of course, had a wonderful time serving as Nasio's teacher. To get the boy to take the quinine he needed to fight a fever, Fernandez told him that the wine or beer we were drinking was medicine and that he could see by our faces that we liked it. The ruse helped get the medicine into Nasio, with much grimacing, but after that, whenever we had beer or wine, he felt sorry for us, shaking his little head and clucking in sympathy.

It was quite a job to get him to drink milk, but we managed by adding a little sugar to it and after a time, Nasio also ate cheese, bread and soup but he still kept his passion for banana peels and mud, which gave him severe stomach aches every time he got hold of them when we weren't looking.

Nasio had the run of the village but understood that only we were bound to feed him. This meant that, like most Indians, he ate something every two hours or so, though never much at a time. He would dart into the storehouse, find what he wanted, then show it to my wife or me before squatting down and consuming it. We couldn't discourage the practice, we discovered, or he would go back to eating banana peels and mud to satisfy his hunger. Fortunately, he was putting on some weight and that was the main thing.

His faith and trust were boundless. After he cut his knee the first time, and I taped a bandage on it, he came running to me with all sorts of minor bruises on which I had to put extra large bandages or he would demonstrate his displeasure vociferously. It was a long time, however, before Nasio would trust the domestic animals around the village but he quickly learned about them from Fernandez and, finally, even dared chase stray dogs out of our house. In fact, Nasio was an excellent little watchdog himself, for in no time he learned which Indians were welcome in our house and which should stay outside until I came to speak to them.

Nor was it long before the child learned to eat with a fork, although we were never completely at ease when he had a knife, too. It was obvious that he had not inherited his father's ill nature but he often lost his temper. When one old Indian who worked for us teased the boy about Fernandez, his adored friend, Nasio grabbed a knife longer than he was tall and, with murder in his eyes, flew at the man. No one dared discipline the boy, which he seemed to sense at the outset, but whenever we learned of similar contretemps we worked out a system of penalties he seemed to accept as fair and he tried hard to behave.

To watch this little savage become civilized was a fascinating experience and we also discovered that he had several talents, one of them music. I had given Nasio a mouth organ which immediately became his most prized possession. Whenever the mission bells were rung, he would grab it and harmonize with the bell tones. He also seemed to have a strong sense of major and minor keys, for he played and danced his own little harvest dance to the major scale or looked sad and walked slowly to music in a minor key.

The boy woke with the sun while we liked to sleep longer on those chilly mountain mornings. So each day we would find Nasio sitting on our doorstep, playing his mouth organ and patiently waiting for us to get busy and show him more exciting things. Once we opened the door, Nasio always began a gay song and started a little dance in which he insisted we join him – and there really are few better ways to start a day on a mountainside in the Andes than dancing to a mouth organ played by an imp of an Indian boy!

At the mission nearby, the monks and nuns were taking care of several Indian children and we were glad that Nasio liked to go down and play with them. Even though the youngsters couldn't understand each other, the boy had great fun playing games and trying to catch the pigeons and ducks sunning themselves around the pool in the patio. It was fortunate he was happy there because we knew we would have to leave him when we started off on our expedition across the Andes. When I talked over the situation with the monks, they readily agreed to take care of Nasio for us but they insisted that before we left there should be a christening.

On the appointed day, therefore, Esther and I put on such finery as we had and dressed Nasio as best we could for the occasion in one of my shirts which she had shortened, held around his middle by a bright, woven belt. Nothing could induce him, however, to put on shoes or sandals.

The ceremony was impressive, Nasio was awed at being the centre of attention and Father José put every facility of the mission at the disposal of the village. The day ended with a lavish meal, Nasio just managing to eat comfortably by standing on a chair at the head of the table, where he conducted himself with complete decorum.

One of the hardest things we have ever had to do was to say goodbye to little Nasio. Although we told ourselves and him that we would come back and get him, we never saw Nasio again. Several months later we received a very sympathetic letter from Father José informing us that an epidemic of influenza had taken the lives of several of his wards, and that Nasio, too, had died.

The news affected us both deeply and Fernandez was beside himself with grief for several days. But it was some comfort to feel that at least we had been able to make the child's last six months happier than they otherwise would have been.

CHAPTER FIVE

WE were back again with 'our' Indians, the diminutive Maracas. The new trail our men had been working on was finished. They had done such a good job of it, in fact, that we were able to ride up the mountain in six hours, whereas the last trip had taken three days. In some places it was a little hard to get through and we had had a few tense moments, but on the whole it was a good trail for that part of the country.

We knew that we should have to spend several weeks with the Pygmies in order to make sure of their friendship, bargaining a little and handing out more gifts, so that they would definitely agree to go with us to meet the Sicacao Indians. At least we had the advantage of having a fairly permanent home now, however primitive it turned out to be. It was large enough for us and our men. They had made a wing to serve as a storehouse for our supplies. The new house was to be our headquarters for all our expeditions deeper into the Andes. I was glad to see that it had remained quite dry inside despite the recent torrential rains.

Yes, it was a good house. The walls were made of cane stalks, tightly bound together, and there was also an outer fence of cane to keep out the jaguars. The floor, of course, was stamped-down earth but now we had one room to ourselves. The outer room, where our men were quartered, opened on to a fair-size yard which they preferred to use for sleeping.

When we arrived we found that a couple of Indian families had also moved in. Lazaro – at least that's what we called him – a very intelligent Indian, who looked more like a Japanese, was there with his wives, who were sisters. One, very young and exceptionally well built for a Pygmy, had a wild look about her but she was always smiling. The old one had undoubtedly once been prettier than her sister. She was very hospitable and made a charming hostess. And they had plenty of callers almost from the first day they moved in.

Their Indian names were too difficult for our men to remember so we called them Eloise and Mariana. Eloise had two babies, one named Chi-chu-che, a name we thought too cute to change. The other was an adorable child whom Eloise herself named Esther, in tribute to my wife.

This family had faithfully guarded our house and the belongings we had left behind while we were away and now they received some special glass-bead necklaces in payment. They were exceedingly pleased with their newly acquired necklaces but proceeded immediately to unstring them. It was much more fun to string beads the way they wanted them, especially if there were plenty of their favourite green and blue colours.

In addition there was a childless couple living with us – little Chipach-chitka, whom we called Pastora, and her husband who was just about as lazy as Lazaro. But he had great respect for her. Even though she wasn't exactly beautiful, she seemed to have a great deal of 'it'. Men would sit at her feet adoringly whenever her husband wasn't around.

Pastora had spent several weeks in Becerril, so she knew how white people did things, and I have to admit she had learned well.

She had also assumed a *grande dame* air which was quite impressive. Never, I am sure, had a one-handled pot been emptied with more ceremony than when Pastora emptied one – always in the presence of many admirers.

Several other Indian families had moved over from the village as soon as our house was finished and had built lean-tos close by along both sides of the stream. In fact, we found that a whole new village had sprung up around our house.

Miro, too, was now our neighbour. It hadn't taken him more than a day to build his simple wind-break as everyone had lent him a hand in putting it together. Not even primitive man can get along working alone. And the communistic society which these Indians maintained made it possible for all to prosper. If one had a bad harvest, the others shared with him. If he had no food at home, he was free to eat at his neighbour's house. It was taken for granted, however, that when he struck good times again the debts he had incurred would be repaid.

Miro was an exception, apparently. He didn't even bother to plant his own section of the cornfield so he was always eating at other people's houses. But he was a friendly sort and no one in the village seemed to hold it against him. They never refused to feed him, at any rate. He sometimes went hunting but had never been known to come home with any quarry. Perhaps he reasoned that as custom prevented the hunter from eating any animal he had shot himself, for fear its spirit would avenge itself on the hunter, it was less work to quit hunting altogether. There was one factor working against his eating meat very often, though. It was also customary for Indian hunters to eat most of what they hunted on the spot as soon as it was bagged. This meant that not much booty ever got as far as the village. Old Menaro, the chief, and father of Lazaro's wives, also had become our neighbour.

We realized very soon, of course, that we had upset the idyllic existence of our Indian friends. It was inevitable. They naturally did not miss glass beads, lengths of cloth and handkerchiefs before they knew of their existence. But now they all wanted more and more and more of everything. Many of the women coveted our aluminium cooking-pots and enamel plates. Whereas they had previously made everything they needed for themselves, they now demanded everything we had.

Lazaro was quite content, nevertheless. He had a hammock, an enamel mug and plate, with a gorgeous parrot painted on it, several knives and a huge collection of empty bottles. Whenever he had visitors, he would take them out and set them up in a row to be admired.

In the evenings we sat around the fire and talked with the

Indians. That way we could hear about the events of the day and managed to pick up several bits of useful information.

One thing we learned was that, while we were away, two of our donkeys had been attacked by jaguars. This was an event they loved to talk about but which we preferred to forget. As for Lazaro he was very relieved, he said, that we had built our anti-jaguar fence as he would not have to worry about his womenfolk any longer. His wives and babies could be snapped up very quickly, he said, as the jaguars were particularly bold up in these mountains. He made certain we understood that he personally wouldn't be frightened to live outside the fence, but it was only natural that he should be with his family.

Whenever Lazaro got into a talkative mood, I listened. It also helped to prime him with a little rum. After I handed him a cup of water with a little rum in it, it wasn't long before he warmed up to whatever he was talking about.

He was quite mellow by the time he got to the subject we were most interested in – a tribe farther south called the Cunaguasaya – the Fever-Water People – because they lived near a river in which the water was unusually warm.

'Have you met them?' I asked Lazaro.

No, he hadn't seen them himself but several years ago a couple of other Indians had come upon them when they were hunting. The Maracas had been chasing a wounded monkey and the other Indians had put it out of its misery for them. Those 'foreign' Indians had been very 'tame' he reported.

I lost no time next day in trying to locate those two Indians. One, I discovered, had died. As the other was lame and couldn't guide us, I tried to get him to describe the route. I was intrigued for I had never heard of the Fever-Water Indians up to that moment. However, I believed they belonged to the Catatumbo tribe which were continuing their fight against foreign oil company engineers. The river waters there were feverishly hot. So much I knew. I decided we would make one attempt to find them before starting off eastwards to the Sicacao territory in Venezuela.

Lazaro promised right away to go along with us – he had absolutely refused to meet any Sicacao – but when he sobered up he decided that even this trip was risky. He warned us not to go too far south. As we watched his older wife prepare a little omelet of birds' eggs in a large curled leaf, he slowly cleaned his nose with a straw, all the while regaling us with stories about the frightful horrors we would find in the Fever-Water country.

'It's dangerous because you don't even see those terrible beasts at first. They look like enormous crocodiles with horns on their heads,' he told us in a mysterious voice. 'When a crowd of Indians was hunting along a cliff over there, one fell behind to tighten his bowstring. When he looked up again, his comrades were out of sight. Instead,' and here Lazaro paused dramatically, 'he found himself looking straight into the jaws of a frightful monster. The other Indians had walked right into its huge jaws,' Lazaro assured us. 'Its gape stretched right across the trail. And while that scared Indian watched, he saw how his poor comrades stuck their arrows out through the sides of its stomach. He was so horrified he turned and ran for his life and couldn't talk for weeks afterwards.'

I gathered that this Indian was probably the one that had died as no one could confirm this story. Meanwhile, Micael was asking why the Indian didn't kill the beast.

'You can't kill them,' Lazaro told him solemnly. 'If you shoot at one it rains day and night until the mountains are covered by a flood and everybody is drowned. And no one is alive today, naturally, who has ever seen that beast,' he added as a sort of anti-climax.

Here we had both a dragon and the story of the Flood, I thought to myself, writing as fast as I could in order to get down Lazaro's exact words.

Micael thought for a moment before he came up with something to settle Lazaro's account.

'Well,' he said at length, 'if we come on that monster and it eats up any of us, Don Gustavo will give it medicine so it will get sick and vomit up everybody again,' and he demonstrated with strangled gurgles just how sick the monster would be.

Lazaro was delighted at this simple way of getting rid of the danger. He roared with laughter and called to all the other Pygmies to come over and hear about it.

Indeed, Lazaro was in fine form that night. He was now telling us about the first people ever to come to the Maraca country. 'It was a tall white man, as white as Don Gustavo,' he announced, 'and a woman.'

'Was she tall too?'

'Yes, she was. They were our ancestors.'

'Then how have we become so small?' someone asked.

Lazaro couldn't explain that. He stood up in his hammock, peeled some bark off a tree and threw it on the fire. There was a strong wind blowing through the forest that night and this special bark had the power to quiet the wind, he said, under his breath. After that, Lazaro reported that even before those two people had come here, another completely different tribe used to live in the mountains, the Atantoche. Now they had disappeared without a trace.

'What happened?' I asked again.

'Nobody knows,' he replied. 'It was a long, long time ago.'

Lazaro was sleepy now. His wives, who had been quietly picking the lice off each other, now took off their capes, stretched their naked little bodies, then lay down with their feet towards the fire and pulled their capes over them again. Lazaro crept in between them. It was warm and comfortable and apparently they were used to his snoring for they soon fell asleep.

We left the circle by the fire to go to see how Opapsimu was getting along. He had a bad fever and had dragged himself over to our house to get some medicine. After a few doses of quinine he had felt better but still looked ill when he decided to leave for his own village.

People are so much the same wherever they are. Our house had become a regular clubhouse or community centre. Old Nerón, knotty and stiff with rheumatism, came over every evening to have a chat, a bite of food or, preferably, a drink. He always sat in the same corner on a rug as worn and shabby as any café settee. There he listened to the village gossip, served up by the women, or told the same old stories of his younger fighting days. No one tired of listening no matter how many times he repeated himself. Every evening he 'killed' several enemies, snapping his bowstring significantly to emphasize these crucial moments. Nerón looked so savage that one readily believed every blood-curdling adventure. Yet, as the evening wore on and it was time to go home, he was very nervous about going home alone for fear a jaguar might get him.

Wise old Monaro, Lazaro's father-in-law, came less often. He was a fine type, respected by all and as friendly as he was reserved. He was also an excellent craftsman and the only one who remembered how to make arrowheads of bone. He braided beautiful designs on his spear shafts of snake markings patterned in different coloured heavy threads. Monaro was also the only Maraca who knew bird markings. He never bragged about his youthful exploits but neither was he afraid of jaguars. While Nerón could sit up all night singing magic songs whenever any of the animals was known to be lurking about, Monaro, who lived in the next hut to his, was quiet.

There was also one greedy married couple in the village. They never missed a chance to be at the head of the line whenever they thought they could get something for nothing. My wife had ordered a cape from the woman, who wove beautifully. But she needed first this, then that to be able to get to work on it. If we gave her those things, the work would go faster, she insisted. She was far from stupid and knew that we didn't have much time. Otherwise the Indians seemed to have little understanding of time.

A young man, for example, sat for two days and nights at the entrance to our house with three arrows in his hand, without saying a word the whole time. Finally, Lazaro told me he had come to exchange them for a knife. But he was in no hurry.

It was the same with our old friend, Maximo. Every so often he would appear at the door with his huge family of children and some very common exchange gifts in a bag. The children were all naked, although we had exchanged several lengths of cloth with Maximo on other occasions. With affected humility he would ask if perhaps we didn't have a few old rags so he could clothe his poor children. We were always amused at his efforts. But Lazaro, who looked down his nose at the people from the neighbouring village, was furious at Maximo's behaviour. As soon as he and his family had gone their way, Lazaro mimicked them mercilessly.

'Those villagers coming over here are monkeys,' he would say. ' "*Yamara Manta*, give us cloth" they say, "Indian poor, kids no clothes." '

Lazaro's performance was worthy of the best vaudeville and each time he performed the Pygmies laughed long and loud.

His two wives got along together very well but there were a few crises nevertheless. One day when Lazaro went fishing with a few others, he took his youngest wife, Mariana, with him. Her sister, Eloise, who was Lazaro's first wife, knew nothing about it. Several days later when they returned, Eloise was very angry and declared she was going to go home to her father. She refused even to look at her sister.

Lagaro was not a particularly strict husband. He let the women work it out by themselves, crept out and went to sleep by the fire alone as Eloise refused to make any food for him or join him. She did find some food for Mariana, however – a double banana, two which had grown together – which she handed her sister.

Mariana quickly covered her face with her hands, refusing even to look at it, and ran out of the house. Should she eat it, she might possibly have twins, a great misfortune. Gradually, however, Mariana was permitted to take care of Eloise's baby again, they were once more friends, and Lazaro dared come home to his wives.

Mariana was always happy and as playful as a kitten. She would hit upon all kinds of tricks. One night she crept up and bit the tip of the nose of one of my men. The poor fellow flew out of bed screaming, believing a wild animal had attacked him. She loved to play games with us and it was all right with my wife but I declined as often as I could. We had one game she loved. It was very simple. Mariana would plan to get caught stealing – opening our door or a box of stores. When I caught her at it, always on purpose, of course, I would chase her with a stick in my hand. She would then dash away calling 'Gustavo angry,' while I shouted, 'Mariana thief!'

She never tired of this game but I did and at those times she always looked as disappointed as a child. Not only was I very tall compared to the Pygmies but to my men as well and they never tired of trying to inspect my body. I had to show Mariana and her girl friends my legs, my muscles and chest and even satisfy their curiosity as to whether I, too, possessed the chief attribute of the male of the species. I found it was wiser to accommodate them once or twice as nonchalantly as I could. I was able, however, to discourage any new games by letting them believe that my wife would be very angry with them, and they wanted to avoid that at all costs.

Mariana made life rather miserable for some of my men by grasping them about the waist, her little head coming not much above it. She became quite infatuated with one of them who, as a result, went in mortal fear of Lazaro until Providence stepped in. He had to have some loose front teeth pulled by the blacksmith-dentist in Becerril. As soon as the Indian girls saw him upon his return, all love was lost and they burst out laughing, calling 'Potasha' after him – 'the toothless one'. The name stuck from that day on.

The Indians didn't like Negroes. Creoles they were used to, but when the man we had contracted with in Becerril to bring up a load of mandioka roots appeared with his load for the first time, Eloise and Mariana immediately moved their mats out into the yard. The poor fellow was afraid of Indians even though these were so small. But the disgusting names the women shouted after him scared him still more, although he couldn't understand a word they said. He came up the mountain a couple of times more but the women made things so unpleasant that he finally turned over his concession to a Creole, even though he badly needed the money.

They had brewed some corn beer in the part of the neighbouring village that lay out on the moor, and our Indians went over to celebrate.

Mariana had orders to stay home but she sneaked out just the same and joined the party. We knew why. She had her eye on a young man in that village – her 'crush' of the moment. She came home in high spirits, quite drunk, with flecks of corn mash around her mouth. Yes, she'd had quite a lot to drink, she admitted readily. Mariana was very talkative. Yes, Eshemu, had forced himself on her, she giggled.

Lazaro came home much later, a good deal the worse for wear. As he lay in bed next morning with a bad hangover, some busybody whispered the news of Mariana's escapade of the night before, ovbiously implying the worst.

Some time later, Mariana appeared carrying a jug of water from the stream. My wife suddenly heard a frightful commotion in the outer yard and ran to see what had happened. Lazaro had taken his largest and heaviest bow and was chasing Mariana from one side of the yard to the other, trying to strike her with it. When he saw Esther, however, he stopped – just long enough for Mariana to make a dash for the forest.

Soon after that, her sister left the house in a hurry, her baby bouncing in the hammock on her back. Then her parents, old Monaro and his wife, took off in the same direction, followed by three or four others. They had to find Mariana as she would never come home of her own accord, they knew. They had to prevent her from committing suicide because, according to the custom of these little Indians, that was the only escape left for her.

They were gone all day. Lazaro lay in bed, still with a bad headache and in a black mood. We offered him some food but he wouldn't touch it. Towards the end of the day, however, he began to be uneasy and very quietly asked my wife if he could trade her an arrow for some green glass beads. He was very miserable.

It was almost dusk before the little company returned from the forest. One of the women came over to our house and asked my wife if she would come and lead the sinful Mariana home, as the girl was still very frightened.

Esther agreed immediately, but as soon as Mariana entered her own hut, she went to a corner and crouched there. Lazaro pretended not to see her.

On their forest excursion, the Indians had not wasted their time. They brought back all kinds of provisions – snails, mushrooms, coconuts, a yellow plum-like fruit, strands of rushes whose core is very tasty raw or cooked, and small, green wild lemons.

Everyone broiled food and had a feast that night – all but Mariana who remained crouched in her corner, and Lazaro, who lay with his back to her.

Next morning, however, Mariana reappeared, her smiling and happy self again, a string of green glass beads around her neck.

My wife and I were busy all the time making preparations for our long expedition to Venezuela – at any rate we now dared call it that. The handful of trustworthy Creoles I had hired as guides had already arrived and it was a good time to send them on ahead with a few Indians. Led by Montecristo, they could report back on the possibilities of cutting a southern trail. I wanted to see the Fever-Water Indians very much. Although, after the dragon story, I didn't take anything Lazaro said too seriously, we nevertheless had actually located an Indian from another tribe who had once seen them. But even should they fail to discover any new tribe, this side trip would be good training for the newly arrived Creoles and, surprisingly enough, I got even Lazaro to go along with them.

The forest-covered chain of mountains that runs south from the Maraca valley and from which the Maraca River rises is dominated by a peak nearly six thousand feet high. From its summit, on clear days, you can get a glimpse of the lowlands to the southwest and southeast on each side of the mighty Sierra de Perijá. From that vantage point anyone would think it would be possible to go between the high peaks and get into more easily accessible terrain. From up there it certainly looked as if it shouldn't be hard going.

I gave Montecristo a compass so he would not get off course, even though I think he could find his way anywhere blindfolded. Well supplied, he took off one morning with five men and a dozen little Indians.

One week later they were back – completely exhausted. Lazaro had caught a fever but was in fairly good shape none the less. He made us all laugh over his disgust with the compass. Demonstrating how Montecristo had found their way with it, Lazaro declared, 'That little box can't tell anybody where to go. Needle doesn't stay still long enough. Anyway, that way's no good.'

His last statement was very true. Montecristo described it for us – the almost perpendicular cliffs covered by impenetrable jungle were bad enough. But the fog and humidity in the valleys were even more unbearable. They had come upon vast swamps where they sank into soggy moss up to their knees. The Indians confirmed my fears – when you run into moss like that, they said, you can't go any farther. They too had tried but had had to give up.

We tried to figure out another way. To go along the top of the mountain range was not impossible for us, perhaps, but we had to find or make a trail big enough to get our stocks of supplies through to an advance depot to which we could retreat, if necessary.

The Indians are used to poor trails and hard going but they know when a trail is hopeless. Discouraged, we made a couple of short excursions towards the east, in the direction of the Sicacao and at least in the direction of Venezuela.

While we were away, life in the villages pursued its normal course. Our men could not do anything much with their wages as we paid them in knives and cloth. Between trips, they managed to have some fun, however, and each time they returned to their villages, their wives were waiting for them with a special meal or some surprise, exactly the same as anywhere else in the world.

One evening there was a real feast in the village on the open moor as one of Lazaro's relatives was celebrating the naming of his baby son and everyone turned out.

Our house was filled with visitors. Our Pygmy friends brought an offering of roasted ants – the fat female is delicious during the swarming season. To catch them, the Indians dig holes near the huge ant-hills, fill them with water, then fish out the females, which fortunately do not bite. They are brought back alive in calabash gourds and are then roasted in hot ashes. They smell like honey and really should be included in our Swedish smörgasbord.

We contributed to the general good spirits by dealing out a few empty bottles. One old lady, who had never seen glass before, asked if she could hang her bottle from the ceiling so the ants wouldn't eat it to the amusement of the other Indians who by then knew all about bottles, thanks to us.

The dance began that night but the drinking had to be deferred until next morning because the corn beer had not fermented sufficiently. Whiling away the time, the men danced alone in the moonlight around the new-born baby hung in a little sling on an old man's back. The baby was very well behaved and only cried a little when an old woman let two wasps sting him so that he would be strong and brave.

The men lined up in one row, a spear flashing between each of their dark heads. In front of them, a row of *agave* plants – relatives of the century plant – had been stuck in the ground. At the end of every simple back-and-forth dance, the men cast their spears into the plants. Back and forth between the *agave* plants and a row of small fires they danced, singing an odd song in unison. The old man with the baby on his back remained in the centre of the dancing area, close to the cask where the beer was working itself up into a bubbly lather.

Later that night they served it up, but only to the men. With it, cornmeal balls savoured with wasps were set out alongside the spears which, by that time, had been laid in parallel rows on the ground. Each guest had to get his own corn cake. However, as the beer still wasn't really ripe we went home.

Towards dawn, while we were still asleep, the beer apparently had responded to various incantations, for when we visited the field of celebration – which fortunately lay a good distance from our house – we found most of the Indians higher than their mountains. They staggered around us, patting us with indiscriminate pleasure. There seemed to be no end to their affectionate demonstrations.

They also grasped each other around the neck, singing happily. The most casual acquaintances became friends for as long as the effects lasted. It wasn't really much different from some student demonstrations I remember from my school days at Uppsala University.

Sure enough, the Indians spotted a guest who didn't belong to their 'nation'. He was sitting quietly off to one side as he had hurt his leg and was temporarily off guard. Now someone recalled that he had seen an aeroplane flying over the mountain. (We had once tried unsuccessfully to explain to the Indians how white men fly through air.)

The Indians had got it into their heads that as long as this 'stranger' couldn't walk, he should be made to fly. Three Indians formed the plane – one was the fuselage, the other two the wings. Lifting the poor fellow to their shoulders, the Indians careened around the field making roaring noises, dipping and swinging in wide circles. Suddenly they all fell down in a heap, tripped by the root of a tree, and their passenger actually flew through the air off into the bushes, where he remained without a sound.

When the women hurried over to see what had happened they found him peacefully asleep and none the worse for his trip. He had fallen asleep during his 'flight' and remained dead to the world. Next day, he confessed he was very unhappy that he had been so drunk; he had missed all the fun and now probably would never again in his life get to 'fly'.

The celebration continued all day. Towards afternoon, the Indians had reached the mean stage and we began to be a little uneasy. Someone started a fight and two men immediately went for each other with their spearheads. When some women threw themselves between the men to separate them, they only succeeded after they had all received a few stabs from the spear points. Blood ran down their arms and sides and I had to assure my wife that they probably were not as badly hurt as it appeared. I still felt we should remain on the sidelines in any dispute.

Then old Kirichapanchu, an inoffensive man when sober, suddenly went berserk. He attacked everyone in his path with a heavy woodsman's knife I had once traded to him. Fortunately his wife got it away from him and slapped him to his senses before any damage was done.

But that wasn't all! A couple of Indians who happened to be guests in our yard, suddenly took to their bows and arrows when two others, who possibly were jealous, attacked them. We succeeded in separating them and getting 'our' two on the way home again. But when the two victims passed the camp and saw their 'enemies' they again grabbed their bows and stood at the ready.

Montecristo and Micael grabbed two, holding their arms behind them so they couldn't shoot. My wife and I walked over to the other two. I remember feeling relieved then they lowered their bows as we approached. Drunk as they were, I wasn't at all sure what they would do. Now it was clear, at least, that they did not want to hurt us. We persuaded them to go back where they came from and sleep it off. Meanwhile, we remained in front of the camp a while so that if the troublemakers should return their arrows would have to go through us first.

And they did come back. But when they found us still there, they shot off a brace of arrows into the ground in disgust, cursing the while and looking very mean.

We had to guard their intended victims the whole day, keeping watch to see that they didn't start anything else. I wasn't too happy about being forced to take sides. It wasn't wise. But we did manage to prevent bloodshed that day and that was the most important thing. If a real battle had developed, there is no telling how this story might have ended.

We soon realized that more than that, we had won a real victory after all. It was now evident that these little Indians liked and respected us. Under no conditions did they want us to get hurt and they didn't want us to have to be partisans in their battles. Even when they were roaring drunk they liked us. So much had been proved. We felt more secure then than at any time since we had started out on our adventures, and not a little flattered.

A few days later we were startled out of our complacency by reports that the whole neighbouring village was approaching our village on the warpath. Fortunately this was another of the Indians' little jokes for, although the warriors did arrive, painted and armed to the teeth with bows and arrows, they had fixed corn cobs to the tips of their arrows. This was only a question of manœuvres, we learned, and breathed more easily.

There they came, the husky, painted warriors, a little larger than 'our' Pygmies, but not much. It turned out that while this battle was only a matter of 'war games' it did serve a useful purpose by letting off the steam generated during the recent celebrations. Not only that but even though they were just corn cobs, they could smack an opponent a good hard blow.

Lazaro told me about a previous 'game' when one of the 'attackers' had made a mistake and shot his best friend with a real arrow. The Indian had looked to make sure of what he had done. Then, in inconsolable grief, he had cast himself on his own spear to join his friend in death.

From what source do people who have no contact with our world of complex beliefs get their own philosophy, I wondered. They knew nothing of the ancient Greeks, of the martyrdom of the saints or the code of the Round Table. They had no god and no religious beliefs which we had been able to discover apart from their jumble of superstition. And yet, when you accidentally kill your best friend, you too must die for, through your act, you have forfeited all men's friendship.

The battle had begun. Indians from our village met the attack and in no time arrows were whining through the air. The battle lines curved forward and back in attack and defence. Even at sixty to seventy-five feet the impact of the corn-cob-tipped arrows made sharp smacking sounds as they hit the bodies of the antagonists. I also noticed that the fighters swung around to take the impact of the blows on their backs instead of risking painful blows below the belt. And as there were not many missed, I imagine quite a few had difficulty sitting down for a couple of days when it was all over.

A few hours after it had begun, both forces withdrew from the field and the women, who had been standing on the sidelines cheering their 'teams', took over their duties of binding up the wounds and cleaning up the mess before they started making hearty meals for their men.

We knew from experience now that the next few days would be relatively calm. Once sobered up and the fight out of them, 'our' Indians could be counted on to work hard. So we got busy putting the finishing touches on the plans for our biggest expedition – walking every step of the way through absolutely virgin jungle across the mountains into Venezuela.

CHAPTER SIX

TIME to start on our march across the Andes! The season was favourable – at the turn of the year, the roads and earth have dried up and the high grass in the mountains is so dry it can be burned off, making it a lot easier to get through than by hacking a trail.

I delegated twelve Creoles, whom I trusted, to guide us. I didn't want to take more along, certainly not any inexperienced men, as it's not easy to maintain discipline in a troop of South Americans on the kind of expedition we were planning. The experience of another group which had attempted the trip, twelve or fifteen years before, made that plain. They had had to turn back after one week.

All our bearers were collected. In addition to Montecristo, Micael, Fernandez and three men from the Sierra Nevada, the boys were all from Pueblito – two of Micael's brothers among them. And Montecristo, my second in command, was the uncle, or at least godfather, of all of them. This was important because they weren't used to taking orders, but they obeyed Montecristo, however much they might complain, because he was very strict.

As the steadiest and most orderly of the crowd, Luis was left behind to take care of the house, guard our belongings and reserve supplies and to maintain contact with the village below. Lazaro and his Pygmy family also stayed with him.

Finally, there was the monk. Why we should have chosen him to be our travelling companion puzzled everybody, but I had a good reason. Apart from the justice in his coming along, since monks had made so many peace expeditions to the Indians themselves until they could no longer afford it, the monks were the real authorities in this Indian territory. In addition, our men were simple good people who felt safer in the company of a spiritual guide. Fray Carmelo was the right man – a modest and humble toiler in the vineyard, always in good spirits, patient and friendly no matter how sick he was or how hard the going. He was a good influence on our men, saying *Ave Maria*'s with them each evening and telling them funny stories afterwards.

Naturally there was a little band of Indians tagging along. So, like the Spanish Conquistadors, we started out with an armed guard, a monk, the little Indians and our bearers. But I doubt that the old Spaniards ever had such a fine caravan as we!

We tried to profit from the experiences of others, knowing how important it was to have enough provisions and the right kind. In addition to our arms and small ammunition, we had tents, clothes, blankets, medicines, photographic gear and exchange gifts for the Indians we hoped to meet. And all of it had to be carried across the mountains.

That fall we had planted corn in the clearing we had made in front of our house by cutting back some of the forest. Lazaro had faithfully harvested the crop so we could have our own fresh dried corn. We also had left the chickens in his care – the flock had increased alarmingly as 'our' little Indians had eaten neither chickens nor the eggs but had let nest after nest of eggs hatch out. We had given Lazaro a couple of hens for himself in return for his good offices while we were away down at the coast and Montecristo gave him some too, so the first chicken farm in the Andes was off to a good start.

We discovered, on the other hand, that the Indians in the next village were trading the hens we had given them for corn in the town. They had kept the cocks because they crowed and their feathers were more brilliant. This had contributed to reducing their flocks considerably before they got over their surprise that cocks don't lay eggs. Montecristo relished telling us about how stupid the neighbouring Indians were. He had never liked them and his opinion had once again been confirmed.

We didn't take any hens or eggs along with us but we had feasted on plenty of them in Maraca while making our preparations. The two cows we brought up from the village had now been slaughtered, however, and the meat dried in the sun. The Indians had helped us grind quantities of corn and roast the meal.

If we had stuck to our European ways, of course, we could have saved a lot of weight in our provisions by taking food concentrates and army rations. But as we were forced to take into consideration the tastes and habits of our men, we were loaded down with dried meat, rice, *panela* bricks and salt cheese. We also took macaroni, oatmeal, cans of beef, beans and corned beef. In the other packs were supplies of powdered milk, bouillon cubes, coffee, cocoa and saccharine.

On the march, lunch for the men consisted of a bite of *panela* and a bit of cheese. As for us, we ate toasted corn meal mush and honey. Our men didn't like oatmeal so, right at the start, I announced that anyone who was sick would get nothing but oatmeal gruel and bouillon. This served to discourage a lot of simulated ailments. We didn't have a doctor with us, as other expeditions usually do, who would be able to see through such tricks. But to give all our boys their due, I must say that not one of them ever tried anything like that. They were all as determined as we that our expedition should succeed.

Then there were the gifts. I had had to send Fernandez off a week before we started to scout around the province to collect all the glass beads he could find as the Indians preferred them to everything else. But there was a duty on them now and they weren't being imported any more, which meant that it was quite a job to find any. He had nevertheless come back with a good collection.

Micael had his three dogs along, which we called our 'reserve stock'. We all knew what had happened to a previous expedition farther south in the Catatumbo territory led by an American engineer, Willcox. He was making explorations for an oil company and managed to follow a river from the Magdalena country to Catatumbo, a trip he thought would take about ten days. It took more than a month and when his provisions had given out, he and his men had been forced to eat their dogs. When they finally got back to an oil field on the Rio de Oro, they were so famished they all got sick from wolfing the good food their comrades forced upon them.

Each of our men carried fifty pounds of provisions or equipment, a gun and ammunition and his own extra clothing. Everything carried was carefully listed so we wouldn't waste time looking for what we wanted, and each man was responsible for everything he carried. I figured we could last out a month, provided we came on one or more Indian villages along the way where we could get a few extras.

After everything was ready, I set about persuading the Indians I wanted to come with us. You can't pick them out and force them to do anything, of course, so it took some patience. Finally about twenty agreed to join us. As my wife was with me, several of the little Indians wanted to bring their wives, too. In one way it was a good idea as everyone we met would understand that, with their women along, they were on a peaceful mission. On the other hand, they could carry even less than the Pygmy men and we had to stick to the rule that no one should eat more than he could carry himself.

I managed to get the idea across that this was not woman's work and we finally set off for the neighbouring village where we picked up the rest of our Indian guides.

On the last night before our departure, they danced and sang until the sun came up but Esther and I managed to get some sleep. Our Indian Pygmy friends were still at it and very tired when we got up at dawn to get our caravan on the road. A couple of them changed their minds at the last minute and remained behind. That meant we had to unpack their share of salt, sugar and chocolate. Then I found that none of the Indians would carry our personal tent. It was really quite light although somewhat bulky. Fernandez solved that by putting it on his head even though he was carrying his full pack. He was foresighted enough to realize, however, that he wouldn't have to carry it far because we were bound for a place a few kilometres away where we were to pick up another Indian who had promised to join us.

As we started off, at last, the women in the village set up a frightful wail and I was anxious as to whether they would succeed in getting their men to change their minds. Finally, six women, among them a mother with her baby, and a couple of young girls gathered behind my wife and followed us.

At the very last minute, an older Indian came striding up to me, greeting me warmly. He was holding an enormous bunch of yard-long rolls of tobacco from which he refused to be separated. He had enough to last at least a year but he wanted to be sure that he'd always have enough for his sour old pipe. We had already packed a supply of tobacco but without his own reserves he refused to budge. I told him he would have to stay home if he didn't change his mind. He stayed home. This meant one less bearer than I had counted on so I was depending on the Indian we were to pick up along the way.

The Indians were the only ones who knew the way to the land of the Sicacao. They had promised to guide us there but no farther. In fact, as soon as we got to the first Sicacao village they were planning to turn back not daring to go any farther. But it was vital that we go through as many Indian villages as possible in order to add to our supplies, and I needed 'our' little Indians to help carry them. They had prepared us pretty well for what lay ahead – we would have to go down some steep trails and clamber up still steeper ones in order to get to a source of water every day.

Our guides were two old Indians who knew very well where the Sicacao were and they apparently thought it was better to go straight towards our goal without any regard for the kind of terrain lying between us and them. They led us up and down the most difficult passes instead of making detours through the more level stretches. We could have found less strenuous ways ourselves if it hadn't been for that matter of water. Our packs were already heavy enough and I didn't dare take along more than an emergency supply of water.

Up a wood-covered ridge we scrambled on our way to pick up the lone Indian. It was a time-consuming, hot and miserable trek and when we located him at last I found he had hurt his foot and couldn't come with us after all.

Fernandez was a good sport and told me he could manage the tent and his other gear for a while longer. But as the trail became steeper and more impossible, Fernandez suddenly collapsed. His face green under its dark tan, he braced himself against a tree, panting.

In addition to the tent, he had been carrying the medicine chest. There was just one thing to do – divide up everything he was carrying among the others. This meant making a new list, as I couldn't risk not knowing where everything was, and another hour was lost.

When we were ready to start off again, our Indian guides announced they were going to take us through an 'Indian short-cut'. Such short-cuts are not for the likes of us, I remarked to my wife, but we were forced to leave it to them.

It wasn't long before I knew how right I had been. They led us up a steep, forest-covered mountainside which was harder to climb than any I remembered. We had to cut and hack up through every foot of it. But when we finally reached the top, caught our breath and started down the other side, the going was even worse. The side of the mountain looked practically perpendicular. Clambering down through a heavily wooded notch in its side, we had to grab every vine and root we could get a purchase on. It was even tougher for the men ahead who had to hack and saw through the jungle of branches, vines and thick undergrowth for every step they took or, more accurately, slid down that mountain.

There was no doubt that this had once been an 'Indian short-cut' but it had grown over again so thickly it was practically impenetrable. Loose stones were a plague. If we kicked one accidentally, there was the danger that it would hit someone ahead or rather, below, us and hurt him badly.

It was almost dark before we at last came to a river valley. Here, about three thousand feet up, we found ourselves at the source of the Maraca River, after a continuous climb of about ten hours. But that wasn't bad considering that this was our first day and we were not yet in top form. We were so tired, however, that after a frugal meal we didn't even bother to put up our tent but fell asleep under the open sky.

Next day we had to get out of the valley. There was no getting around it so we faced another hard day of climbing to get up to the *páramos*, the cold moors and ridges at the nine-thousand-foot level.

It was a hard climb, too, even though a lot of it was in open terrain. After two hours of scrambling over the stony ridge, we reached the tree line again which meant, at least, that we were once more near water. I was afraid, however, that the hot weather might have dried up whatever water there was. I called over one of the guides.

'Where's the nearest water around here?'

'In the forest,' he told me, 'there's a water-hole. After that it's a long way to the next river.'

'Very long?' I asked.

He nodded.

'Can we reach it when the sun is over there?' I asked, pointing to the horizon.

He hesitated a moment, then showed me with his hands: 'Under the horizon.'

That was too risky, so I decided we would go down and pitch camp along the forest stream which I believed was one of the tributaries of the Maraca River. Our bearers needed a rest, too, so we scrambled down and wormed our way through the forest towards it.

Suddenly, with a terrific roar, an aeroplane skimmed over the mountain so low we could see it plainly. However, we had no way of making our whereabouts known down there in the forest valley. I was interested in learning what kind it was and what it could possibly be doing there. Then I noticed that our Indians had thrown the packs off their backs and were grabbing their bows and arrows. Several of the Indians had never seen a plane before and a couple of them, trembling with fear, shook their fists at the sky while the girls dashed to hide behind my wife.

I succeeded in calming them by saying that the plane had been sent out by our white friends to see where we were and to make sure we were all right. At length their fear gave way to delight at this strange apparition and they waved and waved at the machine until it disappeared towards the south. Only one of the girls remained wary of what she called a 'big wasp'.

'Think if it should sting us,' she whispered to Esther. The 'big wasp' was the sole topic of conversation among the Indians for the rest of the day.

It was quite beautiful there, alongside the rushing stream which flowed over a pebbly bed and threw itself off the edge of the cliff in a little waterfall. Below was a natural pool, wonderful for swimming. At any rate I was silly enough to go swimming in it though the water was icy cold and I was very warm. That evening I came down with a fever but it may have been caused by the bites of the nasty red, almost microscopic *coquetas* which had attacked us all day. They get inside your clothes and thrive on your scratching them. If their bites are very severe, you get as red as if you had scarlet fever. Some of the men let the Indian girls pick them off but we settled for alcohol, which made them release their grip but did little to soothe the itching.

Next day, fortunately, I felt better and we continued up towards the summit where we found ourselves walking across the stony, open moor in the teeth of a cutting wind. One of the men shot a deer up there, a welcome addition to our larder.

From our high position we could see, down towards the southwest, the famed peaks of the Tetari which rise almost twelve thousand feet above sea level. Everyone who has travelled across the savannas at their feet knows them well. But, from our vantage point right among them, they seemed to stretch lengthwise rather than to form peaks which were recognizable. Then, in no time, we could see nothing at all. We were suddenly so surrounded in mist and cloud that we had to depend completely on 'our' Indians.

They made the most of it, leading us another chase up one of their almost impossibly steep and dangerous precipices. We set up camp that evening completely exhausted and knowing that we faced another rugged mountaineering chore the following day.

Our camp was pitched in a wooded valley near a rapids – another of the Maraca River's fourteen tributaries to draw in on our map. Between our little tent and the men's big one the Indians settled down in little groups.

It always amazed us how, almost before we settled down, their fires began blazing up. Each group lit its fire from the pipes they constantly smoked and, although they didn't actually carry dry wood around with them under their capes it appeared as from nowhere. The younger ones collected wood in no time when we could find none that wasn't wet through. Then the cooking pots would appear and the Indians would sit back and enjoy the aromas of food which, to our noses, were anything but pleasant.

Experience had taught us to avoid, if we possibly could, eating their dried meat which, as well as being tough was often slightly spoiled. Even so both Indians and white people find it delicious despite the stomach aches it causes. Our men just asked for more medicine and ate more meat the next day.

Our rations were fairly large and we still had a good supply of provisions. The Indians were not tired out as we were. They danced in the light of our Primus lantern, sang and made a great racket with their weapons. Happy, friendly travelling companions they were, too.

Following the Indians' initiative, the Creole men then demonstrated their native dances until the alarm clock rang at seven p.m. Then all was quiet, for I always set it for four next morning. I was glad I had brought it along as it delighted the Indians, who rushed to begin their jobs as soon as it rang each morning. I suppose I have always regarded an alarm clock as a little magical, myself.

The *páramos* we had passed through were called Socurpa, according to the Indians, and the tremendous cascade to the river below our camp was called Susu. This was an amazing river for it flowed in almost the opposite direction from the one we had left that morning. That one had flowed south to the Maraca, its mainstream, while this one flowed north where it joined another river coming down from the northeast. The Indians called both rivers Tocore, and if I had not had my compass, I should have doubted the evidence.

Next morning we cut our trail out of the valley and it was a tough job. Hour after hour we scrambled and hoisted ourselves up through the jungle. Whenever the undergrowth thinned out a little we thought we were at last reaching the top, but each time, a new height worse than the last one rose ahead of us. Usually we weren't even able to go straight up but had to zigzag, making the distance that much longer. At least we gained time as it would have taken days to cut a trail straight up. At last, when we stood once more on an open ridge, the bearers threw themselves on the ground, panting.

My wife and I were relieved to be able to rest, too. We liked to try to set an example but we had to face the facts. This was the most strenuous expedition we had ever undertaken.

I spent the time counting Indians. A few always came along in our wake. A wild thing would catch their eye and they'd be off after it. Also, I was never sure whether some might not have decided to turn back. Most of the little Pygmies had colds in their heads by that time. Sweating from the exercise, they would let the cold winds cool them off. Even at this six-thousand-foot level, the air wasn't free of pathological bacteria, I figured, or else they'd brought the germs with them. I handed out some cough syrup and both Indians and bearers said they felt better right away. They all believed implicitly in the power of everything in the medicine chest ever since I had given one of the men a laxative.

After that, I went up alone to the nearest high point to have a look around. The air was crystal clear that day and I looked down upon mountains and river valleys for miles around. It was immediately apparent that the previous day's troublesome descent had been as unnecessary as this morning's strenuous climb. If we had gone a little farther north in an arc we could have followed a somewhat longer trail but a much less difficult one to the river where we had spent the previous night.

I had worried for some time that the climbing was getting too much of a strain for our bearers and I soon realized how well-founded my fears had been. We had hiked up and down the most difficult sections there were in these mountains. The river cut a deep gorge between them while the terrain farther to the north was much less broken up. There, the river valley looked like a soft field, but we hadn't been able to see it the day before because of the clouds. There was nothing for it now but to carry on.

Those Indians! They're used to climbing up and down. To go around anything didn't make sense to them. For another thing, they wanted to get to high places as often as they could so they could make sure there was no enemy Indian village in the vicinity. It didn't do any good to reason with them, especially with the two old Indian guides. But they did assure me that there wouldn't be any more such climbs before we reached the Sicacao.

I stood a while looking at the narrow valley where the Tocore ran to meet the Maraca. This one flows southwest and is much longer than the Maraca's mainstream, flowing from a ridge down the other side of which it runs towards the east. The Indians had told me about it – it wasn't on any map we had – and I knew now they were right. I also saw that the valley was thickly forested but that, on its north side, the hills were covered with grass.

We were on our way to the river – how much time was lost by our need for fresh water every night! When two of my men became ill I, too, suddenly got an attack of malaria, although I had been free of it for several months. I was good and scared when I felt the fever mounting. What would happen, I remember thinking, if I had to remain flat on my back for several days? And with two men also running high fevers?

My wife had to give one of them a shot of adrenalin for his heart and two others had to drag him along with them. The situation looked serious. To force a march at that altitude when you have a high fever places a great strain on the heart. I set up camp earlier than I had planned in a rather unpleasant, damp spot – a veritable hole on the river bank from which a tropical rain could have washed us out.

Luckily, the anti-malaria shots I had taken from our supply worked and the fever was gone next morning. Later, I discovered that I had what was called 'every-other-day fever'. But the other two were still very sick.

I sent a team on ahead to open a trail as far as they could and told them to set fire to the mass of tall grass which covered the hillside up there. It was man-high and tough to get through, but fortunately it was dry. Also, I figured that the smoke from the fire would tell the Indians on the other side that we were approaching. In a very short time huge clouds of smoke were rising towards the sky far above the mountain tops.

When the men returned they said they had found an excellent camp site, so I gave orders to move to the drier area. It was none too soon for, just as we were pounding in the last stake of our tent, it began to pour. We had our tents to shelter us and the Indians quickly made a shelter for themselves and for the Creoles out of thick, broad leaves.

In spite of the rain they were all in a good humour. I discovered that Micael had shot two spider monkeys, a female and its offspring, and everybody was looking forward to monkey steak that night. The two young girls in our party rushed forward as soon as they caught sight of the prizes. One quickly cut the hand off one of the beasts, the other lifted the baby monkey by the tail, and together they immediately began roasting both the hand and the still-unskinned baby animal over the fire. Their eyes glistening in anticipation, they tended their roasting of these disgusting steaks and eagerly breathed in the revolting odours of burned hair and scorched skin. Both girls, usually sweet and retiring, were suddenly transformed again into little savages.

My wife retired to our tent, sick with the smell, and at the sight of the youngest girl breaking off a piece of the baby ape's tail and starting to gnaw it. Only the more delicate portions were eaten that night. The main sections were buried on wooden frames and the place carefully marked so there would be something to eat on the return journey. After all, the Indians prefer their meat slightly 'ripe'.

The sick bearer had recovered sufficiently to walk without help, but he couldn't carry any burdens as yet. It was not difficult to rearrange the packs, however, as several Indians had very little to carry by this time and could easily take on a little more. Only the two guides, who had managed to avoid carrying anything at all, went around with empty baskets. But then they were well on in years.

The one whose Indian name had been translated as Maximo and who had often come to our house in the Indian village, now regarded himself as our private guide. He always went directly ahead of us, looking around from time to time to make sure we were there and waiting if we fell behind. As for my wife, whom the men were sure would keep our progress down to a snail's pace, she often walked faster than Maximo and, on passing him, would give him a friendly pat on the back.

Maximo did not like this at all. Each time it happened he would sigh and pant, pointing to his shoulder basket to indicate that its weight kept him back. It was really almost empty, but he always carried our thermos bottle and can of coffee, which he guarded very carefully. He also kept our emergency water bottle – except when it was full. Then he would hang it around the neck of one of the girls, taking it back only when it was empty of its last drop and that much lighter.

Maximo was a fussy, pedantic old fellow who would have made a good government clerk. He shot small birds with especially small arrows and stuck the poor little things on sticks to roast. No matter how small, however, he always managed to pull off little pieces of meat to give to anyone sitting around the fire. He was a miser, really, but as a good Indian he had to share what he had with others.

Little Pastora was one of the party as well as her shadow of a husband. It was hard for her to keep up with us as she had such short legs – she was only about three feet tall. Whenever she fell behind she would sob in frustration, but she none the less kept at it. She had considered herself a well-travelled young woman even before we came and didn't want to miss this chance to see more of the world. Her husband always followed meekly in her footsteps.

The smallest child in our odd caravan also helped bring up the rear. He had scarcely a stitch of clothing to cover him and I was concerned about the cold nights. He also cried when he got too far behind and had to catch up. Finally, Fernandez, who could never stand seeing children unhappy, gave the boy his only extra uniform jacket, which made him a devoted slave to the big fellow.

Also in our train was the gay Chuchu-Maysimo, our 'movie actor', who certainly would have been a star if we had been filming this drama. He was our dentist. In general, the Indians have strong white teeth, but even they get toothache occasionally. When that happens, the tooth has to come out. The patient goes to the dentist, who sharpens a stick thin enough to get to the root of the bothersome tooth. The patient then lies on the ground, another Indian holds his head, the dentist places the stick at the base of the tooth and hits the stick a couple of hard strokes with a stone. The tooth flies out on the ground, the patient spits out the blood, then takes a few quick drags on his pipe. No cases of toothache developed when I had my camera handy so Chuchu agreed to re-enact the procedure, which he did one day with a very unwilling boy taking the patient's role. All went well, however, and I got the picture.

The Indians had time for a lot of little jobs after we set up camp. They collected wood, made the fires and built a lean-to for the night. They made the latter out of branches covered tightly with large leaves which they laid down like shingles. It was excellent protection from the rain – if it came from the right direction. But the shelter could be turned quite easily to keep its back to the wind.

It was fortunate for us that we had reached terrain which was less difficult to cross. It gave our sick-list people and our exhausted bearers a chance to take things easier. If only more of them don't get sick, I thought, everything will be fine.

There was only one other casualty – a bearer who had eaten too much salt meat and had taken not only the laxative dose I had given him but another man's as well and had drunk baking soda on top of it. Suddenly he fell to his knees writhing with cramps, but they passed, and he told me afterwards he felt better than ever.

The Indians seemed to have stomachs of iron. At least they seldom asked for medicine. It makes no difference to them if food is spoiled. In fact, they bury it until it has practically rotted, dig it up, cook it, and eat it with apparent relish although one would think it would poison them for life. Even little children share such food. But the Indians eat only a very little of anything at a time. Our Creole bearers, on the other hand, put away huge portions of food at every opportunity.

Between low hills and through damp forests our caravan pressed on towards the valley and the wood-covered high ridge where the Tocore River rises.

Exactly one week from the day we had set out, we found ourselves struggling up the face of the ridge which, I was pretty sure, lay on the boundary line between Colombia and Venezuela!

All my calculations told me I was right. As we slowly went down the other side, we heard rushing water and came upon a stream dashing down the mountain to the river. It was flowing east!

That proved it! We were on the other side of the Andes, standing on the eastern slopes of those magnificent mountains looking into Venezuela!

CHAPTER SEVEN

WE stood there a few moments looking down from a height of almost six thousand feet. Below us stretched the jungle forest, thick, seemingly impenetrable, looking as it must have looked for centuries, as it had always looked, long before that day in 1936 when a white man and woman dared gaze upon it. Liana vines snarled themselves

148

like giant nets between the trees, hung with huge orchids and festooned with broad-leaved herbaceous plants.

On this side of the mountains lived the Sicacao, but exactly where we should find them I had no more idea than had our Indian guides. They move constantly from place to place. But if this were one of their moving days I knew that we might run into them almost any time.

It happened that the following day, as we were slowly hacking our way down through the dripping jungle mountainside, our Indians suddenly began shouting.

'*Yá, yá, yá, yá!*' they called out, as though they were cheering. Some instinct, or more probably a smell, had put them on the alert. A couple of them began blowing on their bone horns. Some of our men joined in, blowing whistles on the muzzles of their guns. It was a frightful racket. Suddenly one of our Indians gave the signal for silence.

It was quiet a few minutes. Then: 'What was that?' my wife whispered to me. 'Did you hear anything?'

Was it an answer or only an echo? We couldn't be sure until suddenly we heard it again. Without a doubt the Sicacao had heard us and were answering!

Now pandemonium broke loose. 'Our' little Indians made more noise than twice as many big ones. But they broke off at regular intervals to listen for a reply. After all, the only way we could tell if the Sicacao were friendly was to listen for their answer.

There it came! Now we knew they would greet us as friends and also that they would soon be on their way to meet us.

It seemed no time at all before we could see them running towards us over the grass-covered hills in the distance. And when we finally got through the jungle between us and started up the hill on the other side, they set fire to the grass to clear the way and make the going easier.

Although the Indians assured us that the Sicacao meant well in doing that, it almost ended in catastrophe. We had to walk in single file and as the first of our band approached the top of the hill, tongues of fire suddenly burst through the grass with a roar, threatening to encircle them in flames. We had to dash away as fast as we could, beating down the blaze as we went. We succeeded in getting through unscathed, but the line of bearers behind us couldn't see the fire before it was too late unless we could warn them. This we managed to do by shouting at the top of our lungs and signalling to their leader to stay where they were. After a good half-hour the fire burned itself out and we breathed easier.

Now the Sicacao were crowding around us with joyful whoops and much noise. They immediately set about exchanging bows and arrows with our Maraca friends. I noticed, however, that the latter gave only one of their arrows for three Sicacao. They are of much finer workmanship, with long, sharp steel heads, while the Sicacao people apparently had little iron for theirs, having had no contacts at all with white people.

The exchange of arrows was in itself a sign of peace. Everything was going beautifully! The oldest Indian, whom everyone called Papashi, or grandfather, couldn't do enough for my wife and me. He took up a position in front of us and began clearing the path for us as he was to do from that day on. He was a perfect gentleman, carefully helping Esther over streams and sometimes even cutting a special trail for her.

All together we climbed down to another narrow valley through which a rushing stream cut a deep gash between the steep slopes on either side. We had to zigzag constantly, crossing the stream from one side to the other, which was a nuisance for those of us wearing boots. But Papashi always made sure we were right behind him.

We carried on four hours without seeing any habitation and when it began to get dark I gave orders to halt. We would have to set up camp there, no matter how damp and unsuitable, and we'd have to have it done before it got much darker.

Papashi was very much upset and tried to explain something, but his Sicacao language differed from the Maracas' about as much as Norwegian and Swedish and I couldn't make out exactly what he was trying to say. He gesticulated urgently, indicating that his house wasn't far. But I couldn't quite believe him. Distance is so relative with these people.

I put a couple of men to work preparing camp although I could see they weren't any more enthusiastic than we were. The place was damp, stony, and smelly. Meanwhile, Esther and I planned to have a little coffee break. But when we looked around we saw that Maximo had disappeared with our thermos and the coffee as well.

It was really thanks to Maximo, however, that we didn't have to spend the night there. Two bearers, whom I had sent off to look for him, came running up about a half-hour later with the thermos bottle but without Maximo.

'We found old Papashi's house,' they yelled to us. 'Come on!'

It developed that Maximo had trusted Papashi more than we did, had gone on ahead and soon arrived at the village. He had already installed himself quite comfortably and the bearers found him contentedly eating cornballs surrounded by interested women and children.

'It's only fifteen minutes from here,' the bearers insisted again. 'We can pitch camp there easily.'

So I gave orders to pack up again and the men lost no time

loading. Sure enough, it was just as Papashi and the bearers had said – very near.

The old Indian's hut stood on a hillside planted with corn and a relative of the banana plant. It was an excellent site, dry and protected. Even though the path down to the river was so slippery that the men bringing up the water fell several times and often had to start all over again, it scarcely mattered because we were so relieved to be able to settle down for a while. Our tent now stood alongside Papashi's simple shelter, which seemed to please him enormously.

According to him, the Sicacao tribe was very broken up – it was almost a day's hike between their family villages. But he said that whenever they felt like living in a big village again they would.

By late evening several hundred Indians had gathered around our little camp. They sat there quietly and a little too seriously, I thought, as I looked out of my tent over a forest of bows and arrows. But this was just the natural caution of people who had never seen white people before and I really couldn't blame them either as we were not looking our best, to say the least.

They could have wiped us out in a very few minutes and our packs of provisions represented a fortune to them, but we had been greeted as friends and would remain so as long as we were guests in their village.

Here came some carrying great bunches of green bananas and vegetables. Big pots were put on the fires which now lighted up the sea of faces and, as we still had some dried meat left (which brought a murmur of approval) the soup was soon steaming and smelled quite good.

As our Pygmy Indians were planning to go home next day, they proceeded to stuff themselves like little pigs. We also gave them some rice to take along and the Sicacao gave them corn. Before we went to sleep that night the Sicacao had promised to take care of us after our Maraca friends were gone.

The night passed all too quickly but we made the most of getting some sleep, well knowing that the following evening was sure to be a lively one. No newcomer could refuse the welcoming party nor did we really want to miss one. However, I remember thinking just before I went to sleep that I was glad there wasn't enough time to brew any corn beer.

151

THE next morning we climbed up the faces of several of the hills which seemed to be piled on top of each other – they rose endlessly above us – so we could get our bearings. When we had caught our breath and our hearts slowed down a bit, we saw a broad valley stretching out below us – the broadest we had yet come upon in these mountains. Huge grass- and fern-covered hills rose up from it on all sides, with patches of forest between their folds. We could make out several small brooks which, farther down, joined a river flowing east through a narrow notch in the valley. And beyond? Yes, there stretched blue plains – without a doubt the lowlands of Venezuela!

When I asked the Indians how we could get down there, they told me there was no trail. They added that the Yasa Indians' territory lay between us and the plain and that a state of war still existed between them and the Yasas. Two good reasons I couldn't argue with, although I thought the latter conditioned the former in some degree.

The Indians knew that white people, *guatia,* also lived to the east, and told us the river was the Tucuco. But there weren't any Venezuelan villages at the foot of the mountain, they said. I saw it was useless to try to get down there so I asked our new Indian friends about other possibilities.

After much discussion, they agreed to take us to the Manastara Valley, which they indicated lay to the northeast. It was three or maybe four days away, they said – we'd have to sleep three nights on the way. But I couldn't determine whether they were reckoning the distance from the farthest hills of the Sicacaos' valley or from our camp. At any rate, there was no way out to the south either, so we had little choice but to start on our way northeast. There was certainly no question of turning back now, and Manastara lay at least in the right direction. It also developed, incidentally, that it was the Motilon Indians' home territory.

Next morning, then, it was decided. Our small Maraca friends would leave us. They had been eating as much as they could hold, and while I should miss them, it would be a relief not to have to worry about our food stores. My wife and I had a chance that evening, when both tribes were together, to see how different they were despite some similarities of language and culture. The little Pygmy Maracas had pale golden-brown skins and many of them had almost East Asian features – not surprising, really, as it is generally believed that South America's Indians came from Asia originally. The older men had beards, not as thick as, for instance, our Spanish monk's, but straggling wisps of hair on upper lip and chin. Their arms and legs were slender, especially their legs. They walked with a rolling gait as if it were troublesome or painful. The women, particularly, walked on the outer edges of their soles.

The Sicacao, on the other hand, have soft red skins, and the women reminded me somewhat of Finnish or Dalecarlian women – straight and proud, with clean-cut features. They are all medium-size in build, after South American standards – the men, between four and a half and five feet, the women somewhat shorter, and they move more gracefully, walking and dancing.

Our little Maraca guides had brought along a young cock and a hen for Papashi, the old man. In fact they had promised them to him some fifteen years ago and he hadn't forgotten that promise. 'Have you got the birds with you?' were the first words that greeted them. From us he received an axe, a gift which so deeply touched him that he just sat stroking it. I wonder even today if he ever brought himself to use it.

It was time to say farewell. Our friend Chuchu-Maysimo, the 'movie star', seemed quite moved. But Maximo, who knew how useful he had been to us by going up ahead and finding Papashi's house, decided to take advantage of his special standing. He came over to me and, with a teasing look in his old eyes, begged me to give him my trousers – 'at least when you come back to my village again,' he added quickly.

It was a pair of old khaki pants he had his eye on but they were in such bad shape I didn't think they would last more than a few days longer. However, Maximo had coveted them for a long time – every day as we hiked along he had pinched the cloth between his fingers, sighing, 'Such beautiful pants!' What he wanted with them I couldn't imagine but I finally changed and gave them to him. It was the last I saw of Maximo or of the trousers as he walked off towards home, the pants proudly slung over his shoulder.

Just before setting off, however, Maximo had clapped Esther on the stomach, as he had done almost every day of the journey: 'You're too small, too thin. You'll never make it to Manastara,' and he left her, looking deeply concerned.

There they went, starting down through the forest for home, the little Indians we had come to know and love so well. I had given them some letters to take back, and Luis promised to post them in Becerril to our friends in the outside world. I later learned he had carried out his mission faithfully but they were a good six weeks on the way to their destinations.

As Fernandez had fallen ill again the same day we arrived in the Sicacao Valley and one of the others was still fairly weak from a high fever, I felt I must tell them, as we were going into unknown conditions from here on, they should feel free to go back with the Maraca if they didn't feel strong enough to carry on. Fernandez was very much upset at my suggesting such a thing, and they both insisted they would go along with us even if they fell down dead on the way.

As I could do nothing to dissuade them, we started off, Papashi and our one-eyed guide in the lead. I knew they wouldn't take us directly to our goal – they always had to visit from village to village along the way to anywhere – but it looked as if we were now on the last lap of our journey into the unknown.

Micael had charge of the provisions, a job he performed with the greatest efficiency, dealing out equal rations to all and turning a deaf ear to all bribes for extras. He also added to our supplies considerably when his well-aimed arrows found their mark. After the bearers had their rations, he would stand four-square and call at the top of his voice: '*Yuca! Coroshi!* Come running all you Indians with your bowls!' He never had to call them more than once.

After each meal we would pack up again and move on along the trail – a curious procession, the wives of our guides behind them and the bearers behind us, followed by a long line of Sicacao, about fifty in all.

Up hill and down dale the trail was miserable, particularly when we had to cross the Indians' fields where we balanced ourselves on the tops of narrow slippery logs placed like bridges across the hummocks of tangled corn stalks. But at least we were on our way once again. Now there could be no turning back for anybody.

CHAPTER NINE

WE were making our way, foot by foot, across terrain where no white person had ever walked before. All of us were immediately conscious of the change of climate on these eastern slopes, more humid than on the other side. Although it did not rain very much we were constantly swathed in clouds and fog. Only on the open hillsides where the sun could penetrate was the high grass dry enough to burn, and the farther northeast we went the damper it got.

We passed one deserted cornfield after the other, thickly over-grown with vines and brambles. The Indians used the few tree trunks lying on the fields as guide-posts – they were all felled in the same direction. As for us, we had to be very careful not to slip off their smooth trunks into the maze of thornbushes growing up between them. The barefoot Indians scrambled along them like little brown monkeys, but because of our boots we had to give up several times and hack out a place to put each foot for every step we took.

We were still very high up. Part of the time the trail led down open slopes but for the most part it went through stretches of forest which, as we approached, seemed to draw their vines tighter as if to defend themselves against our intrusion. Whenever we came to a lookout point and the fog had cleared sufficiently, we were able to see the Tucuo River cutting through the lower valley, flanked on both sides by mighty mountains – one about six thousand feet high, the other somewhat less. To the northwest the horizon heaved with gigantic peaks. Behind them, far to the west, lay Iroca, a Motilon village whose people apparently lacked any contact with the Sicacao.

In every little settlement we came to there were only three or four huts but crowds of Indians always gathered around our camp. They were very reserved and content to sit quietly and stare at us, all the time holding their weapons tightly in one hand. The women and children kept together in their own group but, although they were cautious, they weren't in the least shy and paid no attention when I photographed them.

In one village I was interested to see a tall, well-built Indian with completely white hair and beard. This was most unusual. He looked like an old fisherman. The others told me he was very, very old, and he must have been since his grandchildren had grandchildren of their own. He still looked strong, but he decided against going along with us to Manastara. He didn't walk more than about ten miles a day now, he said, as he felt like taking it easy!

The little glass beads we had with us made a very favourable impression and we dealt them out right and left. All the men who volunteered to go with us received a jack-knife and their wives a little bag of beads or a handkerchief. Our men also let them understand that, when we reached our destination, they would each get a shiny machete. We had a large supply of exchange gifts with us this time, but the knives, machetes, axes, cloth, and baubles weighed a lot and rattled around too. I had arranged that our little Maracas would get their compensation for helping us when they got back home, so we had not had to lug all their 'wages' along, at least, but I was not loath to deal out a large number of items to lighten our packs now.

I knew that the Sicacao Indians planned to take us in a wide arc from north to east so they would not have to get too close to the Yasa Indians' territory. The latter live along the river of the same name which flows south of the Manastara. My wife and I would have welcomed a meeting with the Yasa, but as they were feuding with our friends it was impossible. Anyway, we didn't have enough gifts to woo them all. By this time we had just enough to give to the Manastara when we finally met them.

For days we walked through the Sicacaos' valley and Manastara wasn't getting a bit closer. It was still 'three nights away' when two nights and three days had passed. On the other hand, the old man informed me that there weren't any more villages from this point until we reached the Manastaras' country, so at least the visiting was over and our real march could begin.

The people of Manastara had made peace with the whites, I learned, and some of them lived in the big village at the foot of the Manastara Mountains. The Sicacao said they'd never been there themselves. They knew, however, that the Manastara people got their iron, knives, and cloth, and had also acquired some 'tame birds', from the whites. A vision of roast chicken and fresh eggs rose pleasantly before our eyes. Another thing the Manastara had obtained from the whites was a 'huge animal' like a deer only bigger and fatter, they said, and spread their fingers up from the foreheads to show me how it looked, bellowing a little at the same time so that I would get the idea. I did. And a fleeting dream of fresh milk and butter wafted away eastwards after the first vision.

If the Manastara really had a cow, then they must not only have good relations with the whites but the roads must be fairly good too, I remarked to Esther. We knew from experience that a cow cannot climb most Indian trails. As for Micael, his mouth was watering as, in his thoughts, he pictured slaughtering the cow and eating some fresh meat once again. Our dried meat was not too tasty by this time, I had to admit.

We already knew that the Manastara lived in the area around the Negro River. On the fifth day our guides stopped suddenly and pointed to a mountainside ahead, steeper, if anything, than all the others we had climbed, whose summit was crowned with a cap of clouds.

'That is the way to Manastara,' they announced with a flourish.

I looked at Esther and she at me. It would be a tough job but there seemed no way of getting around it. While we were now 'in training' so to speak, I doubt that we would have undertaken that journey at all had we known that this final pull would be longer and more demanding of our strength than any part of the mountainous country we had yet crossed and which now lay in a blue haze behind us.

'Is it a hard trail to climb?' I asked.

'No! Easy,' the one-eyed one replied.

We looked again at what seemed an unbroken perpendicular wall of mountain ahead of us and asked weakly if there were more like it between us and the Manastara.

'Just two,' they assured us, when we winced. 'We cut through forest for you.'

I asked if we would find water up there if we made it, and they nodded. To be on the safe side, I told the bearers to fill all the water bottles before we started up – an order they forgot, incidentally.

If the white man had the mountain goat's agility coupled with some of the attributes of the smaller monkeys, it would be easier for him to climb the Andes. The Indians had all those qualities and it made little difference to them whether they were going cross country or up and down it.

We had to do our best. That was all there was to it. So a long, thin line of bearers and Indians was soon worming its way up through the man-high bracken, slashing it right and left to form a path.

When I looked down over the Sicacao Valley at one point, I saw huge black clouds building up in the distance. I took a couple of pictures just before they swirled down and enveloped us. Though the caravan was quite far ahead I knew we wouldn't get lost for there was nothing to do but follow the trail the Indians had cut, the only possible way to cross the high ridge we were on. From that height there should have been a magnificent view, but the Indians told us nobody had ever seen it as the weather was always the same here.

It was almost providential that the fog enveloped us, however, because there was a sudden disturbance in the Indian ranks up ahead. Our guides came running back along the line, whispering excitedly to the others who immediately fell silent. They indicated that we too must speak softly, and the one-eyed guide's wives clung together close to my wife, looking very concerned.

The Yasa! Our Indians' enemies were approaching! The Indians were so nervous I was afraid that in their terror they would desert us on the spot. I hastily reorganized the column so that each of my men had two or three Indians in front of him, with two others bringing up the rear to discourage any 'wandering off' into the forest.

We crept along slowly, not talking above a whisper and making signs to each other instead of calling out. The fog was still so thick that those of us up ahead could not see the rest of the line. I could only sense it when they all suddenly stopped in their tracks.

From what seemed quite a distance, we heard faint shouts. The Yasa were evidently unaware of our existence and were on a hunting expedition, calling out to each other so as not to get lost in the fog. If they had been on the war path, Papashi informed me, they would not have shouted but would have managed to run smack into us. Although the fog prevented their seeing us, knowing

Indians I still wasn't sure that they still might not run smack into us, as Papashi had said. And on that high, narrow ridge, there was definitely no room for a battle.

However we looked at it, we were in danger. And I felt we were not only risking our men's lives but were faced with having to turn back to Sicacao. From what I knew of the Yasa, they were not apt to let us through.

I pictured the return trip, shadowed the whole way by Yasa Indians creeping through bushes and hiding in ambush behind rocks and trees for four days and nights.

As things developed, the weather saved us. The Yasas couldn't see us nor could they have heard us, and I decided just not to worry about their sense of smell. Besides, they were busy enough keeping track of each other and getting safely back to their village. Gradually, as their shouts drifted away in the distance, our Indians recovered from their fright and were soon talking and laughing together as if nothing had happened.

But now something else worried me. We hadn't seen any water the whole day long and, up there on the moor, we weren't likely to. Although the guides assured me water was 'near' I knew that word had a fairly flexible meaning for them.

This was the moment when I made the discovery that, despite my orders, none of the bearers had taken any drinking water with him. And they were all extremely thirsty. I had filled our water bottles but between Esther and me there wasn't much left.

We had to find water somewhere. Not only that, the bearers were staggering with fatigue and shaking with cold in the evening dampness. They needed some hot soup very soon if they weren't to collapse or come down with a fever.

What simple, improvident people these half-breeds are! If the sun is shining they think it's never going to rain again and forget to put the covers on the packs. When the rain does come, they're so slow that everything gets drenched through before they get them covered. Now they had forgotten the drinking water. But they didn't complain. Not a word did I hear. Instead, like naughty children, they waited patiently for 'Father' to think of something.

The Indians, on the other hand, understood our predicament, and promised we would soon reach a forest through which a 'river of much water' ran. By that time I wasn't in the least surprised when they also told me that to get to it we had to slither down a mountainside once more.

It was almost unbelievable that we made it in one piece. In the black depths of the wet forest we could only reach out for tree roots and vines to break the speed so we wouldn't break our necks. Our hands were skinned raw from grabbing at rough tree trunks and the stinging spines of bushes as we careened downwards. That some of our men had sat down and slid the whole way was evident when at last we got to the bottom – one whole hour away from the top – and got the Primus lantern lit.

Grovelling through the pitch black forest, the Indians led us to a little clearing where, as they had promised, we heard the welcome rushing sound of a small stream. Warnings about drinking too much water too fast fell on deaf ears.

We managed to get an area cleared for our tent only to find it was so wet that it couldn't be stretched on its poles. And, as not even the Indians could find anything dry enough to make a fire with, we had to be content with cold rations washed down with cold water.

Fortunately, my wife and I had excellent sleeping bags filled with goosedown, and while they, too, were soaking wet they nevertheless kept us from catching cold. In fact, it was more like sleeping in a Turkish bath that night.

Towards dawn we wakened to find a circle of glowing fires dancing around us. The Indians had been up all night climbing into every tree which had dead branches dry enough to burn and were already drying out our clothes and the other damp supplies in the packs.

The patient monk, who had been our quiet but trusty companion the whole way despite several minor upsets, now took a turn for the worse. He had a high fever but not high enough to be malaria, and it puzzled me. Esther persuaded him to take a little soup to help build up his strength and I gave him some pills to bring down the fever. I prayed privately that he would be able to carry on, for it would have been out of the question to leave him behind or even send him back alone with a guide.

The guides now explained that we were to follow this small river – a tributary of the Manastara River – all the way to our destination. That news cheered us a lot because, even though we would have a hard job cutting our way through the jungle in the river valley, it meant we would not have to do any more mountain climbing for a while.

Several of the bearers were weakening by that time and the monk was really ill, I could see. I said to myself at the time that I should not have taken Esther on this trip at all, and certainly never would have dreamed of it had I know beforehand what I knew then. But she had withstood the hardships remarkably well, much better, in fact, than several of our strongest men. As for myself, I felt fine again, which was fortunate, as some severe tests still lay ahead of us on our journey to the country of the Manastara.

THE days that followed were rugged. We had to dig our way through the forest – and what a forest! It dripped with moisture. Tree trunks, vines and stumps were covered with slimy moss and mould; trees and bushes were rotting with decay. Grasp a branch to keep from slipping and as likely as not it would break off in your hand like a matchstick. Day and night the forest thundered as dead trees toppled over, crashing others down with them in our path.

It wasn't really safe to walk or set up camp there but there was little we could do about it. The ground was bare except for its deep covering of wet, dank leaves, although here and there a brave young sprout reached up in desperate defiance towards the sky. And in the tree-clefts, huge sprays of fern joined them in their search for the sun.

In fact, these enormous clumps of bracken fern so dominated the vegetation that one could imagine himself in another age, seeing the forest as it must have looked when anthracite and diamonds were being formed in the bowels of the earth. The entire forest lay gasping like a dying giant, lacking even termites to eat up its skeletons.

Even though it didn't rain, we were soaked through with sweat as we crossed the river, back and forth, trying to find better footing and a breath of fresh air in some rare little open patch the sun could reach. Most of the time, however, we slushed along in the sickly green light of that forest of mouldy trees, which looked and smelled like the stems of a bunch of calendulas left too long in a vase of bad water.

Nor, we discovered, had we entirely escaped a stiff climb up a slippery hillside now and again, because several times it was senseless to fight our way along all the river's meandering loops. At other times, it was impossible to walk along its banks at all.

We could see very little wild life. A bird or two, sometimes a little colony of monkeys which the Indians wasted a lot of time trying to catch. Several times we saw the footprints of bears and once clearly saw where a bear had stretched out on the ground in a patch of dry grass to rest a while. We were hungry enough by then to consider stopping and going on a bear hunt – the thought of those succulent steaks was almost overpowering. But the bears, which I presumed were the very rare black bears of the Andes, kept well out of our way.

Fording the river was not dangerous but very tricky if you wanted to remain dryshod. We were worried that the last pair of boots for each of us might not last if we walked right through the water as the Indians did. It was tempting to try it, though, especially when we had to cross it five or six times an hour.

We had been following the river for three days when I began to wonder if, now at last, the Indians had lost their way. Our guides continued to assure us, in the same breath, that Manastara was very near now but, at times, they seemed at a loss to know which direction to take. It gave me a rather insecure feeling, to say the least.

Reasoning about it later, I decided that because of our growing impatience and shorter tempers, the Indians decided to take us on another of their 'short cuts'. They called it 'just a little climb'. In any case, we shortly found ourselves face to face with another almost perpendicular mountainside. This, without exaggeration, was the worst, the most harrowing climb in all our experience up to that moment!

There wasn't an inch of solid ground to get a foothold on. It was either gravel and sharp stones or slippery moss. Even the weak little bushes couldn't hold on but tore out in our hands as we grasped at anything we could find to haul ourselves up. Our hands and faces were ripped with deep scratches from thorns and burned from the cuts and stings of poisonous leaves. A little snake fell out of its hole and wound itself around my arm like a bracelet, then lost its grip and slithered to the ground where the man behind me crushed it under his boot.

It was one of the few snakes we killed on our journey. I didn't even have time to be afraid and have always thought that the snake was too startled to strike. There was some anti-snakebite serum in the medicine chest, of course, as the deadly coral snake is very prevalent in the South American tropics, but fortunately it was the only medicament we didn't have to use.

We were all well hardened by that time but the ascent of that mountain placed a terrific strain on the heart. Even the bearers were unanimous. 'One more climb like that and we're done for,' they gasped.

I didn't know what to say to encourage them. Between us and our destination all I could see were more mountains. 'Only two,' our guides had said. Maybe they had meant two a day.

Micael had carefully economized our food stores but, by this time, several staples were finished. There was no more cheese, he told me, and the meat was so bad that only the Indians would touch it. I decided to open a few cans of meat I had in reserve and, with the help of some bouillon cubes, we made a really excellent meal for the men who, by that time, had forgotten all their prejudices against canned foods.

The sugar was also gone but we sweetened our coffee with some synthetic sugar pills from the medicine chest. At least we still had plenty of rice and coffee and enough cans of meat for several days. While Micael and I were discussing the food situation quite close to the others, he winked his one good eye at me, letting me understand that there were a few more stores than he had let on officially. 'Better they get used to eating less now,' he said in a low voice, 'than fight for crumbs next week.' Micael was a prince. However he did it, our fifty people still got two meals a day.

Montecristo had his troubles, too. He was responsible for the guides as he knew their language better than we did. But he could do very little about the way they were guiding us and it was hopeless, he told me, to get any detailed information out of the Indians. We hadn't known where we were since the last time we looked out over the whole countryside from the Sicacaos' territory, and only from the compass were we able to tell that we were going along generally in the right direction. Up to the time we had had to make the detour around the Yasas' lands we had been heading due north, but now were bearing off towards the east.

I argued with Montecristo on several occasions but he was always as friendly and patient as ever. He had a firm hand with the Indians as well as his numberless relatives among the bearers. For their part, the boys were good sports and wanted to succeed as much as we did, but I began to hear rumours that they didn't believe there was such a place as Manastara. A couple of them had also been thinking, they told me, that maybe the word 'near' in Maraca language meant 'far away' in Sicacao. When I thought how many simple English words have changed meaning in the United States, for example, I couldn't help granting they might have a point. But I assured them the Indians probably wanted to keep our spirits up.

On the way down another hillside, just as we caught sight through the trees of the river at its foot, we spotted something else – two deserted hunting huts. Inside one were pieces of a basket and a broken arrow shaft, while gnawed bird bones lay strewn around outside.

'Manastara hunting here,' the one-eyed one announced, as though he had known all along that this was exactly what we should have found here.

'How can you tell they weren't Yasas?' I asked him quickly.

He pointed to some spikes in two trees, obviously used to hang a hammock from.

'Monastara get hammocks from *guatia*,' he explained.

'Don't the Yasas ever come here?'

He shook his head.

'And the Manastara never go to Sicacao?'

'Never.'

One young Indian fellow now came forward and announced that he had once visited the Manastara country – the first I had heard of it – and that it wasn't more than a day away from the very spot where we were standing if we started at dawn. The rest of the men were not too impressed by his assurances, however.

Zigzagging across the river next morning, although for only a couple of hours this time, we were brought up sharp at eight in the morning by both guides. From their signal I saw they intended to start straight up the side of another mountain cliff.

I called out to Montecristo to halt the line. 'If we follow the river won't we get to Manastara?' I asked him anxiously.

After checking with the guides, he replied, 'Si Señor.'

'Then why do we have to climb this mountain?'

After this question had gone down the line and the answer relayed back and translated by Montecristo, it was the same familiar, 'This is only a little hill.' But the message added that from the top we could see Manastara.

I wasn't completely persuaded as we had already seen where the Manastara country lay when we were way back in Sicacao. Nevertheless, we assuredly were much closer now and the climb might be worth the effort.

I noticed that the prospect of seeing our goal at least revived a lot of our weary bearers enough to make them agree almost eagerly to the climb. So I gave the signal and the caravan started up what proved to be the most exhausting ascent we had ever undertaken, bar none!

The walls of that cliff were so steep that no one could even stop to rest without hanging on to the rocks and bush-roots with all his main strength. For every foot we wriggled up, we seemed to slide back two. Fortunately the vegetation was fresh and strongly enough rooted to hold and not break off in our hands, and the temperature was very moderate – averaging about seventy degrees. In fact, in these mountains it often gets down to the low forties at night.

The men, even though near exhaustion, were getting excited now and talked continuously about how wonderful this country would be for raising crops. Brother Carmelo, too, could envisage great orange groves like those in his home in Valencia, if only some roads were cut through.

Oranges! Only a little piece of an orange would have tasted like nectar at that moment! We did have a few small wild lemons left which we'd brought from Sicacao, so we sucked them while we caught our breath at a relatively level setback on the cliffside.

Looking straight up from there it seemed to touch the sky, but we made it somehow. In fact, I had to call up ahead to my wife to take it easy, worrying that she was overdoing it. When we at last reached the end of the treeline, there she was, right behind our guides. They were so impressed with her climbing skill that they told her so – possibly the only compliment any Indian has ever voluntarily paid to a white person.

The call was passed down the line: 'From here you can see Manastara!' But when I got to the clearing on the summit, the entire world was washed in swirling, wet billows of cloud.

With dampened spirits we trekked along the top of that high ridge. At least it was fairly level and not too bad underfoot. Then, about an hour later, the sky cleared as though a shade had been raised, and we saw before us a wild jumble of mountains rising from low hills out of the smooth, broad valley at our feet. And through a notch in the middle distance glimmered the blue lowlands we had seen from Sicacao. However, it had taken us not three but eight days to get here!

Jubilant hurrahs broke out all the way down the line of our battered caravan and the tempo of their march quickened as they tramped along the ridge.

We could see no village, however. There were only acres of banana trees in a huge plantation.

'Where is the village?' I asked a guide.

He made a wide half-circle with his arm, which ended much higher than its starting-point. Over there? High up?

I should have known enough by that time not to have asked whether we had to climb a mountain in order to get anywhere.

Meanwhile, down there were bananas and there was water, too. After the past week's constant diet of meat and rice, the fact that we had to scramble down the mountainside to get these didn't matter any longer.

The hills rolling down this side of the range were covered with short grass but near the river they dropped sharply. The descent didn't seem as difficult as the others had been, but perhaps the fact that our goal was now really 'near' made it seem that way.

The plantation had obviously been abandoned and the bananas were still green. My wife and I had never been particularly fond of them in any form, but we all turned to picking and peeling them with a will. They were so green they had to be cooked – which makes any soup almost black – but after filling our big kettles and stewing them with some bouillon cubes they made quite a tasty meal.

We were sitting back to relax after stuffing ourselves when Micael came up with a surprise. He had quietly put aside some salt cheese which he proceeded to dole out for dessert to all but the Indians, since they don't like anything with salt.

On the last leg of our journey, we passed a small lake next morning, following the usual climb out of the valley. It was the first lake we had seen, though scarcely larger than what the Swedes call a 'forest star'. From there we hiked straight off to the east through open country except for an occasional forest glade at the base of the treeline on the mountain's southern slope.

We had not yet seen a sign of any village when our Indians stopped. Then there began such a hallooing that their shouts echoed all around the hills. After waiting for an answer, we followed our guides around a little hill and saw the Manastaras' village dead ahead of us.

CHAPTER ELEVEN

THE village was wonderfully situated, high up in a notch with a view over the entire valley below. Hearty shouts of welcome greeted us. We heard some drums, followed by a couple of rifle shots which sang through the valley. Seldom had we been greeted by a gun salute and I felt a little happier when I spotted a large white rag flapping at the top of a wooden pole. This was a western welcome. Indeed, I was wondering if it really were a Venezuelan village and not the Manastaras' after all.

After tying the small Swedish flag we had with us and a fairly clean handkerchief to my rifle barrel and waving it vigorously, we set out to cross the last bit of forest land which separated us from the village below. It took a good hour's hike, with the yelling and drumming of the villagers dinning in our ears all the way.

Now we could see a few people and they were all wearing trousers. Through my glasses I even saw some men with boots on. This was no Indian village – I'd been right the first time, I whispered to Esther. They must be white Venezuelan planters.

I was wrong, however. When we walked up to the first row of welcomers, I saw they were indeed Indians, all freshly painted for this big occasion. Their joy in greeting us, which seemed boundless, was tempered nevertheless by an astonishment they could not conceal. They had seen white people before all right, but never had they come from our direction. The Indians looked a long time at our well-worn boots and dusty packs, then at the blue mountains behind us, and shook their heads in disbelief.

It was quite difficult to make ourselves understood. They knew only a few words of Spanish and their native tongue was quite different from the Maraca dialect.

Did they have such close relations with the whites in the area that they had taken to wearing clothes, we wondered? They were a comical crew. A few wore large straw hats with their capes and nothing more. Others had pulled thick woollen socks over their bare feet. However, some of their costumes were quite elegant. One, who seemed to be the chief and called himself 'General', wore a tweed jacket and pyjama bottoms, the legs stuck clumsily into husky boots.

The faces of almost all the men were painstakingly painted in intricate designs done in black, which the Sicacao also used. Our little Maracas preferred red paint. These Indians were of the same height and build as the Sicacao and, as they were all suddenly overcome by a shy silence, their paint jobs made them look exceedingly odd.

The women, on the other hand, had painted their faces red with white spots, apparently imitating the white women's makeup. A little later we were to notice further indications of the white man's and woman's influence. For one thing, their huts had clay walls, which were in a sad state of repair, however. The 'crash programme' instigated by the whites several years before to 'civilize' these Indians had not been very successful. They had received masses of presents – cloth, knives, pigs and hens and, as a result, were quite spoiled.

However, we learned they had not got their fine clothes as gifts. An Englishman had come up there from Maracaibo some time back, they told us. On his departure he had carelessly left behind a tin trunk full of clothes which he had told the Indians someone would pick up at the foot of the mountain and send on to him. As was quite obvious, the Englishman never saw his trunk again – these Indians had 'borrowed' all his finery. I didn't laugh at the story. 'Our' Indians would never have done a thing like that. But these people had become so spoiled by the whites in the towns that they were coarse and rude. It was clear we would have to guard our belongings.

Two of my men asked the 'General' about the cow. He looked very much surprised but collected himself quickly. I explained that I wanted to buy the cow. 'It's fairly far away,' he said.

His ugly face took on a sly expression. 'I'll trade her for a rifle – a long rifle,' he added to make sure I understood he didn't mean a revolver. We had a cheap old rifle with us so I offered it to him and he promised to send a couple of Indians after the cow.

In their half-European, half-Indian get-ups, they looked like a collection of clowns and behaved like them, too. They sang, yelled and danced all day and all night, acting as if they were drunk even though they were quite sober. We didn't get a wink of sleep all night, dead tired as we were.

Romantic Manastara had turned out to be a sad commentary

upon man's efforts to bring the 'heathen' the so-called benefits of civilization – in this case the Parajaina tribe in their village of Ayajpaina. But what difference did it make, after all? Far off to the east, beyond the hazy plain, we saw a bright spot we knew must be the town of Machiques in Venezuela!

Next day the Indians continued their feasting and dancing but, tired as we were, I was very much interested in doing business with them as they had a great many items we had not seen previously among any other Indians in these mountains. Among other things, the men decorated themselves with long chains, often beautifully woven, with designs of red and black seeds, which they wore across their chests. I also saw two crudely carved wooden planks, vaguely representing a full-size man's figure, which were covered with painted designs. These were used in their dances and I was very curious about them as we had seen nothing like them on the Colombian side of the Andes.

(Since then I have found that the designs on these painted boards are a form of picture writing, serving as a record or reminder of events somewhat like those which Erland Nordenskjöld studied among Cuna Indians in Panama. At any rate, I hoped the carvings I took back to Stockholm's museum might contribute something to our scientific knowledge up to that point.)

At first the Indians were very choosy and hard to do business with. They seemed to have plenty of knives and of a better quality than those we had brought along. But, when we took out the little bags of glass beads, they had the same miraculous effect we had experienced with them everywhere – the Indians were willing to exchange almost anything for a little bag of beads.

The self-styled 'General' appeared to regard everything in the village as his personal property and he calmly made deals for everybody's account. We ran into complications when the real owner came up to claim his rightful booty but we left him to settle up with his chief.

Our men were beginning to get impatient as the cow had not yet been found. The 'General' explained that the men he had sent to find it were probably having a hard time as it was free to wander all over the place.

Next, I was genuinely concerned over Brother Carmelo's condition. He had braved the trip without a complaint but only his own courage was holding him together, even though I knew he would disagree with me if I told him that. He lay in his hammock, very ill. And to top everything it began to rain and didn't let up until late afternoon. It seemed as if great buckets of water were being dumped on us and every hut leaked in at least five places.

I was determined despite the circumstances to go on the next day and try to reach some white settlement. The Indians had assured us that in a single day we could reach the little town we had seen. I wasn't so sure. We certainly had seen it but I also knew how difficult it was to judge distances from a mountain outlook.

That night it poured again but the Indians went right on with their dancing and yelling. In the dark they kept tripping over the guy ropes of our tent and hitting the canvas until it soon was leaking in forty places. When they stumbled over the last remaining tent stakes, the whole thing fell down over us as we lay on our beds and we were deluged and practically smothered. For the first time in a long while I swore profusely.

With morning the rain stopped and our Sicacao friends prepared to leave us as the first sunlight lay across the mess of sopping clothes and blankets spread out to dry.

We were alone now with our new companions. If the Sicacao were hard to come to terms with in making plans for the next leg of our journey, those Parajainas were impossible. For one thing, they couldn't decide how much pay to ask for going along with us. They didn't want to ask too little. On the other hand they couldn't conceal their eagerness to go with us, so we managed to get a good-sized group together.

The men piled as many packs on the women's backs as they could, managing to carry very little themselves. As for the good 'General' whom I had come to distrust completely by that time, he declined absolutely to join us, using all kinds of excuses. But I insisted he come as the Indians had no leader at all and, even though he apparently had elected himself to that high post, they had to have somebody in charge. At last he agreed, not daring to try to get out of it any longer. But he wanted to be paid just like the others, he said, even though he naturally couldn't carry anything.

I was so fed up by that time that I couldn't argue any longer so he joined our march down to the valley.

The road down was excellent all the way – safe for pack mules and horses – in fact, a much better road than the one we had cut through to our headquarters in Maraca. It was clear that these Indians hadn't built it but that whites had engineered the whole project.

After several hours' hike, we suddenly came on a fairly large house with clay walls. It had obviously not been lived in but was completely abandoned. It also was clear that the Indians knew the house well. We learned they had worked on it at one time and had learned here how to bake clay bricks (adobe) for walls.

While we sat resting on the cool side of the house we suddenly caught sight of some men down on the plain coming towards us. We could clearly make out they were white men – they wore long trousers and carried rifles. Three of them came slowly up the hill followed by another on a mule. They looked nervous and kept their guns at the ready until they were near enough to see us clearly. After that they began to laugh and call out and wave to us, probably having caught sight of my wife and the monk – surely peaceful invaders of their country.

It turned out after they had greeted us, welcoming us to Venezuela, that they had been forewarned by two Indians who had come down to the new settlement half-way to the town. There they had informed a lone white settler that a crowd of men with 'long and short' guns was approaching from across the mountains to the west.

The settler had immediately sent the Indian on to report this astonishing news to the governor in Machiques who was in a quandary as to who might be invading his country from that direction. Even when the Indians told him there was a woman and a 'saint' in the party he decided to be on the safe side and had sent out three policemen to investigate. The white settler had joined them and here they were!

The new arrivals insisted that my wife ride the mule down the steep hillside to the town, but she refused, telling them that Brother Carmelo must ride. As it was, he was too weak to mount and had to be lifted into the saddle.

Before we set off again, I looked around in vain for the 'General'. He had disappeared as soon as he had seen the police approaching I learned shortly afterwards when he finally showed up. He had made up the story about the cow's existence – it had long since been eaten up – because he had wanted to keep us in Manastara until he could tell the authorities himself about our arrival. Someone had beaten him to it and now he was afraid I would tell the police about it or punish him for such 'treason'. When I laughed off the whole thing, I believe I have never seen a more puzzled Indian.

The road was still excellent and the hills nothing remotely resembling what we were used to. However, the lower we got, the hotter it got, and when we came to the rushing Rio Negro, which we had to cross, we ran into some trouble. Several of the men stumbled and fell and we lost a few of our belongings at the bottom of it, among them our prized alarm clock which had amused the little Maracas so much.

In another hour we reached the settlement. The owner offered mules to Esther and me and Brother Carmelo. Although he had only one riding saddle he had pack saddles for the other animals, which was fortunate as they do not have the more comfortable waistline of the horse. The bearers and Indians went ahead on foot while we rested and enjoyed an excellent meal with our generous host.

Our men stared curiously at the white women in the settlement as they had never seen women dressed as these were. It was a very practical costume, really – a variety of beach pyjama with the legs tied tightly around the ankles to keep out the sand flies. As for us, we didn't give the sand flies a second thought. We were covered with so many kinds of bites and deep scratches that a few more didn't make the slightest difference.

Once mounted on our mules, which fortunately were not very lively, the monk and I had all we could do to hang on, having neither reins nor stirrups. While it was difficult, it wasn't a very long trip. After only three hours we came to a large cheese farm surrounded on all sides by lowing cattle waiting to be milked, and found our men already seated around a crude table laden with huge quantities of fresh cheese and oranges.

The farm lay on the plain where trucks came several times a week to take the cheeses to town. Although there was no road, the ground was level and hard enough for fairly heavy trucks to make the trip. We were cheered at supper by the news that as soon as he had learned from the Indian of our arrival, our host had sent one of the policemen back to town not only to confirm the news but to ask the governor to send out a truck to pick us up so that we wouldn't have to walk the last few miles.

After looking at the sky, we decided to remain on the tin-roofed verandah among the piles of highly aromatic cheeses and wait rather than go out to meet the truck. And we were glad we did, for one of the worst downpours we had ever experienced suddenly broke loose, sweeping in under the roof from all directions.

Towards sundown when the rain stopped, I had no illusions about the ability of anyone to drive a truck through such weather. But not much later, a man approached, soaked to the skin but grinning a welcome. The truck was stuck all right, as I had feared, but he assured us it was on the other side of the river, only a few miles away and maybe a few of our men could come with him and help pull it out of the mud?

I decided instead that we should take all our gear along and see what we could do when we got to the vehicle. The Manastara had already indicated their intentions of leaving us and going back up their mountain and we were not going to miss their company. They had managed to steal several things, including Esther's raincoat which she had last seen on an Indian woman as she ran off towards the first hill.

It was fairly dark but, with our Primus lantern firmly tied to a pole, we started off for the river and the truck.

When we got to the river bank, our men decided to carry us over so that we could arrive in town in as presentable a condition as possible. They had often carried Esther and me across rivers and sometimes we had all tumbled into the rushing waters in a heap. This time, however, all went well. The truck was finally freed and loaded and even Micael's dogs, which we had not had to eat, were put on board.

It was very dark by that time but the governor's driver got the truck started off down the road and somebody shouted, 'Long Live Civilization!'

At that moment the left rear wheel slithered into another hole and it took the best part of an hour to pull it out. Nevertheless, at about 10 p.m. on the night of 7 February 1937, we rattled in great style into the cobbled main street of Machiques.

CHAPTER TWELVE

AT that time of the evening a little town like Machiques normally lies dark and silent as everyone goes to bed early, but now there were lights in every window and crowds of people gathered in the streets, shouting greetings and waving to us. It was a great day in the history of the town, they said – the first time an expedition had ever crossed over the mysterious western mountains into their country!

We were driven directly to the governor's house where we found him waiting for us. He welcomed us very cordially and apologized for not having come himself to pick us up at the cheese farm. He had actually started out in his own car but the rain had forced him to turn back, he told us.

We were overwhelmed. He had planned an official reception for us and put a large house at our disposal where Brother Carmelo also had a room of his own. Our men were quartered in a government building and, in general, were quite stunned by the reception accorded them. After we were settled in and had done what we could to look fairly presentable, we were taken by one of the town's high functionaries to a restaurant where we found a huge banquet spread in our honour.

When we had finished dinner and it was the men's turn to sit at the long tables, they didn't appear. The man I sent to get them told me they felt they were too dirty and ragged to be seen in such a fine restaurant. I relayed this news to the governor with my apologies but he laughed heartily and in the next moment went over to get them himself.

We were up early next morning and Esther and I went in to see how the monk was. He still had a high fever but the rest in his small room overlooking the garden had done him good. It was quiet there. We gave him some medicine and went back to our room where a long line of visitors was already waiting for us. In fact, it looked as though everybody in town had come to shake our hands and hear the account of our exploits from our own lips. Fortunately, the outer room was a large one and had been supplied with an unbelievable number of chairs so we did not have to repeat our story oftener than once every half-hour.

Only much later in the day did the governor bring up the matter of our entry permits to Venezuela. He said the authorities had agreed to inform the governor of Maracaibo of our arrival and that we should not expect to have any trouble with our papers. I was grateful that we were not going to jail. Entry permits were hard to get, the political situation was in a periodic state of tension and the only papers we had were our Swedish passports and Colombia identity cards.

It was a long exciting day and we got to bed very late. However, early the following morning, with everything loaded in another big truck, we were driving towards the city of Maracaibo.

Once there, our trusty bearers began to realize for the first time, apparently, that they were famous. People pressed around them everywhere they went. They were interviewed on radio programmes, newspaper reporters dogged their tracks and they were received by the President of Maracaibo himself.

We did not feel particularly tired but, oddly enough, it was difficult to walk up the two flights of stairs to our room at the Maracaibo Hotel. Esther and I had to take them so slowly, resting on each landing, that I began to wonder if we really had strained ourselves more than we realized. Esther told me that maybe we should have stayed at home, safe and cosy by our own fireside instead of climbing all over the Andes like mad. But when we found that the stairs had the same effect on Montecristo and the others we felt less embarrassed.

Esther and Montecristo had fared the best of all of us and my bout with malaria had cleared up nicely. When I found that the others didn't seem to be suffering any ill effects from our adventures, I decided we could safely plan other expeditions from our little headquarters back in Maraca.

Our men and Brother Carmelo, too, now wanted to get home as soon as possible. They didn't feel at ease in the big city and refused to go out on the streets unless the worldly-wise Fernandez was with them. I managed to rent a bus and arranged with the driver to take them down to the Goajira Peninsula. From Rio

Hacha on the coast they would have no trouble getting home. Only Fernandez remained with us as, with his malaria, he had to be hospitalized.

As things turned out, the American doctor at the Gulf Oil Company's hospital in Maracaibo wouldn't let Esther and me leave either before he had practically turned us inside out with X-rays and all sorts of tests. He didn't find anything wrong with us, which seemed to annoy him, but the job took two whole weeks, which rather annoyed us.

The city of Maracaibo, which lies on the large lake of the same name, climbs up the low hills on one side of it. It has long been an important place and in the centre of the city the houses look as if they had been squeezed together to make room for them all. There were few gardens, although some large country villas were being built on the city outskirts. Here the large oil companies have their plants, their own company housing, hotels, swimming pools, tennis courts, playing fields and clubs, surrounded by brilliant tropical gardens. The refineries also have their own excellent hospitals.

The bay of Maracaibo is streaked with oil and tower drills sprout out of the surface of the bay as far as the eye can see. Oil tankers constantly slither in and out of the city harbour, while fishing boats and small sailboats and canoes of every description line the shore.

One sees quite a few Goajira Indian women in their long brown or black capes and square-cut black hair. They wear glittering jewellery and some still paint their faces.

Maracaibo is one of the hottest places on the face of the earth. In fact, they say that not only do you never need a blanket there but that they wrap their dead in blankets to keep them from freezing in hell. Fortunately, the climate was fairly comfortable at that time of year and a fresh breeze blew in from the mountains most of the time.

At last it was time for us, too, to say good-bye. We rented the same bus which had taken our men to the coast and crammed it with all the impedimenta we had collected as well as the new load of provisions we had bought. The authorities couldn't have been kinder. The President phoned ahead to each place we would stop and even arranged a hearty farewell luncheon for us before we started off.

Along the shore of Maracaibo Bay the villages are still very primitive. The half-civilized natives build their houses on stilts and go from one to the other by canoe. These gave the first Spanish explorers a name for the country – Venezuela – which means Little Venice.

The road had ended and we were driving across open country now. At the Limon River, a ferry took the bus across safely although there were moments we were afraid it wasn't going to make it. It was a fairly small craft with a platform up forward on which the bus balanced precariously the whole way across. While it would have taken only a few minutes to go straight over, the ferry had other errands along the shore and it was almost an hour later before we reached solid ground and could breathe freely once more.

The river is noted as a habitat of crocodiles and, apart from our anxiety over perhaps losing our hard-won collection of specimens, we did not relish the idea of a swim at that time and place.

We drove through the little village of Sinamaica and soon were on the desert-like Goajiro Peninsula with its lumps of cactus and its dust. Here and there was an Indian hut and we saw several of the well-built, handsome, naked Indians we had visited on a previous expedition. They are much darker than the others of their tribe as they live in constant sunshine with little shade to protect them from its burning rays. We remembered this peninsula only too well from the time we had taken a mule caravan across it under the most trying conditions. In fact, we always thought of it as the worst, most exhausting trip we had ever made. Now, even after what we had just been through, we still thought so.

This time we were able to travel faster but it was a hot, dusty jolting trip from one government control station to another where we replenished the gas tank. We crossed the border without difficulty although, at one point, we had to spend some time until the guard was made to understand how Fernandez, in his Colombia state police uniform, happened to be coming *from* Venezuela. Even though the man let us continue, he remained very doubtful and was still shaking his head as we drove off.

The whole Goajiro coast is a fabulous bathing beach with sand so hard packed that the bus could drive along it as fast as its limited horse power would let it. Before evening we were in Ria Hacha and learned that we could continue the very next day to Valledupar.

CHAPTER THIRTEEN

EVERYONE crowded around us as we walked through the streets of our favourite little town. Luckily, Montecristo, who arrived ahead of us, had reported on most of our adventures. But people still stopped us everywhere we went, to shake hands and ask for more details.

There were the men and girls coming back from their swim, towels slung around their necks, all chewing on their toothpicks.

The black washerwomen, balancing unbelievably heavy loads of wet wash on their heads and smoking their long cigars backwards – the burning end in their mouths – carefully turned their heads and welcomed us back.

In Valledupar we had to say farewell to Fernandez. He was very sick still and didn't dare go back up to the mountains with us again. We were very sad and missed him – more than anyone we had ever known. We stayed only a short time in the town as I had the luck to find a driver who would take us the whole way down to Becerril. In this way we could take all our packs and supplies with us without having to round up a mule caravan. Along the way – over rough country as there was no road there yet – we picked up Micael and some of the other men.

That truck had been ready for the junk heap for some time and how it held together on that trip remains a mystery. It rattled and banged until everything under the hood as well as on the body, which wasn't already loose, came loose, too. We all hung on for dear life and without Micael would never have made it. He was very handy with pieces of steel wire, and he also knew the way by heart.

In Becerril we found a small troop of acrobats who had been sent there by mistake – there certainly was no audience in that village which would appreciate their show. They looked upon us as their deliverers and, after putting on a performance for us in sheer relief over seeing white people, we saw them off on their way back to civilization in the truck. I learned later that they had got lost and wandered for several days without food and were almost eaten up by mosquitoes. Only by chance did they come upon some shepherds who set them on the right road again.

As for Esther and me, we were back in our little house in Maraca the next afternoon.

I really should have gone down to Barranquilla first to make my report for the oil company, but I thought it was important to inspect our camp and get the roadwork started. I wanted to cut a small road through to the east to make it easier to get up there with supplies. Then, when I came back again from the coast, it would be simpler to organize the expedition I had planned to the Cunaguasayas' territory.

The little Indians greeted us warmly and were delighted to start work on the road. After a couple of days at our camp, things were so well under way that we could leave for the coast.

This time I wanted to try a new route. Instead of going north, we planned to ride south to a little place called Chiriguaná. From there we could follow the river to the coast. I heard that it was possible to phone ahead from Chiriguaná for a motor-boat and, if this were true, it would indeed make the trip a lot shorter. Now we had to ride mules, however, as there were no trucks or similar automotive wonders in Becerril.

The trip across the plains to Chiriguaná was hot and the place itself an oven. We had to wait several days before the motor-boat we had had to telegraph for arrived from the Magdalena River. It was an odd vessel, so flat-bottomed that it didn't seem to promise much security in a storm.

Once aboard, we forgot our worries, watching the thousands of birds which live along the banks of the Cesár River. On each side lay the bodies of crocodiles, all swarming with vultures. The reptiles are avidly hunted for their skins, which bring high prices, but as only the underside is used, the rest of the beast is left to rot. Also from the heavy overhanging branches a few gaily patterned snakes slithered down on the deck roof of our boat.

After a short while we came out into the huge Zapatoza Lagoon. This is a strange body of water, so shallow that anything but a flat-bottomed boat would ground anywhere. With heavy clouds hanging over its grey surface, it made us wonder if this were the way the world looked before sea and land were separated.

The shores were covered with thick, green foliage, as were its small islands and jutting points. Fishermen had their shacks here, and there seemed to be as many fish shimmering in the shallow depths as there were crocodiles and birds. Here, too, men hunt on horseback the wild ducks which live in the trees.

From the middle of the lagoon it was almost impossible to see land. Yet the men constantly had to measure the depth with long poles. As it was, we barely cleared several mud bars.

Although we were paying the rent for the boat, we had two fascinating fellow passengers. The captain had insisted on taking them along as they were relatives of his, he said. A rather plain señorita with her duenna were accompanied by masses of baggage and a cage stuffed full of canaries with which they must have intended to start a bird-shop.

We were well out on the lagoon when a storm of hurricane force blew up. Esther was the first to see the ominous cloud approaching and point it out to the captain. With fear in his eyes, he quickly made for the shelter of the nearest island, and just in time!

The wind churned the shallow water to a boil, trees keeled over into the water and the thick palm-leaf and even tin roofs of the fishing shanties, peeled off into the wet maelstrom like poplar leaves.

Although we lay in the lee of the island, the wind's force was so strong that it took two men on land to hold the boat's ropes so that it wouldn't be drawn helplessly out into the lake. While we did what we could to balance the fragile craft, huge hailstones

suddenly rattled down on the upper deck and spattered like birdshot into the water all around us. Hail in the tropics? We looked
at each other not believing our eyes.

It was cold by then and our teeth were chattering, so that we
could not console the señorita whose canaries had all died suddenly,
whether from the cold or from being hit on the head by hailstones
we didn't know.

A heavy rain followed the hail and the roof of the boat provided
little protection as it swirled around us. Although the storm lasted
only a couple of hours, we were so soaked that we spent the night
in a fisherman's hut, which fortunately still had its roof intact.

Next day, when our boat pulled up at a spot on the Magdalena
River, we were overjoyed to learn that a riverboat was going down
to the coast that same evening.

Determined that our return trip should not take as long as had
the trip down, I inquired about the possibility of flying part of the
way back. Yes, a plane was leaving El Banco on the Magdalena,
not as soon as I had hoped but it was luck just the same.

After a fairly bumpy flight it set us down right next to the motor-
boat I had wired ahead for and, in less than five hours, we were
back in Chiriguaná where the truck I had ordered was waiting for
us. We had made the trip from Barranquilla to Becerril in one day
– and ordinarily it took a week!

We were the only ones, of course, who were always in a hurry.
Our South American friends teased us about it many times. But
this time we had a special reason. We had brought along two big
chunks of ice for the people of Becerril, who had never seen it.
People crowded all around us to touch and taste what was left
of it. But when Esther chipped off some pieces and gave them to
the children to suck, they spat them out. 'It burns!' they cried, and
it took quite a little diplomacy to settle that crisis.

Next morning we were 'home' in Maraca with our 'little' Indians
once again.

CHAPTER FOURTEEN

DURING our absence a good deal of progress had been made on
the road and the section between the mountains was finished. I
was glad because I had to make a preliminary expedition in that
direction for the oil company. We were also very anxious to find
those 'fever Indians', the Cunaguasayas. Every day was important
as the rainy season was approaching. I decided to ride ahead towards
the east with a couple of my men and four pack mules. Montecristo

was to take off at the same time to see if he could find a way through to the south.

The Indians were eager to go along on both expeditions. The fact that we had actually come back – and they remembered very well where they had left us – impressed them immensely and increased their devotion, if that were possible. Even old Lazaro, who had first told us about the Cunaguasaya, offered to join Montecristo's party, dragons or no dragons.

There were a good many preparations to make before we could start. I had a few new bearers who had to be trained. Micael had to go back to tend his fields and I knew I should miss him. Then, we had to kill a cow I had bought in Becerril and the meat needed time to dry.

It began to rain harder and harder. The Maraca River rose and brimmed over its banks. We had to wait five days to get the cow up from the town, and it wasn't very comfortable in our house either. The roof leaked in several places and the sand fleas, seeking shelter from the wet outdoors, did everything they could to make us miserable.

They weren't the only uninvited guests, however. There were rats (which we did succeed in exterminating), ants of every description which regarded our food stores as theirs exclusively, scorpions, and snakes. We killed masses of every kind of creepy, crawly thing which came into the house out of the rain, as well as a lot of their relatives outside it.

Luis was sitting on a camp stool one evening talking with us when he felt what he thought was our dog's nose on his leg. When he put his hand down to pat it, he jumped. It was a snake which was slowly climbing up the leg of the stool. Miraculously it didn't strike him. Esther had similar good luck. When she took the canvas cover off a box of stores, a coral snake, awakened from its nap, wriggled out, coming straight at her.

As is well known, this beautiful snake is the deadliest of them all. Related to the cobra, its venom affects the nervous system, causing paralysis and usually death. It is generally quite short, but this one was almost three feet long, beautifully marked with bands of black and red, with a narrow yellow stripe on each side of the black one.

As the Indians never killed snakes, we had to smuggle out the dead body and bury it deep in the forest. Killing a snake, the Indians believed, would bring a curse of sickness on them. Because of this, we couldn't even keep the skin in the house. They reasoned that snakeskins were bad for the eyes. They were very much frightened of snakes and several times called on me to conduct an execution. Apparently the curse didn't cover us when the chips were down. Several of those snakes were huge, particularly a big rattlesnake one of our men shot one night. It was the largest I have even seen, measuring four and a half feet from stem to stern.

These episodes were sidelines, however, compared to the battle we had to wage against the jaguars. As many of the Indians as could slept inside our jaguar-proof fence, which now had a strong door, and a few rifle shots persuaded the animals to keep their distance. Otherwise, life was peaceful until, completely unexpectedly, something happened which cast a black shadow over the final days we lived with these happy people. It aroused all their savage instincts and came close to costing us all our lives.

My men and I were ready to set out for the interior. Esther was to remain behind and watch our headquarters as we daren't leave two fairly inexperienced men alone there. Luis was a good fellow, but very much afraid of the Indians as so many of his people had been killed by them. The other was José, a half-grown Indian boy who helped with chores such as cutting wood and fetching water. He was of another tribe, but had been brought up at a mission in the mountains. All the others who weren't with me left with Montecristo, leaving only the old people, the women and children behind.

From this point on I hand my pen to my wife:

'That morning I went out to the outer room as usual to have my coffee. Two Indian families were settled in there. We were very good friends for they had lived with us practically ever since our house was built. I don't think I am exaggerating if I say that we loved them more dearly than almost anybody we knew back home. More honest and loyal people than they it would have been hard to find. We were especially fond of Lazaro, his wife, and two children – a sweet little boy, Chi-chu-che, seven, and his baby sister they had named after me.

'I didn't see anyone but José in the front area. Luis was down the hill washing dishes in the stream and the child was playing with some others just outside the door while José watched them lazily.

'I went back to our private quarters but hadn't been there more than a minute when I was startled by the sound of a shot. My first thought was that Luis had shot a bird on his way home, but when I rushed out into the hall, I saw José standing there with a rifle in his hands. He had been strictly forbidden to handle any firearms and had taken this chance to use Luis's rifle. The shot had struck little Chi-chu-che, who stumbled in through the door and fell at my feet as I dashed over to him.

'After grabbing the gun from José, I lifted the child in my arms and, with his mother who had come running in, laid him carefully on a sleeping mat. I raced for the first-aid kit but soon saw that

I couldn't do anything. The boy had been hit in the back of the head and the brains were spilling out of an ugly wound.

'When the last flutter of life left the child, his mother cried out with a frightening scream, grabbed a heavy hunting knife and made a lunge at José, who had remained rooted to the spot as if paralysed. I held the mother back and yelled to José to run for his life. I knew that if there were any more bloodshed, I would almost certainly be their next victim.

'José had scarcely made his getaway when all the women from the surrounding huts came raging over, each brandishing a hunting knife – the knives we had traded to them. They were like crazed animals. When they found that José had escaped, they began to hack and slash at the house – the walls and the poles it stood on. Their knives flashed in the air and I felt their cold steel each time they swished past my cheek.

'I didn't have time to try to save our house from their fury as I had just caught sight of the mother holding a fistful of arrows which she was about to thrust into her breast. Snatching them out of her hands, I managed to prevent having a suicide as well as homicide to deal with.

'Louis came running in at that point, green with fear but still faithful. Between us we kept the mother and her sister from slashing themselves with the knives. But that wasn't all! The two women had reached such a peak of hysteria that they tried to strangle themselves with ropes and banged their heads against stones as soon as we freed their arms.

'There was blood everywhere. The boy lay in a pool of it, and it ran from the wounds the women had managed to inflict on themselves, and the hands, faces, and arms of all the others who had caressed the dead child or clutched him to them were covered with blood.

'I don't remember how I calmed them down except for thinking that on no account must I show the slightest fear. It was the fact that I wasn't too sure if I had succeeded in doing it that worried me, but I had noticed a slight hesitation on the part of the old man – who had brought all the other old fellows with him – when I sharply pushed aside the handful of arrows he was brandishing in my face with a menacing glare. I had to see what I was doing and couldn't with those things right under my nose. It was indeed lucky that I was too busy to be frightened at that moment. At any rate, the old man was so nonplussed that I was able to catch him off guard and ask his help in calming the women.

' "We have always been dear friends," I told them all. I repeated fifty times that José was not a white boy but a bad Indian from another tribe, who was so mean he had run away from his family.

And I let my genuine anger have full sway as I told them that José had been forbidden to touch any guns and had disobeyed that order.

'The old man went over to another and shortly they were mumbling together: "Yes, that tribe was never any good, and if any one of them ever dares come here we'll kill him."

'After that the atmosphere cleared enough so that the old man felt he could safely go off and stalk José. The others retired, shaking their heads and muttering, while the women began the most eerie keening I have ever heard. They kept it up without a break night and day for the rest of the week, and once a week for several weeks after that.

'The mother and her sister sat with the dead child. They wept and stroked his hands and face. In fact, all the women came forward and patted the little body once a day. I put my hand on their shoulders and tried in every way I could to let them understand my grief, too.

'Now, however, I knew I had to act fast. Their tempers had calmed but the slightest thing might arouse them again. Whisperings that our house was to be burned down had reduced Luis to a jelly of fear. Trying to think of some way to get help, I suddenly recalled a couple of elderly white men whom the monks had sent out to teach the Indians in another village only a few hours away up in the forest. I determined to go and get them.

'After telling "our" Indians that I was going to ask the white people to go and catch José and also to tell the child's grandfather, Monaro, the sad news, I fastened all the funds for our expedition and our most important papers in my underclothes. Then I started up through that slippery, snarled mountain forest.

'Luis came with me. In fact, wild horses couldn't have held him behind in that village. Sweating and panting our way up, he kept gasping behind me: "They're after us. They're going to kill us!" But they didn't.

'My news came as a great shock and the white men immediately understood the gravity of the situation. With old Monaro, head hanging in grief for his little grandson, we all went back down to our house. Thanks to Monaro, order and reason were restored and there were no further outbreaks.

'What cheered me most was to find Micael waiting when I got back. He had heard about the accident and had come back to help. I felt much safer – he understood the Indians so well. He said the authorities in Becerril had taken charge of José, which also was good news. Micael had been afraid he would find our house burned down and me dead, he told me. Needless to say, I was very glad to be able to prove his fears unfounded.

'The mother was then making preparations at last for her son's final rest. The little face was painted with red designs – even the eyelids. After that, the knees were bent up to the chest and the arms tightly crossed over them, perhaps unconsciously in a foetal position. Across the feet narrow cloth bands were tied so that the little bones wouldn't fall loose when the body decomposed. One of the boy's feet was misformed, something which had made his mother very unhappy. I had given her a long, white shirt for him to help hide his deformity, and it was pathetic now to see how she carefully arranged the cloth so that the foot was hidden.

'The body – except for the head – was then placed in a cape sewed with strong twine into an almost square package and laid on a wooden frame as if lying in state. Under the head, which remained uncovered, a calabash bowl had been placed to catch the blood, even though there wasn't much by then.

'Next, a special shelter was built – just a sloping roof under which the Indian women prepared another rack with sides, almost like a cradle.

'The following day, the head was carefully bound in strips of cloth like a little mummy, leaving only the mouth and nostrils free. All was then covered with blankets and a little bag filled with the boy's favourite playthings was laid alongside his bow and arrows. At a given signal, all the Indian women came forward and each laid a leafy branch on the body as they mumbled words which meant something like, "Pray for us." They also put a little branch on the body for each of their children, as gifts from each of his playmates.

'Each night after that, the mother set some food and something to drink on the rack so her son would have something to eat "along the way". I tried to discover what the ultimate goal was in these Indians' minds, but was given to understand that no one ever spoke of such things. We were never able, in all the years we worked in the Andes, to discover any religious beliefs among these Indians. Yet there was no doubt in my mind that they had very strong faith in some greater power.

'With the blankets, the gifts, food and drink, a large fire was then lit under the corpse so it wouldn't be cold. The flames were not high enough to burn it but it did speed the drying process. Custom also dictated that the body lie there a couple of months, covered by grass, until it had been purified enough to permit the remains to be collected in a smaller package and taken home to be with the family again, sharing in the home life and festivities the deceased had known best. That was always the occasion for a feast, a special welcoming-home party.

'To my great surprise, however, old Grandfather Monaro sent me a message one evening asking me to see that the body was buried in a grave "like white people". His message said that as Lazaro, the boy's father, was still away, it would be wise if on his return he did not see the little package hanging in his house. If the body were buried, said Monaro, his father would not take his loss so hard. I had to agree, for I had been dreading Lazaro's return ever since the accident.

'So the men made a little coffin from some packing cases and laid the body in it. Then they dug a hole under the grave shelter and put it to rest, covering it over with green branches.

'My next responsibility was to get the mother, sister and grandmother to eat. These Indians always fast for weeks after a death in the family and those who have touched the corpse in any way are not permitted to handle or cook food for months. Although this primitive understanding of the dangers of infection was admirable, it undermined the women's strength to such a degree that I was worried.

'The only thing to do was to feed them forcibly. Luis and I held first the mother, then the other two, by the arms while Micael forced cornmeal porridge into their mouths. They struggled and spat out the food until they saw we weren't going to give in. When they each managed at last to swallow a mouthful, we didn't have any more trouble. I cooked more porridge whenever I thought they must be hungry and, as long as Luis or I fed them, they willingly ate the porridge and drank a little corn beer to brace them for Lazaro's return.'

When Esther finished her story on my return, there wasn't much I could say except to thank all the powers watching over her that she was safe.

Fortunately I got back to Maraca with my party before the other group, including Lazaro, returned. The Indians helped Esther, Micael and me round up all the bows, arrows, knives and ropes in the village. After I locked them all in a big chest, the Indians saw me put the key in my pocket and seemed to approve. We also arranged that before the others arrived, Montecristo was to be tipped off. On some pretext he was to borrow Lazaro's bow and arrows, which he did, so that the poor man returned unarmed to his disarmed village.

The next few days were strenuous. At first, no one dared tell the bereaved father what had happened. As he went around the village, he saw in their faces that something was wrong but no one would say what it was. When he asked for little Chi-chu-che, even his wife called for the boy, pretending that he had just gone out to play. One of the older men at last mustered the courage to whisper the truth to the father.

Lazaro became like a man possessed. We had to restrain him, holding his arms behind his back for several hours. For days after that, we took turns guarding him and, each time relatives from other villages came to offer their condolences, we had to search and disarm them first. I was amazed that, for the most part, the Indians co-operated and obeyed my orders. I told them that we didn't want Lazaro to do anything stupid like going off into the forest to commit suicide, for what would happen to his wife and little Esther? They seemed to agree that it wouldn't do any good, even though it was their honoured custom.

Our last days with the Maraca Indians were overshadowed by their grief. There were no more dances or songs or games. And through the forest on many evenings we heard the rather beautiful long-drawn-out keening cries of the bereaved coming up from the lovely valley. Every night, too, the mother came back to place food on her child's grave – the tasty little things he had liked best.

Montecristo and his men had been gone ten days but they hadn't found the Cunaguasaya – hadn't even seen a sign that they ever lived where we had been told they would be found.

It was obvious that it would take longer to find them than I had figured. I became more and more convinced, in fact, that they must be identical with the dangerous Indians around the Rio de Oro.

Since the accident, it was out of the question to ask any Maracas to join another expedition. It would probably be years before we could even broach the subject. Now, too, the rainy season was upon us and the deluge broke loose with a kind of vengeance as if to wash away the bitter memories of our last days. For we had to leave. With the rains, our expedition was at an end.

We said good-bye to our little friends with real emotion. We didn't know, as we rode down the mountain along the new road we had built, that we would never come back to see them again.

BOOK FIVE

CHAPTER ONE

WE had hoped that with the help of our Pygmy friends we could make contact with the secretive Cunaguasaya or, at least, meet others in the course of our explorations through the Andes who could help us find them. All we knew was that they lived at the foot of the mountains to the south in the forests along the Catatumbo River and the Rio de Oro and that they had definitely not 'buried the hatchet'.

There was no question on that score. During the 1930's their war-like behaviour was confirmed by more than one report from oil prospectors I had met. Oil had been found in their forests and the few prospectors who had survived the Indians' brutal attacks were reluctant to go anywhere near them again.

One of these oil companies had helped finance our trip over the Sierra de Perijá because it was hoped that we could find new oil sources and perhaps meet a group of the same tribe whom we could befriend as a start towards winning over the others. Unfortunately, none of the tribes we met had any connexions whatever with the Cunaguasayas or Catatumbo, as we usually called them.

I started to make plans to go down to the Catatumbo area without much hope of better success, I must admit, but feeling it was worth a try.

This time Esther could not go along as there were no facilities for women at the oil camp. The Colombian Petroleum Company's oilfields are situated in Colombia not far from the Venezuelan border but one had to go to the latter country to get to them.

The hot but charming little mountain town of Cúcuta, where I took the train, was once chosen to be the capital of the centralized republic made up of several neighbouring countries which Simon Bolivar worked so hard for, following his hard-won fight for independence from Spain in 1819. The train passed through some very wild country to Encontrados, a small settlement in Venezuela not far from the mouth of the Catatumbo.

The recent rains had been too much for the river which had overflowed its banks into the town. The train chugged through a lake about a foot deep over the tracks and, when I got off, I found people rowing boats in the streets. Nevertheless, I was met at the half-submerged dock right on schedule by the company's motor launch which was to take me back to Colombia and its tall oil forests.

It was a beautiful boat, modern in every detail even to elaborate mosquito-netted decks and lounge. In addition, it was surrounded by a strong steel net to ward off Indian arrows. Members of the crew were stationed fore and aft with rifles and everyone carried a revolver. It was like a little battleship. And the enemy? A tribe of Indians, desperately trying to defend their lands and riches from the white invader.

I was relieved to hear that the oil company people and the border commission's personnel had strict orders to shoot only warning shots even if they were attacked. And, so far, they had obeyed the order, despite the loss of several of their people to silent Indian arrows.

When the first white conquerors had come four hundred years before, the Indians had been on their guard but had not declared war. It was when the revolutionary general, Barco, gave part of their land to local ranchers in the early 1900's as a concession to his political backers that trouble started. The Indians did not resist right away, although they did not like roads being cut through their land to transport cattle and supplies. It was the peons who drove the cattle and the trucks who started the trouble. They stole from the Indians, attacked their women and burned their villages and, from that time on, the Indians had vowed vengeance on all white men.

This was the situation when the oil prospectors arrived but, in spite of everything the Indians did to keep them back, the invaders kept coming with frightening noise-makers, drilling holes in their forest and clearing stretches of it until it sprouted with a strange kind of tree that thundered and everything stank of oil.

Even Barco had seen the advantage of exploiting this new-found wealth. But it remained for his successors to build the roads to bring in the bulldozers and giant scoops, whose huge jaws snapped up tons of the Indians' earth and carted it away, making a desert of their jungle where they could hunt no more.

The Indians had retreated helplessly before the huge work trucks and noisy motor-boats which darted back and forth on their river and frightened away the fish. Their arrows were impotent against the mighty tractors crashing towards them through the jungle. But they had not capitulated.

How were they to live – to hunt and fish – since the white man had crushed even the birds' eggs along the river banks which they liked to eat and killed the birds, who died when their feathers got stuck together with oil. It was too late to make peace.

After a very pleasant day's trip in unaccustomed luxury, we all debarked at our destination. Bright lights glittered in the distance. It was odd and unexpected to see these signs of civilization after having left human habitation so far behind. We were coming into one of the company's largest and most modern installations. The street lights between the small houses and shops lit up the jungle of oil rigs in the background. The real jungle had been cut back over a wide area and the ultra-modern town through which we were walking provided a dramatic contrast to the Creole villages and even to the coast cities I was used to.

The workers lived in enormous airy barracks, while their bosses each had his own well-furnished bungalow. There were electric lights everywhere, hot and cold running water, showers in all bathrooms, electric fans, refrigerators, a library, doctors' offices, radios, new automobiles and every kind of modern gadget invented up to that time, it seemed to me. In the directors' offices were radio telephones to maintain direct contact with the field and 'intercom' connexions between office and home. All this in the midst of the primeval jungle whose people survived by bow and arrow!

Almost as soon as I arrived I was made aware of that fact. It had happened only a short time back, they told me. Some Indians had come one night to snoop around – watching the men take a shower seemed to have some fascination for them – and they had come upon two white men a couple of minutes' walk from the camp. Zing! And one arrow went through one man's arm while a second pierced the other man through the chest.

The company photographer (whose sole assignment there was to take and develop pictures) snapped both men just before the doctor reached them. That this picture was shown me almost as soon as I arrived I took as a diplomatic move to discourage me in case I still hoped to befriend these Indians.

Then, there was Jensen. I had met him before at a Thanksgiving Day party in Barranquilla. He was a Danish-American who prided himself on being a Viking. His comrades teased him by telling him they'd heard only about Swedish and Norwegian Vikings. Even though Jensen knew they were teasing, he plainly didn't like it.

He took a motor launch up the river one day which had no anti-arrow screening, even though he had been warned against it. And sure enough! A hail of arrows stuck in both sides of the boat before he'd been gone fifteen minutes. Only one hit him, though, in the arm. He finished his business, took the boat back to the dock and, much later, went over to see the doctor. It was impossible to pull out the arrow as its barb was so deep it would require an operation to remove it. The doctor sent him off by boat the next day up to the big company hospital where it was found that infection had set in from old blood on the tip. When they told Jensen they would have to amputate his arm, he refused. Next day he was dead.

The oil company's people had tried various ways of protecting themselves. They had surrounded several camps with electrically wired fences, like prison camps. They also imported a quantity of bullet-proof vests for those who had to go on expeditions into the jungle. But they proved unpopular. Apart from their weight, it was impossible to wear them because of the oppressive heat, so everyone was left to take his chances with Lady Luck and the Indians' arrows.

It was incredible to think that we were sitting in the middle of a jungle when we sat down to excellent European meals, cooled by electric fans and sipping from glasses clinking with ice cubes. The food couldn't have been better, with all the fruit and vegetables one could wish for. In fact, nothing was lacking that a European or American is used to, although only two minutes away lived people who had never tasted milk.

The Indians are there although you seldom see them. They move silently in the shadows of their great trees, keeping constant watch against further encroachments, knowing they are powerless to do more than slow down the march of the oil rigs. In my opinion, it's best for them that they feel the way they do. I do not believe they would gain anything from civilization for, when a free man loses his pride, he loses more than his land. I have only to think of those miserable half-civilized Indians Esther and I ran into above Machiques to hope that this brave tribe will remain free and full of fight no matter how hopeless the prospects.

I was taken on some very interesting car trips to see the oil rigs and also to inspect a small coal mine which supplied the electric power for the settlement. It was sunk in a narrow forest valley overgrown with tangled liana vines through which the big coal scoops plunged down to be filled by the sweating, panting men digging coal below the jungle floor.

In some outlying camps, where work had to be stopped for a few days at a time, the Indians were quick to stage raids. In one camp they slashed all the canvas covering the barracks after they had looted them of everything they could carry away. In another camp they found a store of guns and ammunition – the white man's 'fire weapons'. When some distance away, they set fire to their loot to make sure the white men would never use them again. A brace of bullets killed two Indians. After that, they never touched either guns or ammunition again, which was a relief to hear.

It took a lot of ingenuity to protect work tools, however. They were kept locked in big iron boxes, but in more than one camp the men would return to find the storage box looking as though it had been dynamited and all the tools gone. With what seemed incredible strength, the Indians had managed to break the locks with hammers and crowbars they had stolen previously. As they had no use for the tools, it was probable that they traded them for necessities with other tribes or perhaps with Creoles. Anyway, they had to make a living somehow. I secretly congratulated them for their enterprise despite the kindness of my hosts. That their plan was plain sabotage was clear, however, when they once stole several packets of paper money for which they could have no use whatever.

At the harbour entrance to the oil city was a sign: 'Women Not Allowed'. Esther would have laughed at the various reasons they gave me for the sign – danger of Indians, bad climate and 'primitive' living conditions. I did not comment further than to explain that the presence of women in any camp was an indication to the Indians of peaceful intentions. I told some of the oil men about our first visit to the Motilons with little Sif. However, the hope that lit the men's eyes at the prospect of importing some women to round out their barren life was quickly dimmed by a flat refusal by the company's manager to consider such a thing. The camp had no facilities for women, he said, and that was that.

It was a fact that the weather there was almost unbearable – heat and high humidity and a rainy season bringing as much as five thousand millimetres a year. Even the Indians couldn't hold out against that much rain but withdrew up to the mountains.

Periodically there were terrific hurricanes and electrical storms. I recalled that when we were in Maracaibo we had seen tremendous lightning flashes coming from the direction of the Catatumbo forests.

Taking advantage of the Indians' temporary retreat meant that the oil men had to work overtime to prospect and expand their operations under the most strenuous conditions. When the Indians returned, the company's men, for their part, retreated behind their steel fences and the small lookout posts they had built like bird nests in trees surrounding the camp.

The pipeline taking the oil from these forests down to the mighty Magdalena River is, in many ways, one of the wonders of the world. Almost two hundred miles long, it runs westwards over the Andes at the three-thousand-foot level, then drops abruptly to the river where waiting tankers line the shore. As there were no roads through the jungle, all the rig construction materials, barracks and personnel had to be flown in and parachuted down where it was impossible for a plane to land or take off.

Only people who know those jungle-clad impenetrable tropical mountains and those steaming, fever-ridden marshes, over which evil vultures flap in slow circles, and those clever Indians lurking in wait for their unsuspecting 'enemies' can understand what that Barco pipeline represents. It is a triumph of modern engineering and American ingenuity. Despite its enormous cost – thirty-two million dollars were required before the pipeline, costing another sixteen million dollars, could even be laid – the company considered every cent well invested. The thick greenish-yellow oil yields twice the amount of high-grade gasoline per barrel as ordinary black petroleum.

No one should think that the oil men hadn't tried to befriend those Indians – and they're still trying. But the first prospectors had been a tough lot, working on the principle of kill or be killed, and the Indians hadn't forgotten it. The companies certainly want peace. The precautions they have to take – steel fences, lookouts, high insurance rates, high wages and hospital maintenance, cost huge sums every year. They have tried leaving gifts for the Indians, even parachuting boxes full of cloth, beads and the other things they like – all to no avail. A priest put his picture in some of the packages so the Indians would know what the donor looked like and so would recognize him when he visited them. But the directors felt the project was too risky and called it off, as they did several other ingenious plans to make contact with the 'enemy'.

Another attempt to try to reach them through friendly members of the tribe who lived farther to the north was similarly unsuccessful. The latter hadn't the slighest desire to get to know their warlike cousins any better and refused to co-operate.

While I was there, members of the border commission were working in the area to define the boundary between the two republics. In their own interests, they too tried to win over the Catatumbo savages. They took with them a list of the Motilon words Esther and I had learned, including that magic word, 'Yacano!' But the Indians' reply was a couple of arrows aimed at the two leaders. Altogether, the commissioners brought back from that trip an interesting collection of about five hundred Indian arrows.

I was forced to change my theory that the Catatumbo Indians understood the Motilon language, even though they should have, being members of the same tribe, as most people believed. But the more I saw for myself and heard from the oil workers, the more convinced I became that they had a quite different culture.

They build houses sometimes forty-five to fifty feet long in which a whole village often lives under the same flat roof, the families separated by low partitions. They go about completely naked except for a primitive G-string, wear their hair long and, most amazing, do not paint their faces.

It had proved impossible to learn a word of their language even from the handful of prisoners the men captured from time to time.

All the prisoners committed suicide the moment a guard's back was turned, and even when he was looking he was often helpless to prevent it. That is, all but one, a little boy who gradually became 'tame' enough to become a sort of mascot to the men. But by the time someone got the idea that he might learn some useful Indian words, the lad had forgotten his own language completely and spoke only Spanish – a great loss to science.

There were numberless stories of Indian attacks to brighten a hot evening in the company mess. MacLane, a geologist, had gone out one day with a work gang to take some tests and had to pass fairly close to an area the Indians regarded as their front-line defence. MacLane felt tired and sick so he told the men to go on ahead while he rested in his hammock. The men warned him of the danger but he was a stubborn Scot with a temper, so they left him.

When they returned, they found him still in his hammock, his body bristling with arrows like a porcupine and his intestines hanging on a tree branch over his head.

Almost in the same moment, the entire group was attacked. One man, a German named Wiesner, got an arrow straight through the liver. His companions fled back to camp but when they returned with reinforcements Wiesner was dead, another arrow sticking out of one eye. The Indians had taken all his clothes and disappeared.

In recent years they have also improved their skills of sabotage. They fell trees over newly cleared roads, waiting until months of work have finally made it possible to get trucks through. The crews sent out to remove the tree are promptly bombarded with arrows. At night, when the men work because it is cooler, they have to light their way with flashlights, which make them excellent targets, especially their legs.

Farther south where there were no oil fields, the Indians had adopted a policy of armed neutrality against the inroads of the Creole settlers. And there were many stories of Creoles and Indians fishing together in the same river, although each group sat respectfully on its own side. The Creoles would yell warnings to the Indians whenever they planned to use dynamite. After the explosion, the Indians were then free to haul in all the fish on their side of the river.

This relatively peaceful situation encouraged the oil company directors to send an expedition to the Indians in the Mercedes and Tarra areas. If contact could be made with them, maybe they could serve as arbiters and put an end to the Indian war against the companies, they reasoned.

The expedition was led by an American ethnologist, Preston Holder, who took with him the Colombian explorer, Reichel Dolmatoff. With the help of the white settlers, they managed to make contact with the Indians in that area – close enough to see them and call out friendly greetings. They even got a glimpse of the interior of one of their huts. But it grew more evident every day that the Indians were becoming increasingly withdrawn and cautious. They paid no attention to the gifts set out for them and retreated from their huts as soon as the white group came into view. At length, they seemed to lose patience with such cat-and-mouse tactics and Holder and his men began to find crossed palm leaves lying on the trails into the forest – an indisputable sign of war. There was no help for it. The expedition had to turn back.

It was true that they had not had time enough. In other sections of South America constant peace overtures, sometimes taking years, have ultimately been successful.

Nevertheless, Holder and Dolmatoff made several low flights over the Catatumbo and Rio de Oro areas and took some excellent pictures of the Indians' huge houses, lying on heights near the river and surrounded by huge plantations. They reckoned it must be a day's march between each village. As they flew farther north they noted that the huts were once more round, with conical grass roofs and that the fields were much smaller. These differences seemed to confirm that the Catatumbo Indians were not of the same tribe as our Motilons in the Sierra de Perijá and thus were not Caribs at all.

Every attempt to come to terms with the natives of the Rio de Oro and Catatumbo has failed. The war begun a generation ago goes on between the oil companies and the Indians living at the foot of the Andes. And that, perhaps, is the most extraordinary thing about them!